AA

ORDNANCE SURVEY
LEISURE GUIDE
EAST ANGLIA

O S

Produced jointly by the Publishing Division of
The Automobile Association and the Ordnance Survey

Title page: Norwich Cathedral

Opposite: A fishmonger's at Southwold, Suffolk

Introductory page: beside the River Ant, on the Norfolk Broads

Editorial contributors: Dr Tom Williamson and Liz Bellamy (Shaping the Landscape), Chris Durdin (A Paradise for Birdwatchers), Celia Jennings (East Anglian Churches, Traditional Buildings, Gainsborough, Constable & Others), Christopher Hanson-Smith (Gazetteer), Clive Tully (Box features), Joy Boldero (Walks), East Anglia Tourist Board (Directory).

Original photography: S & O Mathews

Typeset by Avonset, Midsomer Norton, Bath.
Printed in Great Britain by
BPC PAULTON BOOKS LTD
A member of the British Printing Company Ltd.

Maps extracted from the Ordnance Survey's 1:625 000 Routeplanner Map, 1:250 000 Routemaster Series and 1:25 000 Pathfinder Series, with the permission of Her Majesty's Stationery Office. Crown Copyright reserved.

Additions to the maps by the Cartographic Dept of The Automobile Association and the Ordnance Survey.

Produced by the Publishing Divisions of The Automobile Association.

The contents of this publication are believed correct at the time of printing. Nevertheless, the Publishers cannot accept responsibility for errors or omissions, or for changes in details given.

First published 1989
Reprinted 1993, 1994 (twice)

© The Automobile Association 1989
© The Ordnance Survey 1989

Originally published by The Automobile Association and the Ordnance Survey as The Leisure Guide series.

EAST ANGLIA

Contents

Using this Book

The entries in the Gazetteer have been carefully selected, although for reasons of space it has not been possible to include every community in the region. A number of small villages are described under the entry for a larger neighbour, and these can be found in the index.

Each entry in the A to Z Gazetteer has the atlas page number on which the place can be found and its National Grid reference included under the heading. An explanation of how to use the National Grid is given on page 82.

Beneath many of the entries in the Gazetteer are listed AA-recommended hotels, restaurants, garages, guesthouses, and campsites in the immediate vicinity of the place described. Hotels, restaurants and campsites are also given an AA classification.

SELECTION ONLY

For some popular resorts, not all AA-recommended establishments can be included. For full details see current editions of the AA's annual guides and the AA *Members' Handbook*.

HOTELS

1-star	Good hotels and inns, generally of small scale and with acceptable facilities and furnishing.
2-star	Hotels offering a higher standard of accommodation, with some private bathrooms/showers.
3-star	Well-appointed hotels; a good proportion of bedrooms with private bathrooms/showers.
4-star	Exceptionally well-appointed hotels offering a high standard of service. All bedrooms should have private bathrooms/showers.
5-star	Luxury hotels offering the highest international standards.

Hotels often satisfy *some* of the requirements for higher classifications than that awarded.

Red-star	Red stars denote hotels which are considered to be of outstanding merit within their classification.
Country House Hotel	A hotel where a relaxed informal atmosphere prevails. Some of the facilities may differ from those at urban hotels of the same classification.

RESTAURANTS

1-fork	Modest but good restaurant.
2-fork	Restaurant offering a higher standard of comfort than above.
3-fork	Well-appointed restaurant.
4-fork	Exceptionally well-appointed restaurant.
5-fork	Luxury restaurant.
1-rosette	Hotel or restaurant where the cuisine is considered to be of a higher standard than is expected in an establishment within its classification.
2-rosette	Hotel or restaurant offering very good food and service, irrespective of the classification.
3-rosette	Hotel or restaurant offering outstanding food and service, irrespective of classification.

GUESTHOUSES

These are different from, but not necessarily inferior to, AA-appointed hotels, and they offer an alternative for those who prefer inexpensive and not too elaborate accommodation. They all provide clean, comfortable accommodation in homely surroundings. Each establishment must usually offer at least six bedrooms, and a general bathroom and a general toilet for every six bedrooms without private facilities. Parking facilities should be reasonably close.

CAMPSITES

1-pennant	Site licence; at least 6 pitches for touring units; 2 separate toilets for each sex per 30 pitches; good quality tapwater; adequate waste disposal; fire precautions; well-drained ground; entrance and access roads of adequate width.
2-pennant	All one-pennant facilities plus: at least 15% of pitches allocated to tourers; separate washrooms; externally-lit sanitary facilities; warden available at certain times of the day.
3-pennant	All two-pennant facilities plus: one shower or bath for each sex per 40 pitches, with hot and cold water; electric shaver points and mirrors; all-night lighting of toilet blocks; deep sinks for washing clothes; facilities for buying milk, bread and gas; adequate roads; warden in attendance by day, on call by night.
4-pennant	All three-pennant facilities plus: at least 25% of pitches allotted for tourers; 2 washbasins per sex for 25 pitches and 1 shower per sex for 35 pitches; all-night lighting of toilet blocks; washing-up facilities; reception office; late-arrivals enclosure; first-aid hut; shop; routes to essential facilities lit after dark; play area; hard standing for touring vans; facilities for the disabled; fast food take-away; public telephone.
5-pennant	A comprehensive range of services and equipment; at least 50% of pitches allocated to tourers; 2 washbasins per sex for 20 pitches; 1 shower per sex for 30 pitches; heated washrooms; café or restaurant; automatic laundry; indoor play facilities for children; facilities for recreation; warden in attendance 24 hours per day; visitors car park.

EAST ANGLIA

Introduction

*East Anglia's watery landscape, dotted with windmills and picturesque villages, has inspired painters and craftsmen for centuries.
It has a unique atmosphere and a charm all its own.
This book explores Essex, Cambridgeshire, Suffolk and Norfolk, together with the Broads and ancient Breckland.
As well as comprehensive coverage of places to visit, it includes feature articles, walks, drives and a directory of practical information.
Backed by the AA's research expertise and the Ordnance Survey's mapping, this guide is for those who know and love the area, and for those discovering it for the first time.*

Shaping the Landscape

The mention of the East Anglian landscape conjures up a range of images – Constable country, the Norfolk Broads, and perhaps, for the more ecologically-minded, the monotonous arable prairies produced by the intensive agricultural methods of the past 30 years. The countryside varies from flat to gently rolling, and while some areas are virtually devoid of bushes and trees, others are well-hedged and wooded. In places the soil is light, dry and sandy, but elsewhere there is some of the wettest and richest land in the country.

The variations in the natural environment have been compounded by the way that the land has been used over the centuries. In the Middle Ages, East Anglia was the richest and most densely-settled region of England, and its large and prosperous population shaped the environment in numerous ways. The distinct landscapes of the region – the Broads, the Fens, the Breckland, and the areas of what is called Ancient Countryside – reveal much about the natural and social history of these areas. The pattern of woods, hedges, fields and villages can show us how different groups of people organised their lives and work; for the landscape of East Anglia is fundamentally man-made.

The Broads

The network of rivers and lakes that makes up the Norfolk Broads is one of East Anglia's foremost tourist attractions. Thousands of visitors flock to the region in the summer months, to enjoy fishing, boating, or just looking at the scenery. Yet despite the beauty of the Broadland and its wealth of flora and fauna, this is a far from natural environment. It is, in fact, an industrial landscape.

In the early medieval period the digging of peat and turf for fuel was a major source of income for the inhabitants of the area. At that time Norwich was the second-largest city in England, and so provided a flourishing market. As the sea level rose, however, during the Middle Ages, the old peat workings became flooded and so came to form the series of lakes that makes up the Norfolk Broads. Many of these lakes are connected to rivers – the Bure, the Ant, the Chet and the Yare – which eventually flow together and enter the sea at Great Yarmouth. There has been a gradual contraction in the extent of the Broads, as they have become

Hickling Broad (below) forms part of a National Nature Reserve, where it is possible to see a wide variety of Broadland features. Windpumps, like the restored one at Horsey Mere (inset), were used to raise floodwater from the Broads

colonised by reed-beds and alder woods. These areas of marsh or 'carr' form a valuable habitat for wetland wildlife.

To the east of the Broads is a rather different landscape, comprising vast areas of flat, well-grazed grassland, criss-crossed by long drainage dykes and dotted with grazing cows. This is another largely man-made landscape, for the area was once a huge estuary. The accumulation of the gravel spit on which Yarmouth now stands eventually caused the waters to silt up, forming a marsh. Over the centuries this marsh was gradually drained, to produce the rich pastures visible today. All over the area there are monuments to this process of drainage, in the form of hundreds of windpumps. Some, such as Berney Arms, Stracey Arms and Horsey, have been restored and are now open to the public. Many more are in ruins, their sail-less stumps standing out against the flat surroundings. Yet the reclamation of these east Norfolk marshes has been insignificant compared with the projects of land drainage instituted in the west of the region, in the Fens.

The Fens

The East Anglian fenland is a strange and haunting place. It has a flatness and an openness which is quite disorienting to visitors from other parts of the country, with great empty skies stretching over plains of dark, rich soil. There are few trees and virtually no hedges. The houses are largely 20th century, and many stand, lonely and isolated, sheltered only by a few garden conifers from the open expanses of arable land. Above the fields run the drainage ditches, their steep grass banks providing a graphic reminder of the lowness of the surrounding land. These flat fenland fields contain some of the richest soil in England, yet despite the intensity of arable exploitation, the landscape has considerable variety and interest, as well as its own curious aesthetic appeal.

There are two distinct types of landscape – the Southern Fen, which is largely composed of peat, and the Northern or Black Fen, which is made up of silt soils. Both were formed by rising sea levels, following the Ice Age. In the Southern Fen, the increase in the water table turned an area of woodland into marsh. The peat created by rotting marshland vegetation preserved many trees, and these great hard, blackened 'bog oaks' are still

being ploughed up today. In the Black Fen the land became covered with fertile silt, deposited by rivers and the periodic incursions of the sea. In the Southern Fen the landscape is more varied, for, dotted across the peat, there are numerous little islands, many of which have been used as the sites of settlements. Villages such as Soham and Haddenham, and the small town of Ely, rise up out of the landscape on these low hills.

In prehistoric times, before the Fens were drained, there was quite dense settlement on the islands and the fen edge. Recent excavations on Flag Fen, near Peterborough, have revealed a considerable Bronze Age village, its wooden houses and artefacts preserved in the peat. In the Roman period, the exploitation of the area was facilitated by the construction of artificial watercourses, which aided transportation and drainage. The Roman Car Dyke is still very impressive in some places (for example, at Landbeach, north of Cambridge). At Reach Lode, between Cambridge and Newmarket, there is also a 3-mile long stretch of straight Roman waterway.

Although the population of the Fens seems to have declined at the end of the Roman period, the islands continued to be occupied. In the medieval period, the area was dominated by great ecclesiastical estates, such as the monasteries of Ely, Ramsey and Thorney. These wealthy landowning institutions initiated drainage and reclamation schemes, through the construction of ditches, banks and sluices. The meres and marshes were also exploited for fish, wildfowl, sedge, peat and reeds. In addition, the drier areas of the marsh, the 'summer lands', were used for grazing in the summer.

Morston Salt Marshes are evidence today of medieval Norfolk's major salt-making industry. Fishing and thatching provided other livelihoods on the Broads and marshes

By the 17th century more ambitious land drainage schemes were undertaken, often by groups of investors known as 'Adventurers'. These involved the construction of long, straight cuts, which would speed the flow of water to the Wash. The most important scheme of this type, headed by the Earl of Bedford, began in the 1630s, using the skills of the Dutch engineer Cornelius Vermuyden. Two of Vermuyden's waterways, the Old Bedford River and the New Bedford River, are still striking features of the landscape; in wet weather, the land between the two, known as the Washes, forms a reservoir for flood water.

For a while, these drainage projects seemed successful, yielding considerable profits. But as the water was removed from the southern peat, the land compacted and shrank, falling below the level of the cuts and rivers. The drainage courses had to be embanked, and a pumping system was established to bring water up from the reclaimed fields. In the 18th century this was achieved through the use of windpumps, like the one which has been re-erected at Wicken Fen nature reserve. But from the 1820s, the work was taken over by a number of large steam engines, each connected to a network of 'Engine Drains'. One of these old engines can still be seen at Stretham, south of Ely, but most have now disappeared, replaced by diesel engines or electric pumps. It is a salutary thought

East Anglia's fenland once covered a vast area of low land that was filled with deep layers of peat or silt soils, and the drainage system of the Fens had to be constantly maintained. Below, men reinforce the banks of a drain ridge by passing mud from shovel to shovel. Massive steam engines gradually took over the job of windpumps; the one at Stretham, Cambridgeshire, has been restored, along with its engine house (above)

that without the constant maintenance of this drainage system, the whole landscape of the Fens would become submerged once again.

Ancient Countryside

The oldest landscapes in East Anglia may be found in the south and east of the region, in Essex, the central and eastern parts of Suffolk, and the south and east of Norfolk. Here the countryside has an ancient feel, with winding lanes bounded by thick hedges. Large old houses are scattered amid fields and woods, and where modern agricultural methods have not obliterated the long-established hedges and boundaries, the fields are small and irregularly-shaped. This landscape has been formed over thousands of years, by generations of farmers.

In some parts of the region the landscape reveals that as early as prehistoric or Roman times the land was not only divided into hedged fields, but was also laid out in a vast grid, along a series of long parallel boundaries. These grids are clearly visible on old maps, and their ancient origin is often shown by the way in which they are crossed by Roman roads. Odd, irregularly-shaped corners and triangles have been left, however, showing that the fields were obviously laid out before the roads. This pattern is particularly noticeable in the area around Scole, Billingford and Dickleburgh, in south Norfolk.

Elsewhere, the evidence for landscape planning can be seen on modern maps, and even in the countryside itself. In the landscape around the parishes of the South Elmhams and the Ilketshalls, between Halesworth and Bungay in north Suffolk, there is a very regular system of fields, laid out parallel to the Roman roads. This landscape probably dates from Roman times, and is visible to the walker or driver as a series of long, gently-meandering north–south lanes, intersected by shorter and more winding east–west roads. Even more impressive is the landscape of the Dengie Peninsula, to the east of Chelmsford in Essex. The entire Peninsula – an area of almost 100 square kilometres – is divided into a huge grid.

Other parts of the Ancient Countryside were not laid out in the prehistoric period, but were gradually shaped from the Middle Ages onwards, as the area was slowly divided up into fields. The piecemeal progress of land enclosure in this area is revealed today by the irregular pattern formed by the fields, and the antiquity of the landscape is indicated by its hedges. Throughout the Ancient Countryside area, the hedges tend to be large and dense, and composed of a multitude of species such as hazel, dogwood, maple, ash, oak, elm and spindle.

Between the fields are ancient woods. Many of these are remnants of great primeval forests, but they have been shaped by the intensive management techniques employed from the Middle Ages onwards. In Bradfield Woods, near Bury St Edmunds in Suffolk, and Wayland Wood near Watton in Norfolk, visitors can see the ancient techniques still being used. These are traditional coppice woods, in which the majority of trees are cut back to a short stump every five to 10 years, to produce a regular crop of straight poles for use as fencing or firewood. The light airy woods of Bradfield and Wayland are strikingly different from the shady environments that we nowadays associate with woodland, and give a good idea of what the medieval woodland landscape would have looked like.

One of the characteristic features of the area of Ancient Countryside is its dispersed pattern of settlement. The villages are strung out, with a multiplicity of isolated farms and small hamlets between them. Many of these farms have strange, archaic names derived from their medieval owners or occupiers. Some are still surrounded by moats which, in the Middle Ages, would have served as a combination of a security and drainage system, a status symbol, and a water supply. The hamlets are often distinguished by names ending in 'end', 'green' or 'street'.

In part, this dispersed settlement pattern derives from that of the Roman period, or even the Iron Age. But in some places, such as Norfolk and north Suffolk, it would appear that the settlement pattern changed considerably in the 12th and 13th centuries. At this time, many houses moved from their original sites near the church, to form straggling lines of cottages around the common. Sometimes the whole village moved, leaving the church isolated. Sometimes only part of it shifted.

The pretty south Norfolk village of Fritton, where the houses were set around an area of common land

At Wacton, Fritton and Morningthorpe in Norfolk, the houses are still set around a central area of common land, but in most places, commons were enclosed in the last century. Where enclosure has taken place, there are often two lines of building. The 19th- and 20th-century houses are built next to the road, while earlier houses are much further back, showing what was the line of the old common edge.

The hamlets and villages of this region are characterised by their old and interesting houses. Many are timber-framed and there are still a lot of thatched buildings. The number of medieval, 16th- and 17th-century houses is indicative of the prosperity and security enjoyed by the farmers of this region in the past.

Planned Countryside

Most of the land in East Anglia has been altered by the activities of man in the past, but only in the area of Ancient Countryside was the basic fabric of the landscape the product of farming in the Middle Ages or earlier. Elsewhere the pattern of fields and roads is much more recent and is known as Planned Countryside. Between the Ancient Countryside of the central and eastern parts, and the Fenland to the west, there is a broad swathe of countryside which was largely shaped in the 18th and 19th centuries (although some parts have been shaped since). This was the land which, in the medieval period, was farmed as open fields.

Under the open field system, there were comparatively few hamlets and isolated farms, and farmers tended to live in compact villages surrounded by large arable fields. The villagers held small strips of land in each of these fields, and the pattern of agricultural exploitation was organised on the basis of communal decisions. Although there were open fields throughout East Anglia in the Middle Ages, it was really only in southern Cambridgeshire, west Suffolk and west Norfolk that a comprehensive system of open field farming was employed. The open field landscape would have formed a very striking contrast to the Ancient Countryside nearby, for there would have been few woods, trees and hedges. The open field village, with its houses clustering around the parish church, would have been isolated amid a vast expanse of unhedged arable land.

On heavier soils, the land was often ploughed to build up a series of low ridges, following the slightly sinuous profile of the open field strips. These ridges seem to have been used to facilitate drainage, and in some areas, where the fields were

Norfolk women open field harvesting, 1922

used for pasture or enclosure, they have survived as ridge and furrow earthworks. With the spread of arable farming in the region since the war, many of these earthworks have been ploughed up, but they can still be seen in some places. There is a fine series in the landscaped park around Wimpole Hall in Cambridgeshire, now managed by the National Trust.

The enclosure of the open field landscape began to take place in the late Middle Ages, but it was really only in the 18th and early 19th centuries that it occurred on a very large scale. As the agricultural environment was reorganised and the land was divided into hedged fields under the control of individual farmers, not only the pattern of property, but often also the network of roads and tracks, was extensively redrawn. As a result, the landscapes produced by the enclosure of open field parishes have a regularity about them which cannot be found in the countryside that evolved gradually. Straight roads and geometric fields are the hallmarks of 18th- and 19th-century enclosures, together with flimsy hawthorn hedges.

Although former open field areas are still characterised by fairly large and compact villages, they now also usually contain a number of isolated farmhouses. After land enclosure had taken place, many of the more prosperous farmers moved out of the villages, and built themselves stout new farmhouses on their newly enclosed land. These farmsteads are very different from the old, rambling, timber-framed and often moated structures that characterise the areas of Ancient Countryside. Their symmetrical form, slate roofs and solid brickwork display their 18th- or 19th- century origins.

Breckland

It was not always the enclosure of open fields that led to the formation of geometric landscapes in the planned countryside. Some were the result of the enclosure of open heathland. The most extensive geometric landscape is the Breckland of Norfolk and Suffolk. This area was densely settled in prehistoric times, and this led to the conversion of the land from deciduous woodland to open heath. At Grime's Graves, 7 miles north-west of Thetford, there is a network of more than 1,700 pits, dug by our neolithic ancestors mining for flint. Probably most of the flint was made into axe heads for felling trees, the land cleared being used for crops. The importance of the area in the Bronze Age is revealed by the numerous round barrows that are still visible in the landscape today.

By the Middle Ages, however, the poor quality of the land ensured that the area was sparsely-

At Thetford Warren, (above), it is still possible to imagine part of the great open forest that once covered Breckland. This was cleared by Neolithic man. The tools he used for this came from the flint mines at nearby Grime's Graves (left and below), probably the most important prehistoric site in East Anglia. Excavations carried out here since 1879 have revealed a mound of levers and pickaxes which are more than 4,000 years old. The site was once the centre of an industry involving 'knapping' (breaking) flints

populated, with villages concentrated on the fringes of the heath and in the valleys of rivers, such as the Lark and the Ouse. The central Breckland was used largely for sheep pasture, and there were numerous rabbit warrens – hence the frequent occurrence of 'Warren' in the place names of this area.

After the medieval period the population declined further. The towers of ruined medieval churches have become a characteristic feature of the area. In the 18th and 19th centuries much of the heathland was enclosed, as attempts were made to extend cultivation. It was at this time that long lines of Scots pine were planted, to shelter the enclosures and to stabilise the light sandy soils.

Much land was not brought under cultivation until the early 20th century, however, when large tracts of heath were turned over to the production of conifers. Nowadays, Forestry Commission plantations dominate the Breckland landscape, but some areas of open heath still survive. The nature reserve at East Wretham is open to the public, but most of the remaining heath is used as a battle-training area by the army.

In recent years East Anglia has become one of the world's most productive farming regions. The contribution of the 20th century to the scenery has been huge arable fields, from which woods and hedges have been removed to make room for enormous machinery. But concern about agricultural surpluses has brought about a change in policy, with farmers being subsidised to 'set aside' land rather than farm in the most productive way. Just what effect this will have on the landscape of East Anglia remains to be seen.

A Paradise for Birdwatchers

East Anglia's reputation varies from that of an arable desert to Britain's chief area of wild-life, with wetlands and rare birds. The truth lies somewhere between the two; certainly there are huge fields of cereals and sugar beet, but parts of the region – both inland and especially by the coast – are truly outstanding for their natural history.

Norfolk

Norfolk's reputation for flatness is exaggerated. Apart from the Fens in the west, and the grazing marshes in the east, much of the county is gently rolling all the way to the marshes, dunes and intertidal flats of the north Norfolk coast.

Cley and Salthouse marshes lie at the eastern end of this stretch of the coast, the whole of which is internationally recognised for its wildlife. A combination of reed-beds, grazing marshes and shallow lagoons makes the Norfolk Naturalists' Trust (NNT) reserve at Cley one of the top birdwatching places in Britain. The reed-beds shelter breeding bitterns and bearded tits and there

The crossbill, a parrot-like finch, is resident in some of Norfolk's conifer plantations. Common seals inhabit the Wash in great numbers, and are also frequently seen off Blakeney Point

is a growing colony of avocets in the 'scrapes' – shallow, artificial lagoons. The reserve's location on the north coast, where East Anglia juts out into the North Sea, must account for the presence of the many birds that may be seen here, as they move down Britain's east coast in autumn or fly directly across the sea from Scandinavia. The variety of waders can be astonishing. Between July and September, wood and curlew sandpipers, spotted redshanks and little stints are regular visitors to the area. Rarer waders, like Kentish plovers and Temminck's stints, are annual visitors. Wintering species are equally varied and include snow buntings, which feed among the seedheads of the yellow-horned poppies on the shingle ridge.

Just to the west lies Blakeney Point, a shingle spit still growing westwards, which is remarkable for its wildlife. Access to this National Trust property can be gained either by walking along the shingle ridge from Cley Eye, or by boat from Morston. Both common and grey seals breed here, and there are large colonies of Sandwich, common and little terns. The Point also attracts migrants, with 'falls' of bluethroats and wrynecks in most autumns.

The woods at Wells-next-the-Sea, mid-way along the north Norfolk coast, are largely of Corsican pine, planted to stabilise the sand dunes. In 1984 and 1985, the car park by the woods became famous when parrot crossbills bred here, drinking in puddles a stone's throw away from an ice-cream van. Sadly, the colonisation was short-lived. Sometimes the birches and pines are seemingly full of birds, not least in autumn, when scores of blackcaps, goldcrests and redwings are outnumbered only by birdwatchers, searching for the latest rarity.

There are fine saltmarshes at Brancaster and on nearby Scolt Head. The latter is a shingle island not unlike Blakeney Point; like the Point, it also has large tern colonies. However, access across the creeks is tricky, and a local guide is essential.

In recent years Titchwell Marsh reserve, run by the Royal Society for the Protection of Birds (RSPB), has rivalled Cley in its variety of birds.

Marsh harriers breed here, and can be seen quartering the reed-beds beyond the freshwater and brackish lagoons. The peaty remains of an ancient forest litter the foreshore, which is a good haunt for estuary waders like turnstone, sanderling and knot.

The coast turns south into the Wash at Holme next the Sea, and here, at the western end of the north Norfolk coast, lies Holme Bird Observatory. Like many bird observatories it can be windswept and empty of birds one day, and full of migrants the next. In 1987 black-winged stilts raised their young here, the first successful breeding of this species in Britain since 1945.

As well as having the distinction of being East Anglia's only seaside resort that faces west, Hunstanton also has magnificent chalk cliffs. Fulmars nest here, and the cliffs are a good spot for winter birdwatching, especially seaduck like eiders and scoters in the mouth of the Wash.

Great numbers of waders can be found in the Wash from August until May. The best place to see them is the RSPB reserve at Snettisham, where thousands come to roost at high tide on shingle banks and islands in the gravel pits by the seawall. Waders moving ahead of the incoming tide at sunset here are one of the most unforgettable wildlife sights in East Anglia.

The Broads

The Norfolk and Suffolk Broads are not as natural as they seem, for they were created by peat-digging in medieval times. They have deteriorated dramatically since World War II, the cause being mainly poor water quality. There has also been a similar deterioration in the once vast grazing marshes of the Broads, as they have been drained and ploughed for cereals.

However, outstanding areas of wildlife do still remain. The waterways and reed-beds at Hickling and Horsey are probably the best in the Broads; in June it is easy to spot swallowtail butterflies and marsh harriers here. The problems of Broadland are well-described in the NNT's Broadland Conservation Centre at Ranworth. Nearby, a solution has been found at Cockshoot Broad, which has been isolated from the polluted river, and had years of accumulated mud pumped out;

Egyptian geese on the lake at Holkham Hall; the Swallowtail butterfly survives only in fens surrounding the Norfolk Broads

now the waterlilies and dragonflies are returning.

Two good places to visit in Broadland are How Hill, near Ludham, and Strumpshaw Fen, east of Norwich. Both provide a variety of broadland habitats: open water, fen, reed-bed, grazing marsh and carr woodland. Two of the chief attractions at How Hill are the view and the swallowtail butterflies in the formal gardens by the house, now used as a study centre. Strumpshaw Fen RSPB reserve is not only a good place for birds like marsh harriers and Cetti's warblers, but also an outstanding area for fen plants like marsh helleborine and grass of Parnassus. At Buckenham Marshes, adjacent to Strumpshaw, there are thousands of wigeon in winter, and the only regular flock of bean geese in England.

Away from the coast and Broads there are also many fine areas for naturalists. Try visiting a few commons: Syderstone for natterjack toads; Foulden Common for nightingales; Roydon, near King's Lynn, for wintering birds of prey; and New Buckenham for green-winged orchids.

The stately homes of Norfolk have fine grounds. Access to the beech woods at the National Trust's Felbrigg Hall near Cromer, and to the footpaths round Mannington Hall near Aylsham, is no problem. Holkham Hall has a herd of fallow deer. There are also Egyptian and Canada geese on the lake there, and hawfinches are often seen under the beeches by the entrance gate.

Breckland

In the heart of East Anglia, straddling the Suffolk and Norfolk border, lies Breckland – often known as the Brecks. The sandy soil and climate of dry summers and cold winters makes this area unique in Britain. The Brecks are now dominated by the conifers of Thetford Forest. These have their own special wildlife: crossbills and coal tits, along with the last remaining red squirrels in East Anglia; roe deer and red deer, fallow deer and muntjac also live here. The cleared forestry areas attract woodlarks and nightjars. The full range of forestry habitats can be enjoyed on the Forestry Commission's bird trail from Santon Downham.

Away from the forest, the heaths are sometimes heather, sometimes grass and sometimes lichen-dominated. The biggest heath – the army-run Stanford 'battle area' – is out of bounds, but others, such as Cavenham and Knettishall Heaths in Suffolk, are nature reserves. East Wretham Heath in Norfolk (NNT) has a good range of Breckland habitats, including meres with fluctuating water levels. But to see the classic Breckland bird, the stone-curlew, Weeting Heath is the place to visit. They are often inactive during the day, being largely nocturnal, but their eerie cry can be heard at night. They may fly many miles, often to sheep pastures, in search of earthworms and dung beetles.

Suffolk

Inland Suffolk has, by and large, a pleasantly undulating landscape with many areas of interest to the naturalist. The boulder clay woodlands of west Suffolk, Cambridgeshire and north-east Essex are noted for their oxlips. Cowslips and primroses may also be found flowering in April and early May, so beware their hybrid, the 'false oxlip'. There is a particularly fine group of ancient woodlands at Bradfield, where the ancient coppice rotation has been reintroduced by the Suffolk Wildlife Trust. Over the border in Cambridgeshire, Hayley Wood is the finest of the oxlip and bluebell woods, and a Cambridgeshire Wildlife Trust reserve.

The Suffolk coast, which, like north Norfolk, is an official Heritage Coast, has its fair share of famous reserves, and is every bit as charming as Norfolk. Between Benacre Broad in the north, and the Stour Estuary in the south, there is a string of superb wetlands, including the internationally-famed Minsmere RSPB reserve. Mainly inland, but adjacent to the coast in parts, are the Suffolk heaths, known as the Sandlings, much reduced from their former extent, but still worth a visit.

Blaxhall Common and the heaths at Hollesley are good places to listen for nightjars, or to look for silver-studded blue butterflies.

Walberswick National Nature Reserve, south of picturesque Southwold, has some heathland, but is better known for its vast reed-beds. Westwood Lodge gives good views over these, and is one of the best places in East Anglia to see birds of prey, including marsh harriers that breed here, and hen harriers that winter here. Minsmere, near Westleton, also has reed-beds, heath and woodland, but its greatest attractions are artificial lagoons with islands, known as the Scrape. This area attracts an astonishing range of wildfowl and waders at all seasons, in particular the RSPB's emblem bird, the avocet, which recolonised in Britain here, and at Havergate Island nearby, just after the war. Havergate is part of Orford Ness, a shingle spit not unlike Blakeney Point in Norfolk. Avocets overwinter here, whereas they usually leave other parts of East Anglia to go to the milder estuaries of south-west England.

The Suffolk estuaries have their attractions, but the biggest numbers of birds are found in the south of the county, on the Orwell and the Stour. Sadly, the Orwell is threatened by port expansion at Felixstowe. Also at Felixstowe is Landguard Common, where the bird observatory often records rare migrant birds. Wild flowers on the shingle include the scarce sea pea and the edible – but protected – sea kale.

Suffolk rarities: Breckland is one of only two places in Britain where the Military Orchid flowers (below), while in late May the only known British haunt of the Fen Raft Spider (bottom), is found at the nature reserve at Redgrave and Lopham Fen

The extremely rare Fen Violet was recently re-discovered at Wicken Fen. The Norfolk Hawker Dragonfly is found only on a couple of Norfolk Broads

The Suffolk-Essex border runs down the middle of the Stour Estuary, then inland along the River Stour, through 'Constable Country' in Dedham Vale. The Estuary is one of East Anglia's most charming, and is still largely undeveloped. There are various access points both in Suffolk and Essex, and one recommended route is through the sweet chestnut coppice of Stour Wood to Copperas Bay, not far from Harwich. Particulary special among the waders of the Stour are the black-tailed godwits; although they are strictly-speaking wintering birds, their numbers build up from July onwards. Pintail, wigeon and brent geese feature prominently among the Estuary's wildfowl, and there are scores of mute swans which feed by the mills at Mistley.

Essex
As it is closer to London, Essex has more urban development than elsewhere in East Anglia, but some fine woodland remains, including the Royal Forests of Epping and Hatfield. Epping's old pollarded trees are superb, and the elusive hawfinch can be found near hornbeams. Hatfield Forest, near Bishop's Stortford, has many ancient woodland flowers, including stinking hellebore and bird's-nest orchid. Access to these and other Essex woods is generally easy. There are many country parks and open-access woodlands, notably Belfairs Wood (Southend), Thorndon Park (Brentwood) and Hockley Wood (3 miles north-west of Rochford).

Only small areas of heathland remain; the largest, at 62 acres, is at Tiptree. A curiosity here is an abandoned football pitch, which has reverted to heath. The Danbury Ridge has some heath, especially on Danbury Common, but it is mainly covered by woodland, including hornbeam on Lingwood Common and in Blake's Wood. The Roman river valley south of Colchester has an attractive mixture of heathy areas, woodland, and wetland habitats.

Essex's two huge reservoirs at Abberton and Hanningfield inevitably attract many wildfowl. Abberton is the better of the two, and the best viewing places here are the road causeways.

The estuaries of Essex are head and shoulders above the rest of the county in terms of wildlife interest. All have large numbers of brent geese: Essex is at the centre of the limited world winter distribution of the dark-bellied subspecies. Some feed on the estuaries, especially on eel grass, but they also come over the seawall regularly on to winter cereals, where once there was pasture. Coming south from the Stour there is Hamford Water, which is generally difficult to reach except at Walton-on-the-Naze. The scrub here attracts many migrants. The Colne Estuary includes the Essex Naturalists' Trust headquarters at Fingringhoe Wick, where old gravel workings have been developed into a superb nature reserve. Here, a large range of dragonflies has been recorded, and a new wader 'scrape' attracts passage birds. Nightingales sing in the thorn and willow scrub.

The Blackwater Estuary competes with the Stour for all-round interest as far as wildfowl and waders are concerned. It also has the best-remaining coastal grazing marsh, at the RSPB's Old Hall Marshes. Winter also brings hunting hen harriers, short-eared owls, and twite flocks on the saltmarshes. Maplin Sands became famous briefly, during the third London airport controversy, but was eventually saved for the birds; it is, however, out of bounds, along with Foulness Island, due to Ministry of Defence use. Finally, the Thames is immensely important for its wintering birds. The Southend Flats can be viewed from Southend pier, but the most dramatic sights can be seen further west, either from Two Tree Island or from the pubs and cockle sheds at Old Leigh. It is not unusual to see as many as 10,000 brent geese here in late autumn, feeding on the flats, or swirling in majestic flocks.

Cambridgeshire

Cambridgeshire lies inland, and away from its intensively-cultivated areas there are some of the best wetlands in England. In the south of the county, springs run through the chalk to feed the old watercress beds at Fowlmere, attracting water rails and kingfishers. The Ouse Valley around Huntingdon has many attractive watermeadows and gravel pits, the best of which are the ancient Lammas meadow (private land which could be used as common pasture from Lammas to spring) at Port Holme, Godmanchester, and the pits at Little Paxton.

Most of the fens in the north of the county have been drained, leaving mile after mile of rich black soil. Among the best of the remaining wetland is the National Trust's Wicken Fen, which has been kept wet only with difficulty, as the surrounding land has been drained. The mixture of reed-bed, scrub and fen is botanically very rich, and the birds found here include a winter hen harrier roost.

In order to prevent the lower-than-sea-level fenland from flooding, there are two large washlands by the Rivers Nene and Ouse. These are flooded with surplus water, mainly in winter. The resulting wetlands are outstanding for wintering wildfowl. In summer, breeding waders like snipe and redshank can be seen on the grazing marshes. At the Nene Washes, east of Peterborough, birdwatching is difficult without disturbing the birds, but it is much easier at the Ouse Washes, thanks to the reserves of the Cambridgeshire Wildlife Trust, the RSPB and the Wildfowl Trust. In winter, wigeon can be seen in tens of thousands, and there is no better place in East Anglia to see pintails. But above all, it is the wintering swans that make these washes so valuable and exciting. Whooper swans come here from Iceland in their hundreds, and some 3,000 Bewick's swans from Siberia represent about 10 per cent of the world population. These flock on to surrounding farmland during the day, but large numbers concentrate at Welney Wildfowl Trust, just over the border in Norfolk. Black-tailed godwits and ruffs have both returned here, to breed in Britain, but sadly, late spring floods in recent years have led to rather erratic breeding success. Nonetheless, the Ouse Washes have probably the finest wetland of the region, making a fine conclusion to a tour of East Anglia in any season.

Left: the short-eared owl is often abroad in daylight, and hunts its prey on the open heaths and rough grasslands of East Anglia. Wildlife and RSPB reserves abound in the region. The black-tailed godwit frequents wet-meadow nature reserves, such as the Ouse Washes in Cambridgeshire and the Welney Wildfowl Trust in Norfolk (bottom)

East Anglian Churches

It is said that one can see the towers of 60 Suffolk churches from the top of the church at Bradfield St George, near Bury St Edmunds. Although this may be a slight exaggeration, it does point to one of the most striking aspects of the East Anglian landscape. Norfolk and Suffolk have well over 1,100 medieval churches between them; Essex, which was rather more sparsely settled in early times, has slightly fewer. Cambridgeshire has more than 100 churches, among them some unique treasures.

There are many parish churches, and two of England's greatest cathedrals, in the region, as well as some haunting reminders of the great wealth of the monastic houses. The Cathedral Church of the Holy and Undivided Trinity at Norwich is the crown in that city of striking churches. Early in the 7th century the See of East Anglia had Dunwich (Suffolk) as its headquarters; it was moved 50 years later to Elmham, on the borders of the Waveney, which forms the boundary between Suffolk and Norfolk. It was not until 1095 that the See moved to Norwich, and Bishop Herbert de Losinga began building the Norman Cathedral. The piers of the nave stand like great oak trees, their branches formed by the superb vaulting dating from the 15th and 16th centuries; this replaced an earlier roof destroyed by fire. The rounded apse houses the oldest bishop's throne in use in any English cathedral, two ancient stones which pre-date the building by at least three centuries. The massive Norman tower supports a 13th-century spire, the tallest in England after that of Salisbury. Spires are something of a rarity in East Anglia; the round flint towers of the small Saxon and Norman churches, or the flint and stone flushwork towers of the 14th and 15th centuries, are a much more familiar sight.

Ely Cathedral does not have a spire, but it does have a famous 'lantern', which crowns the great church and can be seen for miles around, from anywhere in the fens. Begun in 1083, it took over two centuries to complete.

Even with all the resources of the East-Anglian woodland at their disposal, its 14th-century builders still had difficulty in finding timbers sufficiently long and thick to construct the inner tower; they even had to modify the design, to adapt it for the use of timbers that were shorter than required.

Two of the country's greatest cathedrals are to be found in East Anglia. At Norwich (left), the golden weathercock soars 315ft above the ground, and there are more than 60 carved Tudor misericords in the choir (below). The 'Cathedral of the Fens' at Ely (above) dominates the surrounding countryside for miles, representing a superb architectural achievement of the middle ages. The Octagon is an engineering masterpiece in its own right

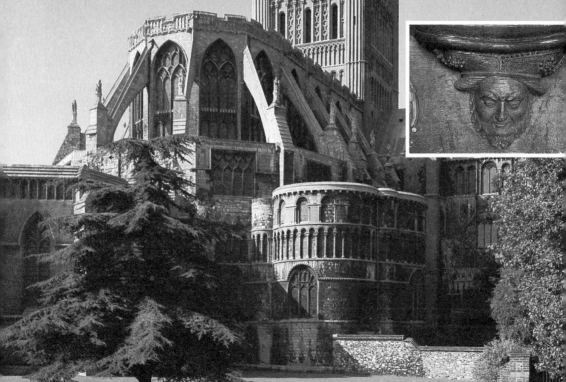

In Colchester it is worth seeking out the ruins of the great priory church of St Botolph, the first English house of the Canons Regular of St Augustine, whose influence was widespread in East Anglia in medieval times. In Colchester, too, the Saxon tower of Holy Trinity dates from about the year 1000. The great abbey at Bury St Edmunds has little left to remind us of its Norman glory, apart from a bell tower at its entrance, but some idea of the beauty it must once have had can be found in perhaps the most spectacular of East Anglia's monastic ruins, the Cluniac priory at Castle Acre (Norfolk), which has retained its delicate Norman arcading on the west front. Today, though, all we can expect to see of most of the great monastic houses are ruins, and sadly, ruins of parish churches are also not uncommon, particularly in Norfolk. Many churches were abandoned in earlier centuries, sometimes for reasons of economy, and sometimes because of depopulation. Their ruins still stand, adding a romantic, if melancholy, atmosphere to the East Anglian scenery.

The first churches

After Christianity was brought to the region by St Felix at Dunwich, St Botolph at Iken, and the Irish mystic St Fursey at Burgh Castle in the 7th century, individuals, freemen, or groups of two or three, some of them probably of quite modest means, built churches on their own land to serve the local community. Though many of these churches have been remodelled over the centuries, their location has nearly always remained the same.

St Andrew's Church, at Greensted (Essex) is one of the most famous early churches. It has a nave fashioned out of vertical half tree-trunks, the rounded part forming the outside of the wall, the flat surface within. They have been dated to the mid-9th century, and were already almost 200 years old in 1013, when the body of St Edmund, king and patron saint of East Anglia, rested here on its way to London. The body had been removed from its shrine at Bury St Edmunds, and taken to London to keep it safe from Viking marauders. Essex has an even earlier church: the 7th-century St Peter's-at-the-Wall at Bradwell, built across the ruins of a 3rd-century Roman fort in what was once a romantic, if marshy situation, but which is now dominated by a nuclear power station.

The ruins of 12th-century St Botolph's Priory, Colchester, destroyed during a siege in 1648

Compared with these rare survivals, late Saxon and Norman churches seem quite modern. They predominate in areas where wealthy patronage, or late medieval industry, did not provide funds for modernisation in the 15th and 16th centuries. North Suffolk and the remoter parts of Norfolk have some delightful examples of these simple little buildings, notably at Haddiscoe on the Waveney marshes. The church here also boasts a magnificent piece of Norman sculpture over the south door, as well as later wall paintings inside. St Edmund's Church at neighbouring Fritton contains a Norman version of the martyrdom of its namesake over the altar. Further south, on the River Stour, the delightful little church of Wissington has a splendidly carved south door, near-contemporary paintings of St Francis and some pleasantly odd woodwork.

The unique Saxon church at Greensted (bottom) is the oldest wooden church in the world. Haddiscoe (below), is famous for its round Saxon tower, which has three bands. Its battlements are decorated with flushwork

Seventy angels are carved in the great oak hammerbeam roof at St Wendreda's, March

An example of stained glass in perhaps the finest of the wool churches, Long Melford

The great medieval churches

It was in the later medieval period that some of East Anglia's most impressive churches were built, as the region prospered on the profits of wool and other trades. Where there was access to water power, for example in the Stour Valley, (where the river ran strongly over a clean bed), the opportunity to develop a highly successful cloth industry was seized and exploited. It is in these areas that many of the most famous churches are situated. Everyone knows of the richness of the churches at Lavenham and Long Melford (Suffolk), where wealthy clothiers could afford to import expensive stone, which was mixed with local flint to produce buildings with sparkling flushwork decoration. At the coast, (where fish, rather than cloth, provided wealth), or on the marshes, (where lush fields for grazing enabled dairy farmers to prosper), there are some superb 15th-century churches. The brilliant light over the marshes on a fine day makes the church of Walpole St Peter (Norfolk) one of the most dramatic in England. The interior houses treasures from all periods: marvellous benches of the 15th and 17th centuries, a 16th-century font and a Jacobean pulpit. Not all churches are so richly endowed, but there is no such thing as a dull East Anglian church.

Splendid timber roofs of the 14th, 15th and early 16th centuries are often found, particularly in Suffolk and Norfolk. Any church with a clerestory (giving it nave windows above the aisles), is likely to contain a beautiful roof, lit in daylight from beneath. Single and double hammerbeam roofs were often ornamented with angels; in spite of Puritan attempts at destruction, many still exist. Examples may be seen at Blythburgh (Suffolk), and March (Cambridgeshire). At Needham Market in Suffolk, the little church has a daringly constructed roof of astonishing height and airiness. These breathtaking pieces of architecture are often found in heavy-clay areas, where the oak woodlands were carefully managed to produce standard trees for beams and other large pieces of timber.

Evidence of aristocratic patronage is not particularly common in East Anglia, which in medieval times was essentially an area of small estates. However, in north Essex and south Suffolk, the influence of the de Vere family, the Earls of Oxford, is apparent. Their distinctive crest, showing a star or mullet, can be seen on the churches attached to the many manor houses that they owned; at their family seat, in Castle Hedingham and at Earls Colne in Essex, and at Lavenham and East Bergholt in Suffolk. The

Howards, Dukes of Norfolk, built perhaps the most beautiful tower of all on the Stour Valley ridge at Stoke-by-Nayland (Suffolk). It has rosy brickwork with deep window embrasures, and pinnacles, which, from a distance, give it the appearance of a great crown. The Howards also owned Framlingham Castle, and St Michael's Church there is one of the grandest in Suffolk, full of the tombs belonging to these rather unattractive patrons.

Details and decorations

Some of the smaller churches have a more immediate appeal than their great, almost cathedral-like counterparts. The tiny chantry chapel at Gipping (Suffolk) built by the Tyrrel family, for the singing of masses for the dead, provides one of the most perfect examples of flint and stone flushwork anywhere.

Many otherwise simple churches are treasured for their wall paintings, or their rood-screens, such as those surviving at Ranworth (Norfolk) or Bramfield (Suffolk). Others have richly painted roofs, with light shining through the brilliant but subtle colours of the stained glass windows set high in their walls.

St Stephen's Chapel in Bures, Suffolk, a small thatched 13th-century building, contains monuments of the de Veres, Earls of Oxford

It is often said that medieval church decoration was gaudy; but this is not so. The colour came from nature, from the earth, plants and animals, and was incomparably richer and gentler than the often crude restorations of the 20th century, even when the subject matter was harrowing, as in the 15th-century painting of the Last Judgement at Wenhaston (Suffolk). This is an example of one of the few surviving 'dooms' which were painted over the chancel arch in every church.

There is also plenty of evidence, in the leafy, carved capitals, and in the misericords of fabulous beasts, of a delight in nature. Pagan elements creep in too. Round the bases of many eight-sided fonts stand the so-called 'woodwoses', the wild men of the woods, covered in leaves and holding stone clubs. Cheerful-looking lions often appear, and the Green Man himself (perhaps a cousin of the woodwose) can often be spotted, with leaves growing from his face, among the delicately carved plants and birds.

'Parliamentary Visitors'

East Anglia has always been close to regions of religious dissent. Dissent came from the Continent, and also from the University of Cambridge. After the Reformation, there was plenty of enthusiasm for the removal of anything considered to be even faintly 'idolatrous'. The worst damage was caused by Cromwell's 'Parliamentary Visitors', commissioners appointed by Parliament, and accompanied by bands of thugs, who undertook an orgy of official destruction. William Dowsing, of Stratford St Mary, Suffolk, even kept a journal in which he gleefully recorded what had been destroyed in each church.

1643/4 ORFORD Jan the 25th We brake down 28 superstitious Pictures (stained glass): and took up 11 popish Inscriptions in Brass; and gave order for digging up the Steps, and taking of 2 Crosses of the Steeple of the Church, and one of the Chancel, in all 4.

In spite of Parliamentarian frenzy, East Anglia is still an excellent place for the brass-rubbing enthusiast. In Suffolk, there are good examples of brasses at Stoke-by-Nayland and at Acton (where a fine brass of Sir Robert de Bures may be found),

while there are superb 14th-century examples at St Margaret's, King's Lynn.

The later churches

Most of East Anglia's parish churches date from the medieval period. There are very few from the 17th and 18th centuries; the most distinguished religious buildings of this period tend to be non-conformist meeting houses and chapels, which can be found in almost all East Anglian villages and which reflect the strong tendency towards dissent among the inhabitants over the past 400 years. The Unitarian chapel at Ipswich is an 18th-century building of great distinction, as are the Congregational chapels of Walpole and Wrentham. In Norwich, the 17th-century Old Meeting House and the 18th-century Octagon chapel, admired by Wesley, are among some of the most interesting buildings in that great city. There are plenty of Victorian chapels, too, around the region.

In the 20th century, little has been contributed to church building in East Anglia, although John Betjeman admired the 'Art Nouveau' of New St Mary's at Great Warley (Essex), and the early 20th-century restoration work of Sir Ninian Comper on rood-screens at Orsett (Essex), Eye (Suffolk) and Mundford (Norfolk).

Try to imagine the East Anglian landscape without its churches. They are so much a part of it, and so closely identified with it, that the very idea is ridiculous. It was not for nothing that it became the custom to speak of 'Silly (*seely*, an old word meaning blessed or holy) Suffolk'. At any turn in the road, a traveller in the region may expect to see a tower of simple flint, or a more magnificent one of flushwork, surrounded by houses with thatched or pantiled roofs. All the churches are worth visiting; in some there will be breathtaking surprises. Their churchyards, alone, are immensely enjoyable. Sometimes they are small nature reserves in their own right, full of wild flowers and ancient trees. In the rush to get from one place to another nowadays it would be a tragedy if these marvellous buildings and their delightful surroundings were overlooked.

The ornate chancel of St Mary the Virgin, Great Warley

Traditional Buildings

East Anglia is essentially a domestic area of England. In Suffolk particularly, the countryside is sprinkled with small timber-framed farmhouses. Wherever one looks, one sees steeply pitched roofs, some still thatched as they originally were, others with red or black pantiles, the walls plastered, or occasionally washed, in traditional terracotta 'pink' or ochre.

Stone is a rarity in the eastern counties. Flint, the most common form, is more familiar in churches than in domestic buildings, though Norfolk has many delightful examples combined with red brick. Cambridgeshire has some limestone, and close to Cambridge there is also a belt of sandstone. Cambridge has a complete history of English architecture, with more timber-framed buildings than are at first obvious.

Timber-framed houses

There is an enormous legacy of timber-framed houses in Suffolk and north Essex. These are often the most striking feature of the East Anglian village. Not all are as famous or as remarkable as Lavenham in Suffolk, which was without equal in the days when it was a prosperous industrial town, the 15th-century equivalent of the great 19th-century cloth-making towns of the north. Lavenham's buildings have survived without modernisation because of its industrial collapse, whereas other small towns, such as Dedham in Essex, which were not so dependent on the vagaries of fashion, continued to prosper well into the 18th century. Dedham's High Street has as many medieval houses as Lavenham's, but they can only be indentified by looking upwards. Behind the

Orford Castle is built, in part, from local septaria

charming Georgian façades of brick or plaster, the tell-tale steep roofs of the old hall houses are visible – inside, some of them have scarcely changed since the 16th century.

Suffolk and Essex still have hundreds of these early houses, many dating from the mid-14th century, though nowadays much altered internally. They are easily recognised by their roof lines; a classic example is Valley Farm at Flatford in Suffolk, which is now part of the Flatford Mill Field Centre.

The main building houses the hall, originally open to the roof, its crown post and rafters blackened by soot from the days before the chimney was inserted, when the fire lay on a simple hearth in the centre of the room. At one end of the hall are the buttery and pantry, and a primitive staircase leads to a bedroom above. At the other end is a cross-wing, with a tiny parlour and, above, a bedroom for the master and mistress. This has a jetty projecting over the lower storey, and a little shuttered spy-hole, looking down on the hall. In the eastern counties, houses were built to plan using timber from the great oak woodlands on the clay land, and wattle-and-daub.

Lavenham's remarkable Guildhall, (left), was built in 1539, whereas Valley Farm at Flatford (below), dates from the mid-14th century

Moats and manors

A glance at the Ordnance Survey maps of East Anglia reveals an astonishing number of moated sites. A moat was an essential part of a house, particularly if it stood on heavy clay. Keeping unwanted visitors out was a good reason for its construction, but more importantly a moat drained the site, provided daub for the infilling of walls, acted as source of water supply, provided fresh fish for consumption, and prevented stray animals from coming too close. The trouble taken to build larger moats also suggests that they were status symbols. Hundreds of moated houses survive in Essex and Suffolk alone, many of them small manor houses. East Anglian villages were often divided up in to areas controlled by several different manors. The original manor house was often called Old Hall; the others Over Hall, Nether Hall, Wood Hall, or any number of similar names. The word 'manor' was, however, rarely used. This type of house was, of course, only available to the newly rising middle classes, farmers and merchants who had enough entrepreneurial spirit to take advantage of the economic opportunities East Anglia afforded. A wealthy farmer might have had a fairly simple house, whereas a merchant might have been able to afford more elaborate carvings on ceiling joists

Three perfect examples of the ancient East Anglian art of plaster decoration known as pargeting: in Saffron Walden (right), Ipswich (below) and Clare (bottom)

and exterior woodwork. However, nothing is left of the houses of the poor. Most of them lived in conditions of unbelievable discomfort, in what were little more than mud huts, thatched with straw or heather, which probably had to be rebuilt every few years.

By the 16th century timber was scarcer and more expensive. This was hardly surprising, though, for a yeoman farmhouse of comparatively modest size needed about 300 mature oaks for completion. Plaster began to be used to keep out draughts in older houses, and as a camouflage for inferior and less expensive framing. 'Pargeting', a form of plaster decoration varying from simple 'combing' in swirling patterns to elaborate modelling, now became fashionable, particularly in areas of north Essex and south Suffolk. Some examples of elaborate plasterwork modelling from this period can be seen on the Ancient House in Ipswich, and in Nethergate Street, in Clare, Suffolk.

As timber became expensive, brick became cheaper and more easily available. Little Wenham Hall in Suffolk, a small fortified manor house of the 13th century, is the earliest brick-built house in England. Until the Tudor period, only the gentry

Many great houses are to be found in East Anglia. One of the finest Norfolk manors, Oxburgh Hall (far left) has been owned by the Bedingfield family since it was built. The 1809 engraving (left) shows its massive 15th-century gatehouse. The splendid 16th-century Paycock's House in Coggeshall (below) is now owned by the NT

could afford to build in brick. The Cambridge colleges used local brick in the 15th century, which was cheaper than importing limestone. Norfolk has a number of early brick houses, of which Oxburgh Hall (1482) is the most famous. Here, there are clear indications of the proximity of the Low Countries. Similar influences can be seen at Deanery Towers, at Hadleigh, which dates from about the same period, and at Layer Marney in Essex, built some 30 years later. Black and red diamond-patterning (diapering), moulded brick and stepped gables are characteristic of these buildings, and of many others. All around the East Anglian coast are English versions of the buildings that cloth merchants and fish dealers must have seen on their trips across the North Sea at this time.

By the 17th century nearly every town and village had its own tile and brick kilns. According to the type of clay used, and the method of production, there were great variations in colour: red and white in Essex, Suffolk and Norfolk, yellow and plum in Cambridgeshire. Townsfolk who suffered devastating fires in areas where old timber-framed houses stood cheek-by-jowl, were eager to rebuild in safer materials. Beccles, which was devastated by fire in 1586, rebuilt many houses in handsome red brick.

Norfolk is a county of brick-built houses. Here, by the 17th century, small manors were often amalgamated to make sizeable estates, and the old timber-framed houses were replaced by new buildings. There are also innumerable handsome halls on a slightly bigger scale, but which are not large enough to qualify as stately homes.

Great houses
Of all the eastern counties, Norfolk is the best for great houses of the 15th to 18th centuries. Blickling, built by Robert Lyminge (who also worked at Hatfield House), was constructed in the 1620s. In its first two years of building, more than one and a half million bricks were used, and £5,400 was spent on materials alone – a considerable sum by 17th-century standards. In the second half of the 18th century the house was

extensively altered to the design of William Ivory, a Norwich architect. Another Norwich man, William Wilkins, was responsible for the plasterwork; the beautiful park was designed much later by Humphrey Repton (1752-1818).

Oxburgh, Blickling and Felbrigg can claim to be true East Anglian houses, however much they may have been inspired by fashionable examples from other parts of England, and from Europe. This is not the case with two great Palladian houses of Norfolk; Houghton, the seat of Sir Robert Walpole, the first Prime Minister of England, and Holkham, which was improved by Thomas William Coke, the great agriculturalist. These houses could have been built almost anywhere in England. Two lovely 18th-century Cambridgeshire houses, Peckover near Wisbech, and Wimpole Hall, near Orwell, seem to have closer links with the land on which they were built. Essex has few examples of Palladian architecture. Its larger houses date from earlier times: Ingatestone Hall and Layer Marney are from the Tudor period, while Audley End near Saffron Walden is a superb Jacobean mansion. On a much smaller scale, Paycocke's, at Coggeshall, provides an excellent example of a merchant's house of the 1550s, with its magnificent panelling and woodcarving.

A legacy from the past
Smaller 18th-century houses are easy to find. In that century, white brick became extremely fashionable, partly because it was harder-wearing. It was, however, more expensive than other materials. Inevitably it became something of a status symbol, and it is not uncommon to see a white brick frontage, with sides faced in cheaper red brick. In later examples, slate was imported as a modish replacement for the warm red of local pantiles, but in the early years of the 18th century, slate was often used decoratively with red brick, to sparkling effect. Sherman's Hall at Dedham is a perfect example; the body of the façade is constructed in white brick, the sash windows are surrounded by the most delicate working of red, and, in the centre, there is a white classical

The 166-year-old tower windmill at Cley next the Sea dominates the pretty village. The flint cottages at Sheringham, Norfolk, (below left) and weatherboard cottages at Burnham-on-Crouch, Essex, (below right) are characteristic local buildings

doorcase. Above the door, a deep red-brick niche, one of the distinctive features of the house, shows the play of light and shadow. This is lacking in the otherwise distinguished present-day revival buildings that abound in Dedham.

The pretty waterfront towns of Essex – Wivenhoe, Brightlingsea and Burnham-on-Crouch – have charming examples of white-painted clapboard cottages, a style which never seemed to find favour in Norfolk and Suffolk, where boarding, usually painted black, appears to have been used only for barns, mills and workshops.

East Anglians of the past might have found it difficult to understand the modern enthusiasm for their workplaces; the idea that they were picturesque would have probably astonished them. After all, it took the genius of Constable to persuade us that a mill was a beautiful building, and it was precisely this romantic attitude to every-day life that his contemporaries scoffed at. But to us, the great black barns, with their thatched or pantiled roofs, are as beautiful as the moated farmhouses, and we are reluctant to see them disappear.

East Anglia's social and commercial past has left us some wonderful buildings: the Guildhalls of Lavenham and King's Lynn, the almshouses and charity schools, the maltings, corn-exchanges, assembly rooms and theatres. There are even some fine workhouses. Stow Lodge, at Stowmarket, one of the earliest, is as elegant externally as the houses of many 18th-century men of property. What went on inside was a different story.

All of these were built by local men, in local materials. Recently there have been great improvements in the way such buildings have been conserved and cared for. No-one today would countenance the extraordinary restoration that

Thaxted Guildhall underwent in 1910, when plaster was removed and a new 'medievalising' carried out. There are plenty of architects and conservationists who can advise on restoration and sympathetic conversion, and now scarcely a house stands neglected. No-one, however, can exemplify the East Anglian house as well as Constable. In *Cottage in a Cornfield* there is a tiny, ochre-washed house, with a steeply pitched thatch, standing alone in the fields under a bright blue sky. This scene is common in East Anglia, even today.

Norfolk reed

Thatching has its own distinctive style in East Anglia, as in other parts of the country. Norfolk reed, grown on the fens and marshes of Broadland, is considered the best material for thatching, although wheat-straw is still the most widely used material in other parts of the country, as demand for Norfolk reed exceeds supply. The reeds are cut in standing water in winter, often in snow and ice, which makes the reed-beds firmer to walk on. A good reed roof can last for as long as 60 years. In East Anglia, thatching is used not only for houses and barns, but also for churches. In Norfolk, the reeds used in thatching produce steeply pitched roofs with sharp angles and heavy ridges. In some parts of Essex, wheat-straw is used for thatching, giving roofs a softer, more flowing appearance.

Gainsborough, Constable and Others

Spend two fine days in East Anglia and, even without a specialist knowledge of painting, you will find yourself responding to the brilliance of the light and the enormous expanse of sky. You will also get some inkling of the excitement that impelled two of the world's greatest painters to transform the history of art in this part of England. Long before the time of Gainsborough and Constable, though, artists, wood carvers, stonemasons and stained-glass craftsmen had been at work in the area. Many of them were based in Norwich, producing the works that made Norfolk and Suffolk churches among the richest and loveliest in Europe.

After the Reformation there seem to have been few native-born artists working in East Anglia, although there were a number of local wall-painters and plasterers of varying ability. A number of patrons commissioned monuments by sculptors from other parts of England. Some of these works were very fine, especially those by Nicholas Stone, Master Mason to Charles I, who executed several church commissions in Norfolk, Suffolk and Essex, as well as contributing to the decorations in the great house at Audley End (Essex). Although there must have been some competent painters working in the eastern counties throughout the 17th century, no works were produced to compare with the great flowering of landscape painting across the North Sea, in Holland.

It was to these masters of the Low Countries that both Gainsborough and Constable turned in their early years. The East Anglian landscape, though not, as is commonly assumed, anything like as flat as that of Holland, has some of the same qualities, particularly in the coastal regions where both men were born and started working.

Gainsborough, born in Sudbury in Suffolk in 1727, explored and painted the Stour valley that was to become 'Constable Country'; while Constable, born two generations later at East Bergholt, loved and revered Gainsborough's work. 'Tis a most delightful country for a landscape painter,' he wrote, 'I fancy I see Gainsborough in every hedge and hollow tree.'

Gainsborough

Gainsborough's enormous success as a portrait painter came only after he had left Suffolk for Bath, when he was in his early thirties. But his Suffolk landscapes and portraits have a certain stiffness and formality which is altogether different from, but equal to, the impressionistic brilliance of his later work.

He often referred during later life to his love of the Suffolk landscape, and in his early portraits of

The elegant town house in Sudbury, Suffolk, where Gainsborough was born, is now a fine museum and art gallery, and dates from c.1725

Gainsborough's masterpiece Mr and Mrs Andrews *can be seen in the National Gallery, London*

friends or patrons he was fond of setting the figures against the background of a park, or a distant view of a church, with which the sitter was associated. The delight with which he places Mr and Mrs Andrews, in their best clothes and within the framework of their own property, is obvious. The half-stormy, half-sunlit sky is familiar to anyone who knows Suffolk, and the wheatfield, just harvested, is a reminder of the importance of corn in the economy of 18th-century East Anglia. The tower of All Saints Church, where the couple married, is just visible through the trees.

Gainsborough left Suffolk for fashionable Bath at the age of 32. From then onwards, his interpretation of landscape became more stylised and less immediate, although he continued to prefer it to what he called 'face painting'. Towards the end of his life, with the great reputation earned in Bath and London behind him, he still looked with affection on a picture he said he had begun before he left school (though he must have finished it a few years later, as it is dated 1748). *Cornard Wood*, now in the National Gallery, shows Gainsborough's Suffolk period to perfection. Here there are no fashionable tricks; instead, he gives a direct and dramatic representation of some of Suffolk's great oak woodland, with all the closely observed activities of people at work that both Gainsborough and Constable delighted in.

Constable
Perhaps Gainsborough was being practical when he abandoned attention to the appearance of the countryside and its inhabitants in his paintings, as it was precisely for this that Constable was later criticised as he struggled for recognition in the early 19th century. Born in 1776, at East Bergholt, he showed none of the early promise that had persuaded Gainsborough's father to allow his talented son to go to London. Constable's father, a successful corn merchant, was anxious for John to take over the running of Flatford Mill, in preparation for the inheritance of his considerable business ventures, and it was not until his son was 23 that he allowed him to go, as a rather mature student, to the Royal Academy Schools in London.

Every summer thereafter, Constable returned to Suffolk, riding and walking round his beloved countryside with a tiny sketchbook in his pocket, recording scenes which were the seeds of his great canvases, many of which were not painted until 10 or 15 years later, in a studio in a smoky Soho street.

The passionate attachment that Constable felt for his native countryside stemmed, as he often said, from his happy childhood. He found it uncongenial to paint places or people with no call on his personal affections. Although in his early years he was forced to paint portraits in order to earn a little money, it was only in pictures of his parents, wife (Mary Bicknell, whom he married in 1816), children and friends that he achieved really happy results. This was also equally so with landscape; an early visit to the Lake District produced some merely competent work. He found the area unsympathetic, and it was only in his native region, and later in Hampstead, where he lived with his young family, that he found complete artistic satisfaction.

Fortunately, much of Constable Country is still instantly recognisable. Go to Flatford Mill, as thousands do every year (so try to get there in early morning or late evening), and you will see Constable brought to life. Better still, take the admirable reproductions of his sketchbooks (published by HM Stationery Office) and wander along the banks of the Stour away from the crowds, or drive to Stoke-by-Nayland, where you can stand on the exact spot where he stood, and see the same view, almost unchanged.

In spite of modern development, the countryside today is less of a working landscape than it was a century and a half ago. Then, the river was a commercial waterway, with barges constantly coming and going, locks opening and shutting and watermills and windmills turning. But Constable has in some extraordinary way almost replaced nature here; it is almost impossible to see the landscape except through his eyes.

The pond at Flatford Mill is still recognisable today as the setting for Constable's Haywain. *It has been the setting for many pictures since*

The Norwich School

On 17 February 1803 a group of like-minded people met in Norwich at the house of John Crome, the son of a weaver who had begun as an apprentice to a sign painter. Crome's friends, patrons and pupils formed the Norwich Society 'for the Purpose of an Enquiry into the Rise, Progress and Present State of Painting, Architecture and Sculpture, with a view to point out the Best Method of Study to attain Greater Perfection'. This rather self-conscious approach to art, so different from that of Gainsborough and Constable, nevertheless gave rise to the Norwich

John Crome, who founded the Norwich Society of Artists in 1803, ranks with Constable and Turner as one of the three great landscape painters of the 19th century; his Back of the New Mills *(bottom) was painted in 1814.* Boats on the Medway *(below) is by M E Cotman, another Norwich School painter*

School, of which Crome and Cotman are the acknowledged masters. It was the only English organisation remotely comparable with the great Italian schools of painting, although its modest output of oils, watercolours and etchings can scarcely be put in the same class. Nevertheless, these artists, who like their Suffolk colleagues were influenced by the Dutch masters, produced work which reinforces East Anglia's claim to being an area of the highest importance in the sphere of English art.

Other painters and craftsmen
In the mid-19th century, Thomas Churchyard of Woodbridge was at work painting charming watercolours, particularly of the Aldeburgh area. Towards the end of the century the Suffolk coast also attracted Philip Wilson Steer, who painted some vividly impressionistic scenes at Southwold and Walberswick.

Apart from Steer, the later part of the 19th century produced little in the way of painting in East Anglia, although there is one rather odd artist well worth seeking out. Ernest Geldart was rector of several rural Essex parishes at the turn of the century, and his talent for decoration was let loose on his churches. The lovely, early 12th-century church at Little Braxted was transformed by Geldart's quasi Pre-Raphaelite vision. Presumably, the effect he aimed at was the re-creation of the interior of an early basilica.

Just before World War II, artists and craftsmen began to filter into East Anglia – drawn there, perhaps, almost as much by economic as artistic reasons. Essex and Suffolk were then counties almost untouched by London, and Norfolk was thought to be impossibly remote (and therefore inexpensive). Few of them, however, seem to have taken their inspiration from the countryside, though John Nash, the most distinguished of them, painted a number of sensitive landscapes near his home on the Suffolk–Essex border. Sir Alfred Munnings, the equestrian painter, lived for many years at Dedham, and his pictures of Newmarket are well known. Cedric Morris also set up a school of painting near Hadleigh, and became well known for his vivid flower paintings.

Joseph Stannard (1797–1830) lived in Norwich all his life. He is best-known for landscapes, such as Thorpe, Near Norwich *(above)*

Potters, weavers, etchers and sculptors have always lived in considerable numbers in East Anglia. Great Bardfield and the surrounding Essex villages are full of artists – among them Edward Bawden, one of England's greatest illustrators. In fact, if you travel to the remotest village, or to the most unlikely small town, you will find a studio or workshop which, even if it is not of the standard of Constable or Gainsborough, still demonstrates that East Anglia's soil is one in which creativity flourishes.

Where to see East Anglian paintings.

Essex *The Minories, East Hill, Colchester* Permanent collection includes early Constables. Also has exhibitions of contemporary work.

Suffolk *Christchurch Mansion, Ipswich* Some fine examples of Constable and Gainsborough, as well as numerous minor East Anglian artists, are lodged in this handsome Jacobean house, set in a beautiful park.
Gainsborough's House, Sudbury Gainsborough's birthplace, which houses a number of his earlier works. Well worth a visit, not only for the pictures, but for the atmosphere and the pleasure of the charming small garden.

Norfolk *The Castle Museum, Norwich* The greatest collection of the works of the Norwich School. *The Sainsbury Centre, University of East Anglia, Norwich* One of the most distinguished modern buildings in the eastern counties, housing one of the most important art collections.

Cambridgeshire *The Fitzwilliam Museum, Cambridge* Fine Constables, Gainsboroughs and works by other East Anglians are part of one of the best collections in England.
Kettles' Yard, Cambridge Permanent collection; not East Anglian, but there are often exhibitions of local work.

EAST ANGLIA

Gazetteer

Each entry in this Gazetteer has the atlas
page number on which the place can be
found and its National Grid reference
included under the heading.
An explanation of how to use the National
Grid is given on page 82.

Above: a colourful village sign in Norfolk

The curious 'House in the Clouds' at Thorpeness: a former water tower, now a family home

Aldeburgh, Suffolk

Map Ref: 93TM4656

Despite great inroads by the sea, this resort continues to thrive on a bracing climate and the fame of the annual June festival that is centred on the old maltings at Snape, further up the estuary of the River Alde. Benjamin Britten, the festival's co-founder, is buried in the great churchyard of St Peter and St Paul in Aldeburgh, and a memorial window by John Piper sheds brilliant colour into the wide nave of the church. The flint church tower overlooks the town from a ridge, and was once topped by a lantern-house in which a warning beacon could be lit.

Drawn up on the wide shingle beach lie the two lifeboats stationed

17th-century Blickling Hall is surrounded by notable gardens

here, and the open boats used by fishermen. The 16th-century Moot Hall, of brick and exposed timbers, stands near the sea; where an open market was once held, the Town Clerk now has his office. At the south end of the High Street is a Martello tower, now let as a holiday home.

The varied houses at **Thorpeness**, two miles up the coast, come to life in the summer. The most unusual is a former water tower, now converted into a house, next to a well-restored post mill which was once used for pumping water.

AA recommends:
Hotels: Brudenell, The Parade, 3-star, tel. (072885) 2071
Wentworth, Sea Front, 3-star, tel. (072885) 2312
White Lion, Market Cross, 3-star, tel. (072885) 2986
Uplands, Victoria Rd, 2-star, tel. (072885) 2420
Guesthouse: Cotmandene, 6 Park Lane, tel. (072885) 3775

Aylsham, Norfolk

Map Ref: 88TG1926

Now mercifully bypassed by the A140, this bustling small town – which featured in Domesday – holds a market each Monday, but not now in the market place. This is surrounded by some unspoilt buildings, such as the Black Boy Inn, where horses were once changed on the stagecoach run from Cromer to Norwich.

Wherries once sailed up the River Bure to Aylsham, and there are still imposing mill buildings down by the river. In the churchyard lies Humphrey Repton, the landscape

architect who died in 1818 and wrote his own epitaph. Roses, which he loved, now grow around his grave.

Towards Blickling is the Old Hall, a fine and well-preserved mansion, built in 1689, with an avenue of trees stretching away in front. The hall, owned by the National Trust, is open by written appointment with the administrator.

Lack of suitable building stone in Norfolk has resulted in great houses built of warm, red brick with stone quoins. **Blickling Hall** is certainly one of the finest: it is everybody's dream of a country house, built between 1619 and 1627 in Elizabethan style, with Dutch gables, corner turrets and a dominant clock tower. Now owned by the National Trust, it is open at certain times during the year.

The most splendid room in the Hall is the long gallery, 123ft long and unusually wide, which now houses one of the finest libraries in the country – over 12,000 leather-bound volumes, many printed before 1500. The design of the superb Jacobean moulded plaster ceiling symbolises 'The Five Senses and Learning'.

The gardens draw people back to Blickling time and again; laid out to a basic Jacobean design, they are colourful at all seasons, and are surrounded by acres of woodland. The great, square herbaceous beds glow with matching colours, and beside the wide path, up to the Doric temple, azaleas and rhododendrons are a glorious mixture of red and yellow in early summer. The park itself, which is always open to the public, has a network of footpaths and bridleways which give access to woods of ancient oak and chestnut,

a pyramidal mausoleum, a Gothic tower, and a curving lake, which is a mile long and full of coarse fish.

Barnack, Cambridgeshire

Map Ref: 84TF0704

The medieval quarries on the A1 side of this village at the very northern tip of Cambridgeshire produce a honey-coloured stone known as 'Barnack Rag', which faces a host of important buildings in East Anglia, notably Peterborough Cathedral and Binham Priory. There are excellent examples of the stone in the village, and many houses are worthy of note. Kingsley House is built around a medieval core, and in Millstone Lane there is an intriguing row of Feoffee cottages, with arched doorways. The Parish Church of St John the Baptist has a 12th-century nave, an Anglo-Saxon tower and an imposing array of parapets and battlements. Inside there are some fine monuments.

Walcot Hall (not open to the public), to the south-east, provides a 17th-century backdrop for its lovely gardens, complete with temples and a rotunda.

Beccles, Suffolk

Map Ref: 89TM4290

When Broadland was a marsh, Beccles was a thriving port on the River Waveney, which reaches the sea at Great Yarmouth. Where sailing wherries and the Yorkshire sailing ships known as 'billyboys' once tied up at the staithes or quays, leisure cruisers now abound. Narrow streets called 'scores' lead to the staithes from the town, with its air of solid Georgian gentility. The churchyard gives the best view of the wide sweep of river and the common, to the east. The church itself has a very fine, mid 15th-century double-storied porch, with intricate embellishments; the tower stands on its own, dwarfing the brick Town Hall in which quarter sessions were once held. There is a museum of rural life on the Newgate road; the display includes the original town sign and a 19th-century printing press. The Roman Catholic church of St Benet was built 100 years ago in the Romanesque style, and further out, on the Bungay road, is 16th-century Roos Hall, whose gables and roofline show a Dutch influence.

AA recommends:
Hotels: King's Head, New Market, 2-star, *tel.* (0502) 712147
Waveney House, Puddingmoor, 2-star, *tel.* (0502) 712270
Guesthouse: Riverview House, Ballygate, *tel.* (0502) 713519
Garage: Pageant, Gosford Rd, *tel.* (0502) 713356

Binham, Norfolk

Map Ref: 88TF9839

The ruins of the Benedictine priory, founded in 1100 on the outskirts of this village, are situated in open arable farmland. The Norman nave serves as the Parish Church of St Mary and the Holy Cross. Inside,

The beautiful setting for the Parish Church at Binham – almost all that remains now of the 11th-century Benedictine priory

there is a seven-sacrament font and, on a side altar table, there is the Tobruk Cross, which was shaped from shell cases to commemorate those who died in North Africa in World War II.

The glory of the priory is its west front, built before 1244 from honey-coloured Barnack stone and local flint. Its array of arches and columns creates one of the finest examples anywhere of early English architecture. The ruins of the priory buildings are open throughout the year during daylight hours.

The Aldeburgh Festival

While in America during the last war, the composer Benjamin Britten, originally a Suffolk man, read an article by E M Forster about the Aldeburgh poet George Crabbe. He suddenly realised that he must return to Suffolk, and that he would draw his inspiration there. Indeed, many would say that as you listen to Britten's music, you can hear the sound of the sea and almost perceive the extraordinarily piercing East Anglian light. It was Crabbe's work which inspired Britten's opera *Peter Grimes*.

The first Aldeburgh Festival took place in 1948, founded by Britten, Peter Pears and Eric Crozier. They had been touring in Europe the previous year with *Albert Herring* and *The Rape of Lucretia*, and had come to the conclusion that it was time British operas – which London, Edinburgh and Manchester had refused to support – got a better airing at home. And so the idea of a modest festival of music at Aldeburgh was born. Early events were held in the Jubilee Hall in Aldeburgh and in other churches and halls in the town, but the festival's popularity eventually grew to a point where a large and a permanent concert hall had to be found.

Benjamin Britten, founder of the Aldeburgh Festival which celebrated its 40th anniversary last year

In 1967 the newly converted Snape Maltings, part of a 19th-century industrial complex on the River Alde, were opened for this purpose. The red brick and bare wood inside gave the hall a visual quality which blended with the surrounding landscape, and it had unique acoustics. Although the concert hall suffered a major setback in 1969, when it was gutted by a fire on the first night of that year's festival, it was completely restored within a year.

All manner of wildlife can be observed on Blakeney salt marshes

Blakeney Point, Norfolk

Map Ref: 88TG0046

It is a long way from anywhere to north Norfolk, and this remoteness has been the salvation of a coastline which is now listed as an internationally recognised nature reserve. The shingle ridge of Blakeney Point, amounting to slightly more than 1,000 acres, was the first reserve in Norfolk. It looms across the tidal marsh from Morston quay, where the ferries set out to drop visitors near the old lifeboat station on the Point, or take them right up to the seals that bask on the sandbars.

A 400yd walkway leads over the dunes from the station to the observation hide, from where you can overlook nesting sandwich and common terns in May and June. The wardens thoughtfully rope off the nests – bare scrapes in the shingle – of the oyster catchers and ringed plovers, to stop visitors treading on the eggs.

A boathouse and information point on the quay at Morston provide a gallery with spectacular views up and down the coast. Other ferries ply from Blakeney, a delightful village full of houses with walls of knapped-flint and mellow brick bound by 'clunch', the local word for builders' chalk. Birds are the main attraction on this coast, however; more than 270 species have been sighted on the Point.

AA recommends:
Hotel: White Hart, Bocking End, 2-star, *tel.* (0376) 21401
Campsite: Sun Lido Caravan Park, Essex Barn Restaurant, Rayne Rd, 1-pennant, *tel.* (0376) 25445
Garage: Quest Motors (Gozzett Ltd), 277/281 Rayne Rd, *tel.* (0376) 21456

A fine example of 18th-century decorative plasterwork – pargeting – in Bocking

Blythburgh, Suffolk

Map Ref: 93TM4575

The romantic, floodlit tower of the great church beside the main west road is a reminder of the bustling port that was once Blythburgh – until the river silted up in the 16th century. There was once a mint and a jail in the shadow of Holy Trinity Church, which was recorded in Domesday. The church was built in a commanding position, on a site where Christians have worshipped since AD620. It is a miracle that so much survives to help the minds of admiring visitors 'to be lifted up towards the truth' as a medieval abbot once proclaimed. A great storm of 1577 sent the spire crashing through the roof. Cromwell's troops with their horses were quartered inside the church in 1644, and bullet-ridden angels in the roof are proof of their occupation. Decay and neglect in later years have left their mark, and the least a visitor can do today is leave a donation in the iron-banded alms box that dates from 1473.

Bocking, Essex

Map Ref: 86TL7624

Bocking nestles in the valley of the River Blackwater, two miles from Braintree. In 1006 two Saxon noblemen presented the manor here to a priory at Canterbury, and several manors were created in the area following this gift. Some of these old manor houses remain, although much-modified and adapted; Doreward's Hall is one such building.

The principal trade for centuries was the manufacture of baize, a coarse woollen cloth, using water-driven fulling mills. Baize was superseded by silk and straw bonnets.

In 1809, George Courtauld, a descendant of Huguenot refugees, decided to make full use of the skilled workforce at Bocking for the spinning of rayon, or artificial silk. He built a fine mill here which became one of the most important owned by his company, but overseas competition forced its closure, and it was finally demolished in 1988.

One mill remains in Bocking – a fine 17th-century post mill, rather forlorn amid so much housing. The 15th-century church has an imposing tower, overlooking the river.

Brandon, Suffolk

Map Ref: 87TL7886

The county boundary follows the line of the Little Ouse at Brandon, and beside the five-arched bridge on the Norfolk bank is a tea room. From here, rowing boats can be hired, a pleasant way of enjoying this placid river which was once navigable. Until enlarged for immigrants from London in the

1970s, Brandon was a small village relying on the felt and flint industries. A few flint-knappers remain, who now provide gun flints for muzzle-loaders used by poachers in Africa and 'Old Gun Clubs' in the USA. The knapping used to take place, amid piles of chippings, behind the Flint-Knappers Arms in the village market place, which is now a paved precinct.

The mining and working of the precious flint is not a recent activity. Three miles up the Swaffham road are the fascinating **Grime's Graves** – nobody knows why they are called 'Grime's' Graves, as they were discovered by a Reverend Greenwell in 1869. He dug down into one of 366 circular depressions in the 'breck', and discovered, at a depth of 32ft, an old mine shaft used for working seams of flint. More shafts were found, and it is thought that these were used by Neolithic Man, 4,000 years ago. Sharpened deer antlers, used as picks, have been found here, as well as drawings of elks and other animals. The shafts may be explored by visitors throughout the year.

Just outside Brandon is a country park, with magnificent Scots pines. Also worth exploring is the long avenue of pollarded limes that leads to the isolated church of St Peter which, like so many other buildings in Breckland, is all flint and 'clunch' – lime mortar made from chalk.

AA recommends:
Hotel: Brandon House, High St, 3-star, *tel.* (0842) 810171
Garage: Brandon Car Spares, Heathlings, Fengate Drove, *tel.* (0842) 810146

Breckland,
Norfolk & Suffolk

Map Ref: 87TL88

This is the name given in 1894 to a unique area of about 400 square miles straddling the Norfolk and Suffolk borders, which embraces the largest lowland forest in the country and an inaccessible army training area of around 17,500 acres. The 'brecks' are the stony fields on sandy soil that are surrounded by large tracts of heath, gorse and bracken. Many are enclosed by boundaries of misshapen Scots pines, which are suited to the dry climate and sparse soil. Plantations of conifers now stretch for miles where once there were sand dunes.

The strong winds often produce sand blows, and in one such storm the village of **Santon Downham** was covered. The same fate befell the Anglo-Saxon settlement at West Stow, which has now been excavated and re-built to give a good idea of how people lived in the period after the Roman occupation.

Rabbits – introduced as a valuable source of food – virtually took over the brecks, and were once farmed in warrens. The medieval stone house now standing isolated on the edge of Rishbeth's Wood, 2 miles west of Thetford, was once the lodge of the gamekeeper who looked after the Prior's rights of hunting and warren in the forests. He had the right to cull 10 rabbits per acre each year. More recently, rabbit skins were sent to Brandon, where a large factory once turned them into felt, especially for hats. This is now a flourishing industry in Australia, which still has a surfeit of rabbits. Breckland was delivered from this problem by the advent of myxomatosis.

Outside the Stanford Battle Area, west of **East Wretham**, the brecks are criss-crossed by forest paths waymarked by the Forestry Commission; good starting points are at Santon Downham, Lynford, and King's Forest at West Stow. The Peddars Way, a long-distance footpath, skirts the east side of Breckland and runs as straight as the Romans first built it, from near Thetford to the north Norfolk coast at Holme next the Sea.

To follow this ancient track is to gain an excellent introduction to the flora and fauna of the area.

At **Knettishall**, where the Way begins, there is a 180-acre country park of heather, grass and plantations. Further up and just west of the A11 is **East Wretham Heath**, a nature reserve of 360 acres in the care of the Norfolk Naturalists' Trust, which allows the public to enter daily, except on Tuesday. The meres and thickets of birch and pine are havens for wildlife. Another reserve further north is at **Thompson Common**, renowned for 'pingos', circular indentations from the glacial past which support a variety of water plants. Everywhere there are excellent opportunities to sight red, fallow and roe deer.

History relates that the Peddars Way was built to enable the Romans to keep in subjugation the Iceni tribes that had rebelled under Queen Boudicca in AD61. At **Cockley Cley**, near Swaffham, an Iceni village has been reconstructed on its original site; the flint church nearby is of Saxon origin and dated AD630.

Further west, and built 850 years later, is the moated mansion of **Oxburgh Hall**, once surrounded by undrained marshland and the home of the Bedingfield family since 1482. In that year, Sir Edmund Bedingfield obtained a licence from Edward IV to build towers and battlements, and the Charter, complete with massive seal, survives in the Hall today. Now owned by the National Trust and open to the public, Oxburgh has a gate tower 80ft high, and intricate tapestries worked by Mary, Queen of Scots, during her captivity.

There are few churches of note in Breckland but an exception is St Mary's at **Lakenheath** (near the huge American air-base). Stand in the middle of the nave and look up to admire 60 angels in the roof, look down to see the original hassocks made from matted fen sedge, and then look towards the peerless Norman arch of the chancel.

Thetford lies at the heart of Breckland; this typical woodland is at Thetford Warren

Mills

The windmill at Wicken Fen

Windmills characterise the East Anglian landscape, the low-lying land making it well suited to mills. Not all grind corn, however. While modern electric pumps keep the marshy areas of Broadland and the Fens drained, the original method used the power of the wind to turn scoop wheels. Of the surviving wind-pumps, those at Stracey Arms, Berney Arms and Horsey are perhaps the most impressive, especially when you can climb up them and appreciate the views. You can hardly fail to be charmed by the open-framed timber trestle Boardman's Mill at How Hill, or by the pretty white-painted, timber-clad mill at Thurne Dyke.

Windmills have been an important feature of the East Anglian landscape since medieval times, although none has survived from that period. The oldest-surviving mill in the country is at Bourn in Cambridgeshire, and dates back to the early 17th century. It is a post mill, with sails and machinery revolving around a central post. Later mills, called smock and tower mills, confine the parts which turn to the cap and sails.

Watermills, as well as windmills, were used to grind the region's corn. In Norfolk, Ingworth and Itteringham mills survive as attractive private residences, but at Letheringsett Watermill, near Holt, you can see demonstrations of the ancient craft and even buy some of the flour.

A tide mill has stood on the river bank at Woodbridge in Suffolk since the 12th century, and the present one was working until 1956, when the shaft of the waterwheel broke. Careful restoration has since returned the mill to working condition.

The Norfolk Broads

Map Ref: 89TG31

Ask a 'foreigner' what he or she knows about Norfolk, and most answer that it is flat, and it is where the Broads are found. Both statements happen to be true for east Norfolk and north-east Suffolk, areas which 500-600 years ago were the most populous and often the most prosperous in Britain. Medieval towns like Norwich and Great Yarmouth, with urban populations, depended on the surrounding countryside for food and fuel. Wood was scarce, so turf or peat began to be dug and transported by cart and barge to the towns. The holes made by the peat digging filled up with water, and shallow lakes were formed. It is estimated that 900,000,000 cubic feet of peat was removed to create the Broads, over a period of 300-400 years. The land was then several feet higher than the sea, but it is probable that a great tidal surge in 1287, similar to that of 1953, broke down the banks and flooded the workings.

The artificial nature of the Broads was only proved conclusively in 1951 from borings made in the fens, and even then it was hard to believe that a lake like Fritton, which is 2 miles long, 15ft deep and 200yd wide, was dug by men using simple spades and 'dydles', a form of rake. Baulks, or walls of peat, were left in parallel lines to protect the pits from flooding and to provide access. Traces of these can be seen in aerial views of the Fens.

Today the appearance of the Broads is very different from that of 150 years ago. Two-thirds of the original water area is now silted up, and much of the plant and animal life has disappeared. Pollution from town sewage plants, the run-off of fertilisers from arable land, the erosion of the banks and the

At Ranworth Broad, there is a Broadland Conservation Centre with a birdwatching gallery

churning of mud by thousands of motor boats have all caused a drastic change in the ecology of the region. A new special statutory Broads Authority was established by Act of Parliament in 1988, with effect from April 1989, to exercise control over the 130 miles of waterways and to try to reconcile the interests of all parties involved. Navigation remains the responsibility of the Yarmouth Port and Haven Commissioners. Farmers are now encouraged, through grants, to keep traditional grazing marshes under grass, and vital drainage schemes are to be better co-ordinated. At **How Hill**, Ludham, the Authority has a centre where these policies are explained. There are also information centres at Beccles, Hoveton and Ranworth.

The Broads, despite their decline,

continue to offer enjoyable holidays to many thousands of people each year, and there are several excellent centres where boats can be hired. Six rivers are navigable – the Ant, Bure, Thurne, Waveney, Wensum and Yare – and their waters all flow into the sea at Great Yarmouth. Norwich itself is on the Wensum.

Wroxham on the Bure is a centre for yachting and boat-building. Beeston Hall, 4 miles north-east, is a flint-faced Georgian mansion open to the public and accessible on foot from Barton Broad, via the delightful village of **Neatishead.** **Horning** is downstream on the Bure, and is another bustling boating centre near the **Hoveton Broads.** Further down still is **Ranworth Broad**, the largest in the Bure valley, on which there is the Broadland Conservation Centre and floating bird observatory, approached by a raised walkway. The best view of the Broad is from the top of the tower of St Helen's Parish Church.

Hickling Broad in the north-east of Broadland, although very shallow, is one of the largest. It is a nature reserve, and permits are needed to penetrate the reed banks, which shelter bearded tits and bitterns in season. The Pleasure Boat Inn on the staithe or quay is a favourite rendezvous for yachtsmen and sailboard users. One mile north-west is Sutton Windmill, the tallest in the country, with its milling machinery completely restored. It is one of many windmills and pumps that dot the Broads; many are now restored and working once more. On **Horsey Mere**, joined to Hickling by Meadow Dyke, there is a well-preserved windpump, from whose gallery there are magnificent views of the Broads. Here they are only a mile away from the sea, and

protected by a great sea wall of shingle.

Potter Heigham is well-placed on the north bank of the Thurne, south of Hickling, and is another popular centre with a three-arched bridge and a thatched Norman church with a round tower. The Yare at **Reedham** is crossed by a chain ferry, and 3 miles downstream, where the Rivers Yare and Waveney flow into Breydon Water, is the Berney Arms Windmill, which contains an exhibition on mills. Opposite, on the south bank, are the ruins of Burgh Castle, one of a chain of Roman castles that once guarded the east coast. A monastery was established within its walls before the Normans built their church. On **South Walsham Broad** boats can

land beside delightful water gardens, which belong to the Fairhaven Garden Trust.

Several Broads are now nature reserves, managed by conservation societies which issue permits, such as at Hickling. On **Strumpshaw Fen**, on the Yare east of Norwich, there are observation hides. An old windpump here provides an ideal lookout over Martham Broad on the Thurne, where bitterns can often be heard booming.

Fishing has always been an important activity, and the valuable rights were jealously guarded. Surges of brackish water and pollution have decimated fish stocks in recent years, but good catches of coarse fish can still be had on some waters under private ownership.

Some of the traditional sailing wherries have been restored, and their great red sails continue to move gracefully over the Broads.

AA recommends:
Wroxham
Hotels: Broads, Station Rd, 2-star, *tel.* (06053) 2869
Hotel Wroxham, Broads Centre, Hoveton 2-star, *tel.* (06053) 2061
King's Head, Station Rd, 1-star, *tel.* (06053) 2429
Neatishead
Guesthouses: Barton Angler Lodge Hotel, Irstead Rd, *tel.* (0692) 630740
Regency, Neatishead Post Office Stores, *tel.* (0692) 630233
Horning
Hotel: Petersfield House, Lower St, 3-star, *tel.* (0692) 630741
Hickling
Guesthouse: Jenter House, Town St, *tel.* (069261) 372

Horsey Mere, controlled by the National Trust, is popular with both sailors and winter wildfowl

Brentwood, Essex

Map Ref: 94TQ5993

For centuries, travellers to and from Harwich and London have refreshed themselves at the many hostelries here. The most famous is the White Hart Hotel, dating back to the late 1400s. Another, the Crown, was reputed in 1700 to have been 300 years old, and to have had 89 different owners! The prior of St Osyth founded a chapel dedicated to St Thomas in Brentwood in 1221, and its ruins can be seen beside the High Street. *Brent* is the old English word for burnt, so it is probable that the woodland hereabouts was once fired, either by accident or design.

AA recommends:
Hotel: Post House, Brook St, 3-star, *tel.* (0277) 260260

Bressingham, Norfolk

Map Ref: 88TM0780

The church in this village just west of Diss was rebuilt in 1527, and has bench ends carved into grotesque shapes, including inter-twining plants. This is a suitable motif for these parts, as the grounds of the hall nearby have been transformed into 6 acres of internationally famous gardens. Alan Bloom, the horticulturist, decided to create a massive collection of more than 5,000 species of perennials and alpine plants here, displayed and labelled in 'island' beds. To make it easier to admire this feast of herbaceous design, no less than 5 miles of narrow-gauge railway weave round the gardens. The carriages are hauled by steam engines, including a model of the famous Pacific type 4-6-2. More than 50 engines and roundabouts are on display.

Brightlingsea, Essex

Map Ref: 92TM0816

This is a genuine seaside resort, with considerably more character than sprawling Clacton further east down the Colne estuary. There is bustle throughout the year on the wharves in Brightlingsea, where coasters attract streams of lorries carrying grain for European ports. Shipping rides at anchor in the estuary, and fishing vessels of several nationalities use the old port. There is another flourishing industry – the servicing and construction of pleasure sailing craft, which are particularly well-suited to the creeks of the heavily indented Essex coast hereabouts.

Down by the smart yachting clubhouse, there are unpretentious pubs and a hotel with an engagingly elaborate front. They look across to an island with a squat Martello tower in its centre; stretching up the estuary are lines of bathing huts, colourful and solid.

In the High Street, the main building of note is Jacobs House, half-timbered and dilapidated, but an important relic of the early 14th century. In the narrow streets round about are old cottages, some with clapboard walls. Roman brickwork can be seen in the walls of the Parish Church of All Saints. The incumbent of All Saints also looks after an impressive church to the right of the road at Brightlingsea's northern boundary. There is an unusual wooden turnstile here.

AA recommends:
Garage: Bright Ford Motors, 43 Hurst Green, *tel.* (020630) 2264

Bungay, Suffolk

Map Ref: 89TM3389

Bungay is an interesting and beautiful town. The lock at Geldeston and the dredging of the River Waveney – which here marks the Suffolk and Norfolk boundary – have enabled wherries to come up as far as Bungay. In the past, Bungay was therefore an affluent town, able to rebuild after a disastrous fire in 1688; one of the two market crosses survived, with a roof adorned by a lead figure of Justice. Beside a recent bypass are modern buildings occupied by printers, who carry on a long tradition of printing in the town.

The centre of Bungay is taken up by two churches, with the ruins of a Benedictine nunnery in between. St Mary's, with a splendid tower of buttresses and turrets, has been declared redundant, although it is still used for occasional services. On a terrible Sunday in 1577, Black Shuck, the mythical Black Dog of East Anglia, caused chaos in this church during a thunderstorm. Sightings of Shuck are common in East Anglia, as much now as in the past; he is depicted on the town sign at Bungay. Holy Trinity, with its very early round tower, is now the parish church, and Christians have worshipped here for over 900 years.

Brooding over the town are the 13th-century castle ruins, handed over in 1988 to the local council by the Duke of Norfolk, whose family has owned them for 500 years. There was already an old castle on this site when the Romans arrived.

From Castle Hill, the tower of Earsham Church can be seen upstream. The church overlooks part of the Waveney Valley, where European otters find sanctuary. From the Otter Trust's ponds in **Earsham**, animals bred in captivity are released into the rivers of Norfolk, where they successfully re-establish themselves and breed in the wild. The Trust's ponds are also a haven for wildfowl.

AA recommends:
Hotel: Kings Head, Market Place, 1-star, *tel.* (0986) 3583
Campsite: Outney Meadow Caravan Park, Broad St, 3-pennant, *tel.* (0986) 2338

Twin towers and massive flint walls are all that remain of the original Norman Castle at Bungay.
Left: part of Alan Bloom's colourful heather and conifer gardens at Bressingham

Nelson

England's greatest sailor was a Norfolk man. The parsonage at Burnham Thorpe, where he was born in 1758, no longer exists, although its site is marked with a plaque beside the road.

In an age where social background was all-important to the making of the man, Nelson's was somewhat varied. One of his grandfathers was a baker, while a great-great uncle was Sir Robert Walpole, the first Prime Minister of Great Britain.

Nelson went to school at the Paston Grammar School in North Walsham, and then to the King Edward VI School in the Cathedral Close, Norwich. In 1771 he joined HMS *Raisonable*, but seven years later he was back in Burnham Thorpe, living in semi-retirement on half-pay with his wife, Fanny. During the five years that followed, he farmed 30 acres of glebe land.

On the outbreak of war in 1793, Nelson was appointed Captain of HMS *Agamemnon*, and a good number of the crew were Norfolk men. During the next 12 years Nelson made his mark as England's

greatest sailor, inflicting defeats on Napoleon at the Battle of the Nile and at the Battle of Copenhagen and, above all, at the Battle of Trafalgar in 1805, in which he lost his life.

The 13th-century church at Burnham Thorpe contains several mementoes of this great seaman. The cross and lectern are both made from timbers taken from HMS *Victory*, and flags from the ship

A drawing of how Burnham Thorpe Rectory, birthplace of Lord Nelson, used to look

hang in the nave. Edmund Nelson lies in the chancel, with a bust of his famous son above. If any doubt remains that you are indeed in Nelson country, take a look at the names of all the local pubs – The Nelson, The Victory, The Hero, The Trafalgar.

The watermill at Burnham Overy is now owned by the National Trust

Burnham-on-Crouch, Essex

Map Ref: 95TQ9496

Sailing craft and oysters have lured visitors to this harbour on the north shore of the Crouch estuary for centuries. The High Street leads down to the quays, backed by a terrace of houses that includes the White Hart Hotel. The Royal Corinthian Yacht Club has its headquarters here. This Club has a burgee that flies on yachts in most harbours of the world. The Civic Trust has ensured the preservation of many traditional buildings, some of clapboard, others of Georgian brick. The market place at the opposite end of the High Street has been the site for the Tuesday market since the 14th century.

Oysters from the creeks were sold in the market, and then shipped in barrels to Holland. The church stands on a mound, a mile south of the town. The tower has acted as a homing mark for mariners for years. A tablet in the church is a memorial to the Rev Alexander Scott, Admiral Nelson's chaplain on HMS *Victory* – the only link between this Burnham and the Burnham Thorpe in Norfolk, where Nelson was born in 1758.

The local museum, open in season, displays an interesting collection of artefacts. In the last week of August Burnham Week is held, attracting yachtsmen from all over the country.

AA recommends:
Hotel: Ye Olde White Harte, The Quay, 1-star, *tel.* (0621) 782106
Guesthouse: Buccaneer, 42 High St, *tel.* (0621) 783654

The Burnhams, Norfolk

Map Ref: 87TF8342

It is very confusing to have seven Burnhams all clustered together between Brancaster and Holkham, with the largest, **Burnham Market**, at their centre. A handsome town, it has a wide green, a small stream flowing across the main road, and a range of Georgian houses.

Burnham Overy Town to the north-east has real charm, and there is a brace of mills built over the River Burn. The remains of a preaching cross stand in the village centre. The Norman church sits on a knoll.

Once, sailing craft could load and unload at the mill jetties here, but the inexorable silting-up of the river forced the building of the small village of **Burnham Overy Staithe** a mile down-stream. Here there is a fine watermill, whose wheel remains intact. The line of brick and flint cottages that overlook the mill pool are all part of the hamlet preserved by the National Trust.

Burnham Deepdale and **Burnham Norton** both have churches with Anglo-Saxon towers and Norman fonts. **Burnham Thorpe** is particularly notable as the birthplace of Lord Nelson; Nelson Hall near the church contains many relics, and holds frequent exhibitions of Nelsoniana. There is a wonderful panorama from the hill between **Burnham Westgate** and **Burnham Deepdale** of the Deepdale and Burnham Norton Marshes.

AA recommends:
Holkham
Hotel: Victoria, 1-star, *tel.* (0328) 710469

Bury St Edmunds, Suffolk

Map Ref: 92TL8564

Here is a very old, complete and prosperous market town in close contact with the country round about, and, now it is bypassed by the A45, a visitor can do no better than walk through the town and savour its many historical buildings, which give an atmosphere of serenity. Within the town, which still retains much of its 11th-century layout, there are sharp contrasts between narrow streets, open squares and market places. As an indication of Bury's architectural importance, 980 buildings have been listed as worthy of conservation.

The grandest building was the Abbey, once one of the greatest in

the Kingdom and a place of pilgrimage. It was founded by the Benedictines in AD945 with King Canute's support, to house the shrine of the martyred King (later St) Edmund, slain by Danish invaders in 869. From him, the town has derived its name. In the Abbey Church, on 20 November 1214, 25 major barons of England met the Archbishop of Canterbury, Stephen Langton, and vowed on the high altar that they would force King John to accept a Charter of Liberties. John signed the following year at Runnymede and Magna Carta has formed the basis of representational government throughout the free world ever since. A plaque on the gaunt ruin of the north-east pier of the presbytery records this historic meeting. After its dissolution in 1539, most of the Abbey buildings were dismantled, but some of its former glory remains.

The gateway and gatehouse, rebuilt in 1347, tower over the eastern side of Angel Hill and frame the beautiful Abbey gardens that lead down to the River Lark and the Abbot's Bridge, which once carried a wall across the stream. At the southern end of Angel Hill is the Athenaeum, an excellent example of a Georgian assembly room. Charles Dickens is known to have given readings in the elegant ballroom. He also immortalised the Angel Hotel, an old coaching inn, in *The Pickwick Papers*. At the opposite end is Angel Corner, a Queen Anne house that contains the Mayor's parlour and a superb collection of timepieces of every description. Visiting this museum at noon is a memorable experience!

Bury St Edmunds: the great gateway leading to the Abbey gardens (top); a view down Angel Hill; the interior of the Theatre Royal, built in 1819 by William Wilkins, architect of London's National Gallery

Across the street from the Athenaeum is the cathedral Church of St James, built in Perpendicular style in the 15th century and considerably restored by Sir Gilbert Scott in 1862. The blaze of colour afforded by the ceiling, decorated in East Anglian style in 1982, and the 1,000 embroidered kneelers displayed on the pews, are worth seeing. The Norman tower was once the main gateway to the Abbey Church. Further down Crown Street is St Mary's Church, the fifth on that site, which claims to be the finest parish church in England. It has a superb hammerbeam roof. Beyond it is the Greene King brewery, which also owns, but allows the National Trust to use, the Theatre Royal, a beautifully restored Regency theatre which remains a cultural centre for the town. Moyses Hall, overlooking the Butter Market, is a Norman dwelling-house of flint and stone that now houses the Borough Museum.

Three miles south-west, at Horringer, is **Ickworth**. The Hervey family (pronounced Harvey) has lived on this site since the 16th century, but it was only in 1714 that they came to prominence, when John Hervey was created the first Earl of Bristol. His third son, Frederick Augustus, Bishop of Londonderry, was responsible for the majestic pile that is Ickworth. Capability Brown chose the site; the round house on Belle Isle in Windermere, Cumbria, inspired Ickworth's elliptical design, and the Sandys brothers were commissioned to build it in 1796. For the last 10 years of his roving and adventurous life, the Earl Bishop steadily purchased works of art in Italy, with Ickworth in mind. Nearly all these were confiscated by Napoleon's troops in 1798. In the house there remains a collection of paintings, furniture and Georgian silver to satisfy even the most

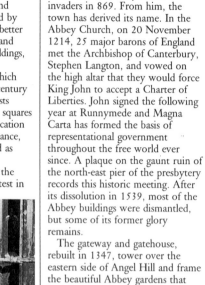

discerning visitor; these items were collected by the Herveys, who were fortunate in having Gainsborough as a local portrait painter. Two curved corridors connect the oval Rotunda, 100ft high, to two wings; the east wing remains the home of the 7th Marquess, but the west wing is now an empty shell.

AA recommends:
Hotels: Angel, Angel Hill, 3-star, *tel.* (0284) 3926
Butterfly, Symonds Rd, Moreton Hall, 3-star, *tel.* (0284) 60884
Ravenwood Hall, Rongham, 3-star, *tel.* (0359) 70345
Suffolk, 38 Buttermarket, 2-star, *tel.* (0284) 3995
Restaurant: Mortimer's Seafood, 31 Churchgate, 1-fork, *tel.* (0284) 60623
Guesthouses: Chantry Hotel, 8 Sparhawk St, *tel.* (0284) 67427
Dunstow, 8 Springfield Rd, *tel.* (0284) 67981
White Hart, 35 Southgate St, *tel.* (0284) 5547
Garages: Tim Brinton Cars, Bedingfield Way, *tel.* (0284) 67344
Northgate Motors, Northern Way Industrial Estate, *tel.* (0284) 63441

Caister-on-Sea, Norfolk

Map Ref: 89TG5212

As the name implies, this was an important Roman station and naval base, on the great inlet that once ran into Broadland. The foundations of a few Roman buildings have been laid bare and are open to view. Wide, sandy beaches and endless caravan parks now ring them. There are still flint-faced fishermen's cottages to be found, and the long-shore fishermen have formed the crews of the Caister lifeboat for generations.

A mile inland are the imposing remains of Caister Castle, built by Sir John Fastolf on his triumphant return from Agincourt – the same knight whose family lived at Blickling, and whom Shakespeare used as a model for Falstaff in *Henry IV*. Today, the moated walls surround a tall tower as well as the hall, which has Georgian embellishments on its walls. A collection of motor vehicles is here.

Two miles away are the Thrigby Hall Wildlife Gardens, a 250-year-old landscaped park.

AA recommends:
Campsite: Grasmere Caravan Park, 7 Bultitude's Loke, Yarmouth Rd, 3-pennant, *tel.* (0493) 720382
Garage: Allens, 2 Yarmouth Rd, *tel.* (0493) 720212

Cambridge, Cambridgeshire

Map Ref: 90TL4458

With its open spaces, famous buildings, peaceful courtyards, river and gardens, Cambridge is one of

Cambridge: punting along The Backs is a favourite occupation; visitors flock to the marvellous interior of King's College Chapel

the most beautiful and famous cities in Europe. In summer, one of the best ways of viewing Cambridge is to punt along the River Cam that flows around the city. From the river, it is possible to savour the breathtakingly grand architecture of the colleges along 'The Backs', and to enjoy the peaceful surroundings of the meadows upstream.

The Romans founded Cambridge. They settled north of the River Cam, on a site now occupied by Castle Hill and the Civic Offices. The A604 to Huntingdon follows an old Roman road that linked both towns. Later, both Cambridge and Huntingdon were Viking trade centres, and Danish longboats moored at the quays where Magdalene Bridge crosses the River Cam today. William the Conquerer built a huge fortress on what is now Castle Mound, in order to harry the Saxons under Hereward the Wake.

By 1200, all the churches in Cambridge had been built. Flourishing trade, prosperity and security attracted several religious orders to the town, and Cambridge became an academic community in the early 13th century when a group of scholars from Oxford arrived, fleeing religious persecution. This marked the beginning of the transformation of Cambridge from a small market town into a city best-known for, and largely dominated by, its university colleges.

Since the 13th century, the University has influenced both the architecture and the character of the town. By 1284, the University's first college, Peterhouse, had been founded. Five new collegiate foundations appeared over the next 70 years. As the University and its colleges became wealthier, they extended to the commercial heart of the town, and to most of the land along the riverside, where many of its great buildings stand today.

One of the famous sights of the city is the Chapel of King's College, which boasts great windows ablaze with colour, as well as a magnificent fan-vaulted ceiling. King's College was founded in 1441 by King Henry VI, but its construction was slowed by civil strife during the Wars of the Roses, and it was not until the middle of the 16th century that it was eventually completed. One of the most charming colleges, Queens', was founded no fewer than three times, first in 1446, then in 1448 by Margaret of Anjou, wife of King Henry VI, and then again in 1465 by Elizabeth Woodville, Queen of Edward IV. Cloister Court, in Queens' College, has mellow brick and half-timbering, an ideal setting for the Shakespearian plays performed here.

No visit to Cambridge would be complete without a trip to the Fitzwilliam Museum, with its priceless collection of paintings, antiquities, porcelain and armour in opulent surroundings. This is one of the oldest museums in the country, dating from 1816.

AA recommends:
Hotels: Garden House, Granta Place, off Mill Lane, 4-star, *tel.* (0223) 63421
Gonville, Gonville Place, 3-star, *tel.* (0223) 66611
Cambridge Post House, Lakeview, Bridge Rd, Impington, 4-star, *tel.* (022023) 7000
Guesthouses: Fairways Guest House, 143 Cherry Hinton Rd, *tel.* (0223) 246063
Lensfield Hotel, 53 Lensfield Rd, *tel.* (0223) 355017
Barnwell Lodge, 627-631 Newmarket Rd, *tel.* (0223) 249791
Restaurant: Midsummer House, Midsummer Common, 2-fork, *tel.* (0223) 69299
Campsite: Highfield Farm Camping Site, Long Rd, Camberton, 3-pennant, *tel.* (0223) 262308
Garages: Airport, Newmarket Rd, *tel.* (02205) 3131
Gilbert Rice, 350 Newmarket Rd, *tel.* (0223) 315435

Selection only: see page 4

Castle Acre, Norfolk

Map Ref: 87TF8115

Earl Warren, son-in-law of William the Conqueror, was given this manor, together with 139 others, and constructed a great castle that covered 18 acres. Edward I was entertained here in January 1297, and would have seen the three divisions of the fortifications, surrounded by an embattled wall 7ft thick. Only the 13th-century gateway and the earthworks survive today, but even these are on an impressive scale.

To the west of the village, beside the ancient Peddars Way, Warren also built Castle Acre Priory for the Cluniac order. Twenty-five monks once lived here in great state, and in 1500 the prior built himself a lavish residence. In 1536 all was swept away by the Dissolution, but today

Hedingham Castle's magnificent Norman keep is worth a visit

the glorious west front of the priory church still stands, almost intact, among the peaceful ruins, a reminder of Norman skills and monastic splendour. Down the valley of the River Nar at West Acre, there are ruins of another priory, founded by the Augustinians a few years afterwards on a scale to match their Cluniac neighbours; here a 14th-century gateway still stands.

Castle Hedingham, Essex

Map Ref: 91TL7835

This is an historical corner of Essex, with the best-preserved Norman keep in England, complemented by a parish church that was built in 1190, 50 years after the castle. The keep, almost 100ft high and the home of the Earls of Oxford for more than 400 years, commands the whole country around, including the village nestling at the

base of the knoll on which the castle was built. Inside the church there is an impressive monument to the 15th Earl, who died in 1539, and his wife. Like several other medieval churches in the vicinity, St Nicholas has a Tudor tower of red brick, and in the churchyard there is a war memorial made from a 12th-century cross.

There are other ancient, but more humble buildings worthy of note in the village, notably the Falcon Inn, and some of Georgian construction, such as the vicarage. Crafts are not neglected either – there is a thriving pottery, and a weaving shed, where silk can be woven on broadlooms in the old tradition.

The castle keep is open in the season, as is the Victorian railway station which is part of the Colne Valley Railway, which runs restored steam and diesel trains on most Sundays.

Just up the main road, the A604, is the sprawling village of Great

Essex play Surrey at the County Cricket Ground in Chelmsford

Yeldham which, at the south end, has a handsome coaching inn built in 1505, the White Hart. At the other end are the sad remains of a great oak tree, kept together by iron bands; it is known as the Gospel oak. An American financed the salvation of this gnarled veteran, but a replacement was also planted nearby, to mark the wedding of Edward VII to Princess Alexandra.

Chelmsford, Essex

Map Ref: 95TL7006

The county town of Essex derives its name from an ancient ford over the River Chelmer, near its confluence with the Cam. The road came in the reign of Henry I, when the Bishop of London built the first bridge, around 1100. In 1591 Chelmsford was described as being 'situate in good and wholesome air', comprising more than 300 houses and many inns.

Village Signs

Carved wooden village signs are a particularly attractive feature of the East Anglian countryside. They often depict some historical event linked with the village, a local industry, a legend or a character. Often the sign is the focal point of the village, located on the green or close to the church.

The idea originated in the reign of Edward VII. The first signs were erected on the Sandringham estate. Individual styles are instantly recognisable, especially that of Harry Carter, nephew of the discoverer of Tutankhamun's tomb, the first of whose brightly-coloured East Anglian signs was erected in Swaffham in 1929.

A different kind of sign is that made of decorative wrought iron. A particularly fine example can be seen at Kenninghall near Thetford. Today, local Women's Institutes are mainly responsible for commissioning the building or restoration of village signs.

Swaffham's famous 15th-century pedlar is depicted on the town's two-sided sign

Between 1789 and 1791 a Shire Hall was built, in the basement of which was the corn exchange. Its architect, Johnson, also rebuilt the church, to replace the one that collapsed in 1800. This rebuilt church, St Mary's, has the stature of a cathedral, and retains the original Perpendicular south porch. A free grammar school was endowed by Edward VI in 1552, and the school house was rebuilt in 1782. Water power led to the building of numerous corn mills along the river banks, to supply flour for the London market. Other industries followed, so that the town, with its excellent communications, became increasingly prosperous. The Chelmsford and Essex Museum in Oaklands Park has displays of the district's history and growth, and includes the Essex Regiment Museum.

Writtle, 2 miles to the west, was on the original highway from London, and has retained its importance because it was from St John's Green in the village that Marconi engineers developed the first regular radio broadcasts. The main green, complete with duck pond, is surrounded by fine Tudor and Georgian houses. The church was severely damaged by fire in 1974.

AA recommends:
Hotels: Pontlands Park Country, West Hanningfield Rd, Great Baddow, 3-star *tel.* (0245) 76444
South Lodge, 196 New London Rd, 3-star, *tel.* (0245) 264564
County, Rainsford Rd, 2-star, *tel.*(0245) 266911
Guesthouses: Beechcroft Private Hotel, 211 New London Rd, *tel.* (0245) 352462
Boswell House Hotel, 118-120 Springfield Rd, *tel.* (0245) 287587
Tanunda Hotel, 219 New London Rd, *tel.* (0245) 354295
Garage: County Motor Works, Eastern App, Springfield, *tel.* (0245) 466333
Writtle
Garage: Oxney, Ongar Rd, *tel.* (0245) 420149

Clacton-on-Sea, Essex

Map Ref: 92TM1714

There were once two sleepy coastal villages, Great and Little Clacton, which have now merged to form a popular holiday town, which backs onto a 7-mile stretch of sand. There are tree-lined streets, formal gardens, an esplanade and a long pier which was erected in 1873 when the railway first brought the visitors here. There remain three Martello towers, a much-restored Norman church, and a Georgian Mansion House; as a comfortable centre for exploring the hinterland, Clacton is ideal.

St Osyth, to the west, is an unspoilt village renowned for its Priory. As it is near a coastal creek,

it was all too easy for the Danish Vikings in AD653 to destroy the nunnery that had been established here by Ositha, daughter of the first Christian king of East Anglia. She later suffered martyrdom and became a saint. The site continued to be used until Henry VIII dissolved the Priory in 1539.

Only fragments of the original Priory buildings remain, but their former splendour can be traced in the surviving gatehouse, built in 1475 and recently restored. The outer façade is decorated with an elaborate pattern of white stones set into black, knapped flints.

Climb to the top of the Abbot's Tower, erected by Lord d'Arcy in 1558 as part of a range of domestic buildings (now demolished), to see the lawns laid out below, and the mysterious gardens with well-tended shrubs and hedges. The mid 16th-century tithe barn west of the gatehouse has a roof supported by an intricate network of beams. In the church of St Peter and St

Paul, the d'Arcy family, who owned the priory from the Dissolution until late in the last century, are commemorated in wall monuments.

AA recommmends:
Hotel: King's Cliff, Kings Pde, Holland-on-Sea, 2-star, *tel.* (0255) 812343
Guesthouses: Chudleigh Hotel, Agate Rd, *tel.* (0255) 425407
Sandrock Hotel, 1 Penfold Rd, *tel.* (0255) 428215
Campsite: Weeley Bridge Caravan Park, Weeley, 3 -pennant, *tel.* (0255) 830403
Garage: Auto Techs, 18 Brunel Rd, Gorse Lane Industrial Estate, *tel.* (0255) 429790

Clare, Suffolk

Map Ref: 91TL7645

There is no better introduction to this large, prosperous village astride the A1092 than a walk to the top of the motte or mound of the Norman castle, built in 1090. A country park surrounds it, and the old railway station is used as an

The remains of St Osyth's Priory are set in attractive gardens and a park, where deer and peacock roam. Clacton's sandy beaches and famous pier are popular with holidaymakers, especially children

information centre. Across the River Stour and over the railway bridge, a jumble of stone and brick walls may be seen. They once formed an Augustinian priory founded in 1248. Two buildings survive; the old infirmary, and the church, which was reconsecrated in 1954.

The flint-built parish church with its 13th-century tower dominates the centre of Clare. Mainly 15th-century, it contains some superb wood carving, but the stained glass suffered at the hands of Dowsing, the Puritan iconoclast who wreaked havoc in East Anglia's churches. Around the church are old houses displaying the ancient Suffolk art of pargeting – the application of moulded plaster to timber frames.

The Ancient House by the church, now a local museum, bears the date 1473 on its plaster, and the intricate, floral designs on gable ends and walls are well-worth discovering.

AA recommends:
Hotel: Bell, Market Hill, 2-star, *tel.* (0787) 277741

Cley next the Sea, Norfolk

Map Ref: 88TG0443

Prounced 'Cly', this is one of the many delightful flint villages that line the north Norfolk coast. It was once a busy port at the mouth of the River Glaven; the Custom House is a reminder of the days when great volumes of wool off the backs of Norfolk sheep were exported to the Low Countries. The chief imports today are migrant birds that are avidly watched and recorded as they nest in the nature reserves on the salt marshes, protected on the seaward side by a great shingle bank thrown up after the devastating floods in 1953. Indeed, Cley is the nerve and intelligence centre of the nation's 'twitchers' (or bird-watchers). It is a 3-mile walk west along the shingle bank to Blakeney Point, and to the east lies Gramborough Head, a small knoll that was once a Roman signal station. There is a well preserved windmill, now offering accommodation, and a church on a grand scale, with a superb south porch and lofty nave.

Local-caught fish being smoked in Cley

Coggeshall, Essex

Map Ref: 95TL8522

The River Blackwater, which is quite small here, divides Little and Great Coggeshall, and was once crossed by three bridges. On the right bank, on the Little side, a Cistercian abbey was founded by King Stephen in 1142. Some of the buildings survive, notably a 13th-century gate chapel and a two-storey corridor. Adjacent to them is the Abbey Barn, probably completed in 1150 and now restored. The result is an impressive timber building, one of the oldest in

The keep of Colchester's early Norman castle now houses a museum

Europe, that displays the wood-working skills of the Cistercian craftsmen. Over 80,000 tiles cover the roof. Grange Barn is now open to the public and is used for a wide range of events.

The old Roman road passes through Great Coggeshall, and the remains of a villa have been found, complete with arched vaults of brick. Beside the road in West Street is Paycocke's House, a splendid example of a timber-framed building, completed in 1505. The original naturalistic frieze bears the initials of Thomas Paycocke, a rich butcher, who died in 1580. Many old houses in the town have survived, displaying traditional pargeting.

AA recommends:
Hotel: White Hart, 3-star, *tel.* (0376) 61654
Garage: S G Saunders & Son, East St, *tel.* (0376) 61255

Colchester, Essex

Map Ref: 95TL9925

Colchester's importance throughout the centuries has lain in its geographical position: it commands the head of the Colne estuary and lies astride the route from London to East Anglia. Its history has been turbulent – in AD60, Boudicca of the Iceni sacked the Romans' first colony, which had been established here; King John employed French mercenaries under Prince Louis to capture the town in 1218, and in 1648 parliamentarian troops under General Fairfax laid siege to it.

In the reign of Elizabeth I, Flemish weavers settled in Colchester and transformed the town's economy. It became a centre of the cloth trade, and Bourne Mill on the western outskirts was one of the first water-driven mills built for the manufacture of baize cloth. The mill remains, with much of the machinery intact, an historic island in a sea of housing estates.

In no other town are so many Roman remains to be found. The small bricks favoured by those master builders are to be seen in every historic building. The great

Norman Castle once stretched from the High Street to the north wall. All that remains now is the keep, which was built directly over the Roman Temple to honour the Emperor Claudius. In the keep is a museum, where an outstanding collection of Roman antiquities are on show.

St John's Abbey, founded in 1097, was finally dissolved in 1539 when the Abbot, refusing to hand it over to the King's men, was hanged on the gallows at Greensted. Roman bricks are found in the 15th-century gatehouse, complete with pinnacled towers. This is all that remains of the original Abbey. The impressive ruins of St Botolph's Priory which, in about 1100, became the first in the country of the Augustinian Order, stand outside the Roman walls. Roman bricks also occur in the rebuilt tower of St Mary's Church, which was once used by the Royalists as a gun platform during the Civil War.

There are several excellent museums in the town: the one in All Saints Church is devoted to natural history, and another on 18th-century domestic life is housed in Hollytrees, a fine Georgian house. Across from the Castle there is the Minories, another Georgian building built around an earlier core, and now managed by a charitable trust as the arts centre. Around Stockwell Street is the old Dutch quarter of the town; here there are several coaching inns with courtyards.

No description of this historic town would be complete without mentioning oysters, which have been cultivated and savoured here since Roman times.

AA recommends:
Hotels: George, 116 High St, 3-star, *tel.* (0206) 578494
King's Ford Park, Layer Rd, Layer de la Haye, 2-star, *tel.* (0206) 34301
Campsite: Colchester Camping Caravan Park, Cymbeline Way, Lexden, 3-pennant, *tel.* (0206) 45551
Garages: Candor Motors, Magdalen St, *tel.* (0206) 571171
Cowies GM, Scotts Corner, Ipswich Rd, *tel.* (0206) 844422

Cromer, Norfolk

Map Ref: 89TG2142

Originally a select watering place where visitors sought the sharp and health-giving breezes off the North Sea, Cromer mushroomed with the coming of the railway. By 1901 the pier had been built, and a week by the sea at Cromer was much sought-after. Today, not much has changed – the old fishing village is still there, among Victorian hotels and boarding houses, and every summer the pier theatre plays to full houses. The lifeboat lives in a shed at the pier's end; there has been a lifeboat on station here since 1804. The longshore fishermen are known locally as 'crabs'. Crabbing begins in March and continues until the autumn storms make fishing dangerous. Cromer crabs are now served throughout Norfolk and are a local delicacy.

Two miles to the south-west is **Felbrigg Hall**, a National Trust mansion that is one of the finest houses in Norfolk, containing its original 18th-century furniture and pictures. First begun as a modest Jacobean house in 1620, a Carolean west wing was added in 1675, followed by a Georgian addition to the east. Finally, a castellated stable block was built in 1825. The

Wyndham family was responsible for this work, but the hall's name comes from the de Felbriggs, whose brass memorials, dating from 1380, make the isolated parish church at Felbrigg very special. There is a large walled garden, which has been colourfully restored and is overlooked by a rare dovecote that once housed 2,000 white doves.

AA recommends:
Hotels: Cliff House, Overstrand Rd, 2-star, *tel.* (0263) 514094
Cliftonville, Runton Rd, 2-star, *tel.* (0263) 512543
Guesthouses: Brightside, 19 Macdonald Rd, *tel.* (0263) 513408

The lifeboat's steep ramp can be seen at the end of Cromer's pier

Chellow Dene, 23 Macdonald Rd, *tel.* (0263) 513251
Morden, 20 Cliff Ave, *tel.* (0263) 513396
Sandcliff Private Hotel, Runton Rd, *tel.* (0263) 512888
Westgate Lodge Private Hotel, 10 Macdonald Rd, *tel.* (0263) 512840
Campsite: Seacroft Camping Park, 4-pennant, *tel.* (0263) 511722
Forest Park Caravan Site, 3-pennant, *tel.* (0263) 513290
Garages: Allens, West St, *tel.* (0263) 512557
East Coast Motor Co, 16 Church St, *tel.* (0263) 512203

Working Boats

With its long coastline and its network of waterways, East Anglia has depended for centuries on working boats. Inland and along the coast, boats were used until well into the 20th century, both to carry farm produce and goods produced by mills and factories, and to bring coal, iron and other materials into the area. Long-distance sea-going vessels have been important since at least medieval times, when men from Lynn, Blakeney, Cromer, Dunwich, Ipswich and other ports went to Iceland each summer to catch cod, and to trade.

The most distinctive working boat of East Anglia is the black-sailed wherry, which is able to carry 13-ton cargoes in shallow waters. Wherries were used throughout the Broads, and were particularly important for transporting cargoes between Norwich and Yarmouth. Only one trading wherry survives, the *Albion*, which is on view at Ludham and preserved by the Norfolk Wherry Trust.

The sea-going equivalent of the wherry was the brown-sailed barge, often called the Thames barge, which could withstand sea storms but was also manoeuvrable on inland waters. Until about 1960, spritsail barges were carrying cargoes of all kinds along the East Coast. The last one to trade under sail, and the last commercial sailing

ship in northern Europe, was the *Cambria*, which was sold in 1970 for preservation, to the Maritime Trust. Spritsail barges were built and owned in considerable numbers on the Stour and the Orwell, where many are still to be seen. The Pin Mill Barge Match is still held in June each year.

The various forms of fishing also gave rise to specialised boats. For herring fishing, there were sailing 'luggers' of Lowestoft and Yarmouth. Introduced in the late 18th century, they usually went out to sea in the afternoons, and after shooting their nets, would join together in groups of as many as 100 luggers at a time, stretching over perhaps as much as 2 miles of water. Luggers were replaced by steam drifters, but today both have disappeared. Models can be seen at the Maritime Museum for East Anglia at Yarmouth, and in the delightful little maritime museum at Sparrow's Nest, Lowestoft. One of the sailing smacks which trawled for

Wherry unloading in days gone by

flatfish and cod in the North Sea is now being restored at Lowestoft. It is known as the *Excelsior*. Numerous examples of the little oyster smacks used on the Colne and Blackwater in Essex can still be seen sailing at weekends, although the professional oystermen now use motor boats.

Lifeboats were established early along this busy and dangerous coast. The first was placed at Lowestoft, on the Suffolk coast, in 1801, and another was placed at Cromer in 1804. A rowing and sailing lifeboat, based on the design of crab boats, called the *Henry Ramey Upcher*, can still be seen in a boathouse at Sheringham. It was a volunteer boat, operated by the fishermen.

In the days of sail, when it was not unusual for many hundreds of vessels to be prevented from sailing by the wind off Yarmouth, a great deal of salvage work and lifesaving was carried out by the 'beachmen' in yawls, large open sailing boats which were launched off the open beaches between Happisburgh and Aldeburgh.

Danbury, Essex

Map Ref: 95TL7705

A long gravel ridge joins Maldon to Chelmsford, and surrounding villages have claimed grazing rights to areas along it for centuries. To the south of the A414 is Danbury Common, which has been used for military operations since Saxon times. There was once a hill-fort here, but with the threat of French invasion in Napoleonic times it was turned into a large army camp. The remains of earthworks can be traced to the west of the Cricketers' Arms, a pleasant inn that overlooks the old cricket pitch.

Today this common and that of Lingwood, north of the village, are used for more peaceful pursuits. There are waymarked walks and bridleways supervised by a National Trust Warden, who also helps to manage the woodland and heath in traditional ways to ensure the survival of rich animal and plant life. At Blake's Wood, adjacent to Lingwood, more than 10 million bluebells carpet the ground in May. In Danbury itself there is a traditional village green, complete with pond and ducks. The church is a landmark on top of the hill, and contains wooden figures of medieval knights.

Debenham, Suffolk

Map Ref: 92TM1763

Debenham is as typical and unspoilt a village as can be found in Suffolk, on the old direct route between Norwich and Ipswich; yet the inhabitants complained about heavy traffic at the beginning of the last century! The River Deben rises nearby. A fire in March 1744, which broke out in a bakery, destroyed 33 tenements. History also recalls that under Priory Field are the foundations of a large priory, once owned by the Prior of Ely in the reign of Edward the Confessor.

The church in Debenham, which has two Anglo-Saxon windows, is renowned for its fine bells, cast in 1761.

Crows Hall, 1½ miles south east, is an imposing early 16th-century moated manor house, with a range of outbuildings once used by Royalist cavalry in the Civil War. At Bedingfield is another moated, timber-framed and brick mansion, Flemings Hall. Neither Flemings Hall nor Crows Hall is open to the public. At Mendlesham a collection of armour reposes in the chamber above the south porch of the church of St Mary.

The market town of Diss in the Waveney Valley retains some old and interesting buildings, especially around the Market Place

Dedham, Essex

Map Ref: 92TM0533

The charming valley of the River Stour and the surrounding countryside has been immortalised in the brilliant oil paintings of John Constable. The silhouette of the tall tower of St Mary's Church in Dedham appears in many of them. The artist was educated at the old grammar school in the village, founded about 1570; the fine building survives. The ancestors of General Sherman, an American

The elegant Shermans Hall in Dedham was the home of the American general's ancestors

Civil War hero, are buried in St Mary's, and the elegant Georgian town house directly opposite is Shermans Hall, one of many period buildings in this popular village. In the Marlborough Arms are some beautiful carved beams, and the Master Weaver's house is half-timbered, built in the 15th century with a courtyard.

Another noted artist, Alfred Munnings, went to live in Castle House on the outskirts of Dedham in 1920, and his widow, Lady Munnings, offered the house as a gallery to the public in 1961. The collection of paintings it contains spans the artist's turbulent life.

The old mill buildings down by the river are now converted for residential use, and boats can be hired from there for the short row down to **Flatford Mill**, where Golding Constable, the artist's miller father, worked. Thatched Bridge Cottage, upstream of the mill beside an old timber bridge, has a National Trust pictorial exhibition that shows the spots where Constable's paintings were first conceived, and then executed. A modern tea garden is next door, beside the original dry-dock in which horse-drawn barges that once plied the rivers were built. In 1914 most were scuttled to prevent them from being used following invasion, and it is planned to display one of these in the dock that Constable once painted, when restoration is complete. Willy Lott's cottage, also restored by the mill pond, is instantly recognisable as the setting for the *Hay Wain*. Valley Farm opposite the mill is one of the best-preserved medieval farmhouses in Suffolk.

AA recommends:
Hotel: Maison Talbooth, Stratford Rd, 3-star, *tel.* (0206) 322367
Restaurant: Le Talbooth, 3-fork, *tel.* (0206) 323150
Guesthouse: Dedham Hall, *tel.* (0206) 323027

Diss, Norfolk

Map Ref: 88TM1179

This is a thriving market town built around a mere or, as the Saxons called it, a *dice*. The facetious John Skelton, Poet Laureate in the reign of Henry VIII, was Rector of St Mary's Church, and was eventually forced to take sanctuary from his enemies in Westminster Abbey. The church is very much part of the town centre, with a tower

surmounted by a lantern and processional arches on either side. Around the market place are many period buildings with half-timbering and jettied upper storeys. On the right of Market Hill is the Greyhound Inn, and the Saracens Head, with its colourful plasterwork, is adjacent to the church. Several modern shop fronts strike a discordant note, however, and there is traffic ever-present. Some fine Georgian buildings remain, however, and beyond the Corn Exchange of 1854 are cavernous maltings, built in 1788 by Lacon's Brewery.

Wingfield College, 7 miles south-east, has a neo-classical façade which hides a great hall of an earlier manor house. Restoration work began in 1971, and a fascinating series of rooms was uncovered, some of which are now used for cultural events. The collegiate church contains fine monuments to the Wingfield family, who founded the College in 1362.

AA recommends:
Restaurant: Salisbury House, 84 Victoria Rd, 2-fork, *tel.* (0379) 4738

Downham Market, Norfolk

Map Ref: 87TF6103

Once a thriving river port on the banks of the Great Ouse, from which it was separated first by the railway and then by a drainage cut, Downham is a quiet market town, built largely from local carr stone. There has been a settlement here since Romano-British times, and for centuries fen roads have crossed at this comparatively high point. Two fine old hostelries remain, and if the main railway line to London and Cambridge is electrified, much new building can be expected. The cast iron Gothic clock tower, built in 1878, stands out in a livery of green-and-white paint.

The higher land extends towards the sea, and is known as marshlands rather than marshy fens. Here along the river bank, four old settlements may be found, the Wiggenhalls. Three of them boast interesting churches, with superb carved benches and welcoming pews.

AA recommends:
Hotels: Castle, High St, 2-star, *tel.* (0366) 384311
Crown, Bridge St, 1-star, *tel.* (0366) 382322
Guesthouse: Cross Keys Riverside Hotel, Hilgay, *tel.* (0366) 387777

Dunwich, Suffolk

Map Ref: 93TM4770

Stand on the sandy cliffs of Dunwich and beneath your feet is a buried town that was once the seat of the Saxon king of East Anglia and one of the greatest and most prosperous ports in Britain. Dunwich grew as a fishing and trading port until the end of the 14th century, but then the sea literally swept away much of the town. In 1386 a great storm caused three churches and many acres to sink beneath the waves. The monastery of the Franciscans, whose ruins can still be seen, escaped the sea but fell victim to King Henry VIII's Dissolution. The only other ruins are those of the leper hospital of St James. All the rest of the ruins have gone: the tower of the last of Dunwich's nine churches fell into the sea in 1918. Beneath the war memorial is the Cooper Brass, a fragment of a memorial to a shipowner and bailiff who died in 1576 and was buried outside the old All Saints' Church, the last to be claimed by the sea.

Today the boats of Dunwich fishermen are still drawn up on the shingle bank; behind them is a beach café which serves some of the finest fish and chips in those parts.

The town sign is a reminder of Dunwich's days as a great port; now fishermen catch cod for visitors

Two miles down the coast is **Dunwich Heath**, 214 acres of heather and scrubland preserved by the National Trust, with guaranteed access to the cliffs and shore. The old coastguard cottages that overlook the neighbouring RSPB nature reserve at Minsmere have been converted into tea and information rooms, holiday cottages and a house for the resident warden. The brooding bulk of Sizewell A, Britain's first nuclear power station, will soon be eclipsed by even larger Sizewell B, but the birds that find sanctuary here appear blissfully unaware.

Leiston, a mile or two inland from Sizewell, is an industrial area on the Suffolk coastline, home to a thriving engineering industry begun during the Industrial Revolution for making agricultural implements. One of the best-known firms, Garretts, was established in 1778 as a blacksmithing business. The company's 'Long Shop' was built in 1853 as an erecting shop for traction engines. This spectacular building is now preserved as a museum. To the north of the town, the imposing flint and brick ruins of 14th-century Leiston Abbey, including the church transepts and cloisters, are open to view throughout the year.

AA recommends:
Hotel: White Horse, Station Rd, 1-star, *tel.* (0728) 830694
Campsite: Cakes & Ale, Abbey Lane, 3-pennant, *tel.* (0728) 831655
Garage: Waterloo Avenue S/sta, Waterloo Av, *tel.* (0728) 830783

Duxford, Cambridgeshire

Map Ref: 90TL4746

Motorists on the M11, glancing west on approaching Junction 10, notice an ever-changing selection of aircraft lined up in front of hangars, some of which date from World War I. In the sky above there could be Sopwith Pups in mock skirmishes with Fokker tri-planes, or Hawker Hurricanes with ME109s. This early military airfield is now the home of an historic collection of civil and military aeroplanes, and army vehicles, under the care of the Imperial War Museum. In the Battle of Britain, fighters from Duxford were often in action; Douglas Bader's squadron was based here.

The pilots who died are buried in the graveyard of Whittlesford church, 2 miles to the north. The small village of Whittlesford, which has grown up around a ford over a tributary of the River Cam over the centuries, has several fine half-timbered buildings, including an old mill house.

AA recommends:
Hotel: Duxford Lodge, Ickleton Rd, 3-star, *tel.* (0223) 836444

East Dereham: Bishop Bonner's Cottage and St Nicholas', where Bonner was Rector in the 1530s

East Dereham, Norfolk

Map Ref: 88TF9813

Although there is a West Dereham village near Downham Market, this thriving market town is usually called Dereham and lies at the heart of Norfolk. A milestone just off the market place claims that London is 100 miles away. George Borrow, the 19th-century author of *Lavengro*, was born just outside at Dumpling Green; poet William Cowper is buried in the quiet churchyard, and so is a French prisoner-of-war called Denarde, who escaped while on his way to Peterborough jail and was shot while hiding up a tree.

The town today is an odd mixture of some fine Georgian buildings in the market place, a few hideous shop fronts and vast maltings, now giving way to development and the inevitable supermarkets. Bishop Bonner's Cottage, with attractive pargeting, stands aloof near the church, a rare reminder of how Dereham would have appeared in the 16th century. The Bishop made a name for himself by sending many Protestants to the stake under Queen Mary.

St Withburga, daughter of the Anglo-Saxon King Anna, who founded a convent here in the 7th century, was buried in the churchyard, and miracles occurred. The Abbot of Ely later deceitfully removed her remains, and the spring which gushed from her desecrated grave is known as St Withburga's Well. The coloured wooden frieze over the road by the market reminds us of the tale.

Three miles north, at Gressenhall, is the Norfolk Rural Life Museum, an excellent place in which to learn about the changing face of the countryside.

AA recommends:
Hotels: King's Head, Norwich St, 2-star, *tel.* (0362) 693842
Phoenix, Church St, 2-star, *tel.* (0362) 2276
George, Market Pl, Swaffham Rd, 1-star, *tel.* (0362) 66801
Campsite: Dereham Caravan & Camping Park, Norwich Rd, 2-pennant, *tel.* (0362) 694619

Elton, Cambridgeshire

Map Ref: 84TL0993

The River Nene flows past this attractive village of stone-built houses and cottages, many with thatched roofs. Coopers Hospital, an almshouse founded in 1663, is noteworthy, and the Black Horse Inn is also worth seeing. It is of Georgian construction, like other houses facing the village green. The church has a high tower and interesting fenestration that lights a mainly 14th-century interior.

Elton Hall is a Gothic building with several contrasting architectural styles, incorporating a 15th-century tower and a chapel, which is equally ancient. Each elevation is different in appearance, but all is not as it seems. The battlements and turret tops were created from wood to save expense, and French prisoners-of-war from the nearby Norman Cross camp were employed for the same reason during the reconstruction, which took place between 1812 and 1814.

Eleven fine rooms are open to view. They range from the sumptuous state drawing room in the style of a French château, to a small room in the medieval Tower, where there is a bust of a gardener who tended the gravel paths for nearly 70 years. The main library is the home of one of the finest private book collections in England, with more than 12,000 volumes that include rare bibles, manuscripts and Henry VIII's prayer book. Every room contains treasures, and family portraits are by Reynolds and Gainsborough; over the fireplace in the small dining-room is a masterpiece of Dedham Vale by John Constable.

Outside, in the old stables, is the family state coach used for Queen Victoria's Jubilee, and in the Victorian rose garden there are 1,000 roses, including old-fashioned scented varieties.

Ely, Cambridgeshire

Map Ref: 90TL5380

For 900 years the Cathedral of the Fens has provided a landmark which can be seen from miles around, dominating the rich, black fields that stretch to the horizon under wide skies. The Normans who built this Romanesque marvel were so skilled that today, masons engaged in a £4 million restoration scheme have found the towering piers in perfect order. Admittedly, the first steeple collapsed in 1322, but it was replaced by the Octagon, 400 tons of masonry suspended, seemingly, without any visible support.

Hereward the Wake

When William the Conqueror invaded England, most of it fell to his Norman soldiers fairly quickly. But in Fenland, a small pocket of resistance remained as a thorn in the Normans' side for a good five years after the Conquest. Hereward's landowning family originated from Bourne in Lincolnshire but, outlawed in 1062, he left England for Flanders. After the invasion, William tried to consolidate his hold by dispossessing rich, powerful monasteries and wealthy landowners. While protecting his family and estate, Hereward's brother was killed at Bourne, and this gave Hereward his thirst for revenge.

In 1069, Hereward was party to the sacking of the Anglo-Saxon monastery at Peterborough. Afterwards, he sought refuge on the Isle of Ely, protected by the treacherous surrounding marshes. It was an ideal base from which to harry his enemy, and easy to defend. Unlike today, the Fens then were wild and desolate marshes.

The Normans made several unsuccessful attempts to besiege the Isle, which included trying to lay a causeway across a narrow stretch of fen, probably at Aldreth or Stuntney. They did break into Ely eventually, but Hereward managed to escape the considerable bloodshed and retribution that followed. What happened to him after that remains unclear, although

Hereward and his companions flee from Ely after the Conqueror's forces finally broke through

he is reputedly buried in the Abbey grounds at Crowland.

Charles Kingsley (author of *The Water Babies*) wrote a novel about Hereward the Wake. Many of our notions of Hereward as a romantic hero are based on this novel.

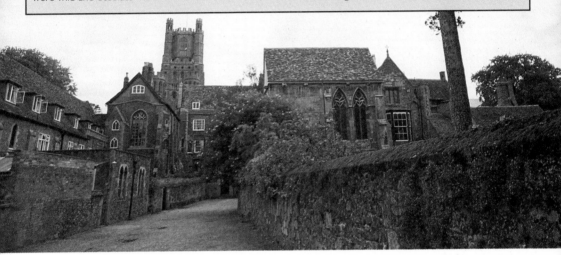

This cathedral is doubly interesting for its setting, in the walls and buildings of a Benedictine monastery that dates back to 970, and for the King's School in its precincts, founded by Alfred the Great.

The Norman nave, with its Victorian painted ceiling, now fresh and weatherproof after a great amount of restoration, captures the attention first, but the 14th-century choir stalls and misericords are not to be overlooked, and the 11th-century figures grouped around the outside of the prior's door in the south wall of the nave are also memorable. A stained-glass museum in the north triforium gives spectacular views of the cathedral.

The best approach to the cathedral is past the parish church of St Mary, begun in Norman times, which is flanked by half-timbered buildings (one of which was Oliver Cromwell's home for 11 years and is now the vicarage) and Palace Green, where there is a large Russian canon. The delightful walk to and from the Great Ouse that washes the shores of the Isle of Ely is also well worth taking.

The Octagon of Ely Cathedral is clearly seen from **Wicken**, a small village whose main claim to fame is the fen to the west – an undrained remnant of the great marshes that were finally tamed by Dutch engineers. The Victorians hunted insects here, especially the lovely swallow-tail butterfly and, fortunately for posterity, ensured that the wet habitat remained in a natural state. In 1899 Wicken Fen, rich in plant and insect life, was declared the country's first nature reserve and given to the National Trust. More than three-quarters of the 740 acres are open to the public throughout the year, and access is made easier by a raised walkway 1km long, suitable for wheelchairs.

Along the route is a small working windpump, the last survivor of the hundreds of drainage

Above: Prior Crauden's Chapel in Ely dates from c.1324

mills in the Fens. It now pumps water onto the fen. There are also flooded brick pits, which are ideal for studying aquatic life. Here there are hides from where birdlife can be watched, and fields which are harvested for reed and sedge in season. In a modern, hexagonal reception building is an illuminated display that shows how the fen has altered over the past 4,000 years.

AA recommends:
Hotel: Fenlands Lodge, Soham Rd, Stuntney, 3-star, *tel.* (0353) 67047
Restaurant: Old Fire Engine House, 25 St Mary's St, 1-fork, *tel.* (0353) 2582
Guesthouses: Castle Lodge Hotel, 50 New Barns Rd, *tel.* (0353) 2276
Nyton, 7 Barton Rd, *tel.* (0353) 2459
Wicken
Hotel: Wicken Country, Cross Tree Rd, 2-star, *tel.* (090857) 239

Epping Forest, Essex

Map Ref: 94TQ49

An invaluable place to walk for those living in north-east London, the Forest covers 6,000 acres south and east of Epping, and is crossed by two motorways, one of which, the M25, was built underground in order to preserve a section of the Forest. In Saxon times, most of Essex was wooded, as many of the place names testify – Theydon Bois, for example. Later, the royal liking for the chase ensured that some woodland was carefully preserved near London (see also Hatfield Forest, page 54). The stag was turned out on Easter Monday to be hunted, by tradition.

In 1878 the Epping Forest Act placed control of what remained of the Forest in the hands of the City of London, assuring public access and a curb on the development that had ceaselessly eroded the Forest's boundaries. A third of the Forest is now grazing land, and the rest is a natural mix of standard trees and underwood, in which beeches, hornbeams and oaks have pride of place. There are numerous paths and rides. Two long-distance footpaths, the Essex and the Forest Ways, begin at Epping and link Harwich and Hatfield respectively.

The town of Epping, which is 1 mile long and was well-served by coaching inns for centuries, is an excellent centre for exploring the ancient Forest on foot or horseback. Visitors have a choice of several centres that interpret the history and life of the area. There are Epping Bury Fruit Farm and Epping Upland, a village which also has a 13th-century church, and Hayes Hill, north of Waltham Abbey at Crooked Mile, where there is a working farm that demonstrates the milking of cows and explains modern farming practice. At Hobbs' Cross Farm, Theydon Garnon, the accent is on domestic livestock and their use to man.

South of Epping, easily seen to the right of the road, are massive Iron Age earthworks, known as Ambresbury Banks. Here Boudicca, leader of the Iceni, was reputed to have made her last stand against the Romans. Models of this fort and another at Loughton Camp nearby can be seen at the Epping Forest Museum at Chingford, where a timber-framed hunting lodge erected by Henry VIII for his courtiers has been restored to house it. History relates that Elizabeth I used to ride up and down the stairs, which were adapted to make this possible. A mounting block once stood on the top landing.

The Epping Forest Conservation Centre is at **High Beach**, where the poet Tennyson lived for three years. Here there is a strange grotto known as the Catacombs, built from great blocks of stone.

AA recommends:

Epping
Hotel: Post House, High Rd, Bell Common, 3-star, *tel.* (0378) 73137
Garage: B G Automotives, Half Moon Lane, off High St, *tel.* (0378) 74753
Loughton
Garages: Brown's Eng, Brown's Corner, High Rd, *tel.* 01-508 6262
Dawkins Coachworks, Oakwood Hill Ind. Est, Debden, *tel.* 01-502 0431
Chingford
Campsite: Sewardstone Caravan Park, 3-pennant, *tel.* 01-529 5689
Garage: Connaught Electrical Svcs, 2 Loxham Rd, *tel.* 01-531 3811
Theydon Bois
Garages: Station, Station Approach, *tel.* (03788 1) 2451
Wood & Krailing, High Rd, *tel.* (03788 1) 3831

There is plenty of room for everyone in the 6,000 acres of Epping Forest. Queen Elizabeth's Hunting Lodge at Chingford, from which monarchs viewed the chase, now houses a display relating to the history and wildlife of the Forest

Eye, Suffolk

Map Ref: 92TM1473

It is hard to imagine now that the small River Dove was once navigable from Cromer, but the very name Eye, or Aye (Saxon for island), proves this. The Romans settled here and a hoard of gold coins was dug up in 1781 on Abbey Farm. Nearby is the site of the Benedictine Priory established by Robert Malet, whose father, William, came over from Normandy with the Conqueror and built the castle that overlooks the tall tower of the church. Where mock ruins now crown the castle's motte, there was once a post mill, but this was removed in 1845.

The church is remarkable outside for the 101ft flushwork tower, which Pevsner called 'one of the wonders of Suffolk', and for the two-storied south porch, against which rests a red brick table which was used to distribute the 'dole' or bread each Saturday to the poor. Inside, the rood-screen is a striking feature, erected in 1480 and heavily restored in 1925. The painted figures in the panels are original, and complete.

The half-timbered 16th-century Guildhall by the churchyard gate, the splendid Victorian town hall, and the ancient pubs are also features of the town. There are several fine examples of crinkle-crankle, serpentine brick walls built in corrugations, and peculiar to Suffolk.

Finchingfield's charming duckpond and village green is a deserved favourite with calendar compilers. Felixstowe (left), a major container port, is also a popular, bustling seaside resort

Felixstowe, Suffolk

Map Ref: 93TM3034

This town calls itself the garden resort of the Suffolk coast, and is situated between the estuaries of the Deben and Orwell rivers, facing south. The cliffs have been transformed into hanging gardens, a floral backdrop to 2 miles of promenade, beaches, and the usual array of boating ponds, miniature railways and amusement arcades. The Spa Pavilion provides indoor amusement, while the new leisure centre can offer three swimming pools and associated fitness areas. The resort has a pleasant pre-war flavour quite different from the frenetic bustle of the port, which is privately-owned and has grown since 1966 into a major European container port. Container ships are constantly passing the Landguard Fort, which has guarded the approaches to the estuaries and the port of Harwich since Charles I's time. The Fort, rebuilt in 1718 and strengthened several times since, was the subject of a painting by Gainsborough. Landguard Fort and the nearby nature reserve are both open to the public.

St Felix was the Patron Saint of the East Angles, and in the 11th century, the Benedictines founded a priory in his name on a site where the parish church of St Peter and St Paul now stands.

Felixstowe Ferry, up the coast towards the Deben estuary, is a charming village with a good anchorage, used by both yachts and fishing boats.

AA recommends:
Hotels: Orwell Moat House, Hamilton Rd, 4-star, *tel.* (0394) 285511
Brook Hotel & Restaurant, Orwell Rd, 3-star, *tel.* (0394) 278441
Marlborough, Sea Front, 2-star, *tel.* (0394) 285621
Ordnance, 1 Undercliff Rd West, 2-star, *tel.* (0394) 273427
Garages: French's, 31-39 Undercliff Rd West, *tel.* (0394) 286339
Henly's, Crescent Rd, *tel.* (0394) 283221

Finchingfield, Essex

Map Ref: 94TL6832

Approaching this unspoilt village from the east, the first building to note is the post mill, built in 1775. The old miller's house is down by the roadside. The steep, sloping green has a pond and hump-backed bridge; on all sides there are well-preserved houses of various ages. One road climbs a sharp, short hill to the church. The entrance to the churchyard is through the gatehouse of Holy Trinity guildhouse, built in the 15th century as the village school. The church has several notable features, including its massive tower; the first two storeys of this date from Saxon times. The south door bears original tracery and carving of 1370, but even earlier is the elaborate rood-screen with ogee arches. Look out for the little men playing pipes at both corners, which are a pointer to the screen's Flemish origin.

Framlingham, Suffolk

Map Ref: 93TM2863

From the first Norman kings of England until the accession of Mary to the throne in 1553, the castle at Framlingham was the seat of three powerful families, the Bigods, Mowbrays and Howards. Mary Tudor's standard was flying over the gateway tower when she was told that she was Queen. Here lived Thomas Howard, the first Duke of Norfolk, who won the Battle of Flodden for Henry VIII; when he died in 1524, he was buried at Thetford Priory. Today, the curtain wall and 13 towers, many surmounted by blank Tudor chimneys, hide a hollow courtyard. The well-preserved ruins look down on a large village, and the Victorian buildings of a public school erected, it is said, with money left over from the building of the Albert Memorial in London. The parish church contains a magnificent painted alabaster tomb, with effigies of the Earl of Surrey, beheaded by Henry VIII on a trumped-up charge of treason, and his father. There are other less colourful, but equally fine monuments, and an unusual 18th-century allegorical painting behind the altar.

AA recommends:
Hotel: Crown, Market Hill, 2-star, *tel.* (0728) 723521

Charming cottages in Glandford, once noted for its fishing trade

Glandford, Norfolk

Map Ref: 88TG0441

This is a delightful estate village, largely owned by the family living at Bayfield Hall, a mile to the south. Both the Dutch-gabled museum that houses a collection of shells, semi-precious stones and fossils, and the rebuilt church, owe their existence to Bayfield. In 1906 St Martin's Church was completed, a copy of the medieval building which once stood on the site. Inside, the rich carving of roof, screen and choir stalls, made from local oak and cedar, is overwhelming.

Letheringsett, on the road to Holt, has a water-driven corn mill and a delightful water garden along the banks of the Glaven.

AA recommends:
Holt
Hotel: Feathers, Market Pl, 2-star, *tel.* (026371) 2318
Guesthouse: Lawns Hotel, Station Rd, *tel.* (0263) 713390

Glemham Hall, Suffolk

Map Ref: 93TM3459

Motorists who speed up the A12 should not be put off by the austere façade of this country mansion. Behind it is a comfortable dwelling, now the home of the Cobbold family.

The building dates from the Elizabethan period, although the de Glemhams owned land here as early as 1228. They sold the estate in 1709 to Dudley North. By 1722 the interior of the hall had been converted into the superb set of Georgian rooms which the visitor sees today, full of fine Sheraton, Chippendale and Hepplewhite furniture. The imposing staircase dates from 1720, as does most of the panelling which, in the hall, has been stripped. The Queen Anne furniture is framed by Corinthian columns.

Time must be taken to explore the beautiful rose garden, enclosed within sheltering walls, which contains a summer house, lily pond and classical urns in traditional English symmetry. The wide lawns are framed by avenues of Irish yews; spreading cedars and beeches complete the setting.

The 15th-century tower of St Andrew's Church overlooks the garden. Brasses on the church walls commemorate the Glemham family.

Godmanchester, Cambridgeshire

Map Ref: 90TL2470

The Roman town of Godmanchester, pentagonal in shape and still defined by the ancient roads that encircle it, has charters dating back to 1214. It is not surprising, therefore, to find several ancient farms here, as well as town houses surviving among the thatched and half-timbered cottages.

One such house is **Island Hall**, a large red brick building two-and-a-half storeys high, with two bay wings. This mansion was built in 1747 for John Jackson, Receiver General for Huntingdon (which lies just across the River Ouse). Its name is taken from the island which formed part of the original pleasure gardens to the house.

Now the house has been restored, and is used as a comfortable family home. The main rooms are panelled in fine Georgian style, and contain many interesting items that relate to the family that acquired them. The gardens in their tranquil riverside setting are open and teas are served here.

Grafham Water, Cambridgeshire

Map Ref: 90TL1468

A bold and successful move by the water authority to create a reservoir near the small village of Grafham has resulted in a 2½-square-mile stretch of water that has become a mecca for sailors, fishermen, bird watchers, walkers and cyclists.

The village itself, 5 miles south-west of Huntingdon, has a small, simple church dating back to the 13th century. Next to it is the old rectory, mostly 16th-century.

To the south-west is **Kimbolton Castle**, a Tudor house remodelled by Vanbrugh with an Adam gatehouse. Inside are unusual mural paintings by Pellegrini, and an original Tudor great hall.

AA recommends:
Grafham
Campsite: Old Manor Caravan Park, Church Lane, 3-pennant, *tel.* (0480) 810264
Kimbolton
Restaurant: La Côte d'Or, High St, 1-fork, *tel.* (0480) 861587

Great Yarmouth, Norfolk

Map Ref: 89TG5207

Great Yarmouth was described in 1818 as 'the Margate of Norfolk'. The Romans came as far as Caister to the north, and to Burgh Castle inland, beside Breydon Water. The Normans were also here, and King John granted the town a Charter in 1208.

Around the town in those days was a wall, with no less than 16 towers and 10 gates. Bishop Losinga of Norwich established the parish church of St Nicholas in 1123, which stood until 1942 when enemy action almost destroyed it. Rebuilt after the war, it is now a vast church, one of the country's largest. The market place remains the centre of the town, and King Street, the main shopping

16th-century glass panel in the Elizabethan House Museum, Great Yarmouth

thoroughfare, leads off from it. Close to this street is the remarkable early-Georgian church of St George, with a tower enclosed within the building; it is now used as an Arts Centre. Near the market place is the old Fishermen's Hospital, founded in 1702 to house retired fishermen and their wives.

Fishing was for centuries the main industry here, and Yarmouth was known for its herrings. Over-fishing and Dutch competition caused a decline in fishing, however, and

waterfront. The Elizabethan House and the Customs House are now museums. Behind this grand frontage stretched the Rows, a pattern of narrow parallel lanes where humbler folk lived. An especially narrow horse-drawn cart had to be used here to transport nets and cargoes. No 4, South Quay is a fine Jacobean merchant's house, with a Georgian façade; in an upstairs room here, the Cromwellians finally decided to behead Charles I. It is now a museum of local life and industry. On the seafront there is also the Maritime Museum of East Anglia.

AA recommends:

Hotels: Imperial, North Drive, 2-star, *tel.* (0493) 851113
Cliff, Gorleston on Sea, 3-star, *tel.* (0493) 662179
Two Bears, South Town Rd, 2-star, *tel.* (0493) 603198
Guesthouses: Bradgate Hotel, 14 Euston Rd, *tel.* (0493) 842578
Gladstone House, 92 St Peter's Rd, *tel.* (0493) 843181
Georgian Guest House, 16-17 North Drive, *tel.* (0493) 842623
Campsite: Vauxhall Holiday Park, 5-pennant, *tel.* (0493) 857231
Garages: M & M Tyres & M & M Radiators, 12 Battery Rd, *tel.* (0493) 856062
Trimoco Cars, Station Rd, *tel.* (0493) 603677

Selection only: see page 4

The long sandy beaches at Great Yarmouth offer countless entertainments during the season

tourists arrived in the town. A whole pleasure industry has grown up, and there are now two piers, gardens and parks, a race course and a vast Marina Centre, which has artificial beaches and waves to defy the weather outside.

Apart from herrings, Yarmouth is also famous for its north and south quays, where vessels have tied up for centuries. Two bridges now join the sides of the main channel, and plans are afoot to extend the quays to form a great basin, to ensure safer anchorage and less silting up.

Merchants once lived along the south quay, in fine houses giving the appearance of a Dutch

coastal trade in coal gradually took over.

With the coming of the railway,

American Connections

East Anglia has the largest concentration of USAF bases in the country. There are also scores of old bases used during World War II; many have reverted to farmland, some have become industrial complexes. At Parham, near Framlingham in Suffolk, the 390th Bomb Group Memorial Air Museum is housed in the supposedly haunted control tower, and there is a vast American cemetery at Madingley near Cambridge.

There are strong historical links between East Anglia and America.

1942, East Anglia: American heavy bombers prepare for combat

John Harvard, once a student of Emmanuel College, Cambridge, emigrated to America, where the University of Massachusetts, founded in 1636, was named after him. Christopher Jones, master of the *Mayflower*, lived in Harwich, Essex, and today a plaque can be found on his house in King's Head Street.

The church at Dedham contains an interesting commemorative pew to the people of Dedham, Massachusetts – with whom there are close links – including the forebears of General Sherman, the American Civil War hero. Another pew commemorates the first manned landing on the moon with a quotation from Psalm 8.

In the early 17th century, many Nonconformist weavers, among them Samuel Lincoln, emigrated from the Norfolk village of Hingham to found Hingham, Massachusetts. One of Samuel's descendants, Abraham, became President of The United States, and there is a bust of Abraham Lincoln in Hingham Church.

The brilliant Thomas Paine, 'friend of humanity and enemy of kings', was born and educated in Thetford, Norfolk. In 1774, at the suggestion of Benjamin Franklin, he went to the American colonies, where he edited the *Pennsylvania Gazette* and advocated independence, greatly influencing the American Revolution. The gilt statue of Paine, standing in front of King's House in Thetford, was presented to the town by the American Thomas Paine Society, and commemorates him as a champion of human rights.

JOHN BALL of Colchester Priest A leader of The Peasants Revolt Executed at St Albans 15th July 1381

Dutch Connections

The East Anglian link with Holland is not just in similarity of landscape, or in paintings by the 17th-century Dutch School of artists, which are collected in England and which were imitated by the Norwich School of painters in style and mood. Nor is the link due to the close connections of the ports of Felixstowe and Harwich with Rotterdam and the Hook of Holland.

In medieval times, East Anglia's prime industry was wool, and woollen cloth weaving. When Edward III banned the import of foreign cloth in England in the middle of the 14th century, many Dutch and Flemish weavers settled in East Anglia, bringing their culture with them. Typical Dutch houses can be found in Colchester's Dutch Quarter, and elsewhere, dual-pitched roof buildings with Dutch gable-ends are clues to the identity of their former inhabitants.

For centuries, the Fens were marshy wastes, grazed in summer, but allowed to flood in winter. It was not until the 17th century that sufficient technology existed to tackle the problem. The Earl of Bedford employed a Dutch engineer, Cornelius Vermuyden, to drain around 20,000 acres of land near Whittlesey. His first attempt involved a straight cut, bypassing the Great Ouse and allowing water to drain out to the sea more quickly. After the Civil War, Vermuyden returned to construct the New Bedford River, parallel to the first cut: these two cuts still provide the basic drainage for much of Fenland today.

During the 17th-century Anglo-Dutch wars, the British fleet engaged the Dutch in Sole Bay, off Southwold. Thousands were killed and wounded in the ensuing bloody battle, and yet, just 10 years later, Britain had a Dutch king and the two nations were allies against the French.

The influence of Dutch settlers from the Middle Ages onwards can still be seen in coastal towns throughout the region. These examples are in Colchester

Greensted, Essex

Map Ref: 94TL5302

In Saxon times the land here was afforested, and the first settlers had to make clearings, or 'droves', for their crops and stock. In such a drove a simple wooden church with a thatched roof was built in AD845, dedicated to St Andrew. Part of that building survives today as the oldest wooden church in the world, a claim authenticated by a scientific dating of the oak timbers which formed the walls. The Rector of Greensted's special prayer begins 'Lord, as I sit in this ancient church I can feel that it is a special place . . .' The body of St Edmund, the first patron saint of England, rested here in 1013 on its way from London to Bury St Edmunds. After their return from Australia the Tolpuddle Martyrs were granted tenancies in this parish, and one of them married in this church in 1839. Adjacent is Greensted Hall, a 15th-century house built on the site of a Saxon manor.

Hadleigh, Essex

Map Ref: 95TQ8187

Hubert de Burgh, Earl of Kent, built Hadleigh Castle on the brow of a steep hill that commands a fine view over the Leigh Marshes and the Thames estuary. Only the north-east and south-east ruined corners remain of the 50ft-high bailey, built within an oval fortification that once measured 110ft by 40ft. The ruins were sketched by John Constable, and the resulting paintings can now be seen at the Tate Gallery in London, and in the Mellon Collection in the USA. Hadleigh is a haven of peace from the surrounding developments taking place in Southend and Basildon New Town. The small Norman church of St James the Less has a belfry, added in the 15th century, and remnants of late 13th-century paintings inside, which are well worth noting.

AA recommends:
Garage: Castle Autos, 124 High St, *tel.* (0702) 557372

Hadleigh, Suffolk

Map Ref: 92TM0242

This important provincial town was once a Viking stronghold, and later became one of the most prosperous towns in the country through its wool trade in the 14th and 15th centuries.

Guthrum, leader of the Danes, was defeated by King Alfred, embraced Christianity, and was eventually buried in the Saxon church that stood here in 889. Marked in the churchyard of St Mary is the spot where Rowland

The 15th-century Guildhall in Hadleigh (Suffolk) is open to view

Taylor, Rector of the church, was burnt at the stake during the persecutions under Queen Mary in 1555. The church is not, however, a gloomy place to enter. There is an octagonal 14th-century font, and an imposing Perpendicular east window that blazes with colour when back-lit by the sun. Adjacent to St Mary's, red-brick Deanery Tower, built by Archdeacon Pykenham in 1495, and the half-timbered Guildhall, which was once a school, form the heart of medieval Hadleigh. In the rectory nearby a meeting held in 1833 marked the start of the Oxford Movement.

On each side of the long and bustling high street are well-preserved buildings, financed by the lucrative wool trade. Several display colourful coats-of-arms in relief. The town hall, near the market place, was built in 1851.

Halstead, Essex

Map Ref: 95TL8130

The steep main street of this small town drops down to the River Colne, where a large mill was built by Courtaulds for the manufacture of silk. Its striking white clapboard walls rise to four storeys, and inside there are now craft and antique shops. The old weavers' cottages nearby are also pleasant. The flint church of St Andrew dominates the town, with its 1850 tower; the other two Gilbert Scott churches at Halstead were built a few years before this. In the old Fremlins Brewery Chapel Museum there are some interesting local relics, as well as a fine reredos from All Hallows' in London.

Just east of Halstead are the gardens of Blue Bridge House, once the home of a butcher, John Morley, whose tomb, dated 1732, can be found in St Andrew's churchyard.

Harlow, Essex

Map Ref: 94TL4410

In order to relieve congestion in London, 32 new towns were planned in Essex after the war; Harlow was one of the first to be built. In 1947, 2,500 hectares were set aside, and Sir Frederick Gibberd drew up a plan to enlarge the existing town to accommodate 80,000 inhabitants. Around the town centre are four large residential clusters, each with its own range of amenities. The Harlow Development Corporation was dissolved in 1980; its records are now kept at Kingsmoor House.

Harlow has a giant sports centre, a swimming pool and the Moorhen, a water recreation centre beside the landscaped River Stort. The stable block and walled gardens of the ancient manor house of Mark Hall,

in the Parish of Latton, are now used imaginatively; there is a comprehensive museum of cycles, a 17th-century parterre, a rose garden and practical displays on the evolution of gardening. Another museum, in Passmore's House (built in 1727 on Third Avenue), sheds light on how the area once appeared before the recent development took place.

AA recommends:
Hotels: Churchgate Manor, Churchgate St, Old Harlow, 3-star, *tel.* (0279) 20246
Green Man, Mulberry Green, Old Harlow, 3-star, *tel.* (0279) 442521
Harlow Moat House, Southern Way, 3-star, *tel.* (0279) 22441
Garages: Arlington Motor Co, Potter St, *tel.* (0279) 22391
Motor Sales, Elizabeth Way, Burnt Mill, *tel.* (0279) 412161

Harwich, Essex

Map Ref: 93TM2431

Harwich's name is derived from the Saxon words, *here* (an army) and *wic* (a fortification), evidence that this large town has always been in the front line of coastal defence. Harwich has a strong sea-faring tradition, and is Britain's second-largest passenger port, with a distinguished history. The Romans had an important camp here, and so did the Saxons, who used it as a base to fight marauding Danish Vikings. Edward II granted a charter for a market here in 1318, and in James I's reign, Harwich returned two Members of Parliament. William III used the port for his journeys to Europe, as did succeeding Hanoverian monarchs, and countless travellers since. It is a shame that so many people nowadays head directly for Parkeston Quay on the north side, where the ferries have their

Courtaulds' striking white mill on the Colne at Halstead. Below: cargo and passengers leave daily from the quayside in Harwich

terminal, and ignore the town, which contains much of interest.

The Redoubt, part of a coastal defence system erected in 1808 to foil an invasion by Napoleon, has been restored, and now houses a small museum, as does the Low lighthouse on Harwich Green; there is also a nine-sided High lighthouse. The Guildhall, built in 1769 of red brick, has a handsome doorway. Samuel Pepys was an MP for the town in the days when there was a Royal Naval Dockyard here. Along the sea front are several Victorian hotels; there is no lack of good inns, either.

The south of the peninsula is called Dovercourt. Now the residential quarter of Harwich, this is in fact the older part of the town, and is mentioned in Domesday. It has a pier, sandy beaches and a new indoor swimming pool. For many years, visitors have come here for 'the waters', and bathing machines were all the rage 150 years ago.

AA recommends:
Hotels: Cliff, Marine Parade, Dovercourt, 2-star, *tel.* (0255) 503345
Tower, Main Rd, Dovercourt, 2-star, *tel.* (0255) 504952
Guesthouse: Hotel Continental, 28/29 Marine Parade, Dovercourt Bay, *tel.* (0255) 503454
Garage: Motorfit, 475A Main Rd, *tel.* (0255) 508469

Hatfield Forest, Essex

Map Ref: 94TL5420

This Hatfield, near Bishop's Stortford and in the shadow of the enlarged Stansted Airport, occupied a special place in the great Forest of Essex. Earl Harold once owned it and, after his death at the Battle of Hastings, the Conqueror kept it for himself. It thus became a royal forest and was much prized for its deer, until Henry VI relinquished his hunting rights in 1446. The Forest was gradually whittled down in size until in 1857 approximately 1,000 acres were enclosed; in 1924 the freehold was handed over to the National Trust by the Buxton family.

There is now full public access. Beside the lake, created in 1746, is the Shell House, named for its decorated walls. Here the visitor will find the usual amenities and a warden who issues fishing permits – the lake is well-stocked, with some large carp and pike. The woodland is divided up with rides, and punctuated by open spaces, all of which give the effect of wildness. The Doodle Oak stood here until 1924. It was 60ft in circumference, and more than 700 years old.

To walk through the Forest is to appreciate how ancient woodlands were managed by a programme of grazing, coppicing and pollarding. Fallow deer and the more recent muntjac deer can often be seen, and so can a wide variety of birds, including nesting snipe and kestrels.

AA recommends:
Bishop's Stortford
Restaurant: The Mill, Hallingbury Mill, Old Mill Lane, Gaston Green, Hallingbury, 2-fork, *tel.* (0279) 726554
Garages: Hunts Motor Garage, 26 Northgate End, *tel.* (0279) 507722
Mann Egerton, 123-127 South St, *tel.* (0279) 58441

Heacham, Norfolk

Map Ref: 87TF6737

There are two names that stand out in the history of this old settlement on the Wash. The first name is Le Strange, that of a family living in these parts since the early 12th century, for most of this time at Hunstanton Hall; and the second is that of Pocahontas, the Red Indian princess who married John Rolfe of Heacham Hall (now demolished) and died aged only 22. Her effigy appears on the village sign.

Today, Heacham is known for the lavender farm at Caley Mill, a 19th-century building on the site of an older mill recorded as standing here in 1086. Different-coloured lavenders and herbs are grown in colourful strips over 100 acres here, and there are guided tours and a tea room.

Helmingham Hall, Suffolk

Map Ref: 92TM1857

The visitor to Suffolk may not equate local Tolly ales with the Tollemache family which, in 1886, founded the brewery of that name

The Norfolk Lavender shop at Heacham, where lavender and herbs have been grown, dried and distilled since 1932.
Below: the lake in Hatfield Forest, a mecca for fishermen

in Ipswich. The present Lord Tollemache lives in Helmingham Hall, a moated Elizabethan mansion built by his ancestor in 1510. The house is not open to the public, but its walls of red tile and brick provide a timeless setting for the gardens, which are open to visitors. The 375-acre park has red and fallow deer, and rare breeds of cattle and sheep. The deer have been there as long as the massive oaks; some say for as long as 600 years.

The approach to the gardens is across a small Saxon moat. Here, surrounded by wide lawns and two ancient black mulberry trees, there are the geometric designs of a parterre garden. The traditional kitchen garden has four square beds in Tudor style, full of vegetables in serried rows – like the Coldstream guardsmen whom generations of Tollemaches have been wont to command. Outside the walled garden are yew, apple and shrubbery walks, and a wild meadow garden covered with flowering bulbs and orchids in season.

This is also Constable Country, as the artist once lived in Helmingham Rectory.

Heydon, Norfolk

Map Ref: 88TG1127

The access road to Heydon Hall, a large brick mansion dating from 1581, skirts the village green which is surrounded by houses of varying designs, a pub, a village store and the smithy – all still owned by the family living at the Hall. It is a delightfully quiet setting, overlooked on the north side by an impressive, decorated 15th-century Perpendicular church. Inside are recently uncovered wall paintings, a rare wine-glass pulpit, a Crusader's shield and, up in the clerestory, an original clover-leaf light. The grounds of the Hall contain an ice house.

Nearby, in the direction of

Right: The famous striped cliffs at Hunstanton and, below, playing bowls on the sea front

Reepham, the magnificent 126ft-high tower of Salle Church can be seen, in which the body of Anne Boleyn is reputed to have been laid to rest.

AA recommends:
Reepham
Hotel: Old Brewery House, Market Sq, 2-star, *tel.* (0603) 870881

Holme next the Sea, Norfolk

Map Ref: 87TF7043

The windswept dunes around Holme have known the imprint of Roman sandals and the keels of their coastal craft, as this extreme north-western corner of Norfolk was the point where the ancient Peddars and Icknield Ways ended. From here, it was possible to set off for ports across the Wash and up the east coast in Roman times. The dunes are now splendid walking country, with waymarked paths skirting the golf links, and the 6-acre Holme Bird Sanctuary, where the Norfolk Ornithologist's Association warden issues entry permits on the spot. The wet sand stretches down to the sea, and the black patches visible in the sea water are the remains of the ancient forest of the North Sea basin. The parish church has a Perpendicular tower but a modern nave, which contains one early marble memorial to a revered couple called Stone; the husband died in 1607 aged 87, with no less than 75 grandchildren to his credit!

Along the dunes to the east, **Thornham** has a natural creek where fishing vessels continue to go in search of mussels, crabs and cockles. It is a delightful village with well-frequented pubs where the old game of gnurdling is still played, and there is a cavernous church surrounded by great ilex trees. Inside, the building is lit by a polychromatic screen, unusually depicting the 12 prophets.

The flourishing coastal trade of Thornham was killed off about a century ago with the creation of **Hunstanton** by the railway. Although John Betjeman's favourite branch line from King's Lynn is now closed, Hunstanton possesses two quite distinct features which secure the town a place in the memory of all who go there: its famous 60ft-high striped cliffs, made of successive layers of carr stone, red and white chalk, and its unusual situation, for unlike any other resort in East Anglia, the town faces west. On a clear day you can seen 'Boston Stump', the tower of Boston parish church, 20 miles away, due west, on the other side of the Wash. The sandy beaches of old Hunstanton, to the north, are popular with children, and it is also a favourite place for boating and water-skiing enthusiasts.

AA recommends:
Hunstanton
Hotels: Le Strange Arms, Golf Course Rd, Sea Front, Old Hunstanton, 3-star, *tel.* (04853) 34411
Lodge, Hunstanton Rd, Old Hunstanton, 2-star, *tel.* (04853) 2896
Wash & Tope, 10-12 Le Strange Ter, 1-star, *tel.* (04853) 2250
Guesthouses: Caley Hall Motel, *tel.* (04853) 33486
Claremont, 35 Greevegate, *tel.* (04853) 33171
Sunningdale Hotel, 3 Avenue Rd, *tel.* (04853) 2562
Sutton House Hotel, 24 Northgate, *tel.* (04853) 2552
Campsite: Searles Camping Ground, South Beach, 3-pennant *tel.* (04853) 34211
Garage: Mann Egerton, 12 Lynn Rd, *tel.* (04853) 33435

Houghton, Cambridgeshire

Map Ref: 90TL2872

Two miles downstream from Huntingdon is a small island in the Great Ouse, where there has been some form of mill since Domesday. Although 17th-century Houghton Mill's three waterwheels have now been replaced by flood gates, much of its early Victorian machinery has survived intact, turned by an electric motor, so that corn may now once more be ground into wholemeal flour between stones that were quarried many years ago at Caen in France. Beside the mill, punts can be hired in season, and there is a footpath across to the right bank - which passes through the building.

The village of Houghton, now bypassed, has a traditional square – complete with pump and clock – overlooked by a church with a tall, slender spire. On the opposite bank is the charming village of Hemingford Grey, where the curious, squat tower of the church of St James is topped by eight stone balls. The manor house claims to be the oldest inhabited house in the country; parts of it date back to the 12th century. It is not open to the public.

AA recommends:
Campsite: Houghton Mill Caravan & Camping Park, Mill St, 2-pennant, *tel.* (0480) 62413

Huntingdon, Cambridgeshire

Map Ref: 90TL2471

Another ancient Fenland town: the Romans left traces of a settlement here, while the Danes, who sailed up the Great Ouse, first laid out the streets in a pattern which is recognisable today. The Normans built one of their massive mottes nearby, and today the remains still overlook the ancient river crossing. In the 13th century there were no less than 13 churches, of which only two remain. One of them, All Saints', in the market place, displays construction of several kinds from medieval to Victorian. Near it is the three-storeyed Town Hall, an excellent example of the many Georgian buildings which are to be found in Huntingdon. An early 14th-century bridge spans the river, linking the town to Godmanchester, and the cutwaters were constructed to enable pedestrians to avoid passing traffic. Oliver Cromwell was born in Huntingdon in 1599, and the school which both he and Samuel Pepys attended is now a museum dedicated to items relating to the Civil War. The Protector is believed to have used The Falcon Inn as his headquarters during the war.

From the late 17th century, roads were greatly improved, and as traffic increased, great coaching inns appeared in the town. One such is The George, which retains two sides of its original courtyard.

The sleepy town of Godmanchester near Huntingdon is on the Ouse

Half a mile away is Hinchinbrooke House, a 13th-century Benedictine nunnery with later additions, which is now used as a school. Here there are further associations with Cromwell, Pepys and the Earls of Sandwich. Students show visitors round some of the rooms and delicious teas are served. There is also a 60-acre park.

AA recommends:
Hotels: George, George St, 3-star, *tel.* (0480) 432444
Old Bridge, 3-star, *tel.* (0480) 52681
Campsite: Park Lane Touring Park, Godmanchester, 3-pennant, *tel.* (0480) 53740
Anchor Cottage Riverside Caravan & Camping Site, Church Lane, Hartford, 1-pennant, *tel.* (0480) 55642

The old schoolhouse in Huntingdon (left) is now the Cromwell Museum. Christchurch Mansion in central Ipswich (below) contains outstanding collections of china, glass and other decorative arts

Ipswich, Suffolk

Map Ref: 92TM1644

The county town of Suffolk, Ipswich is predominantly Victorian. Comparatively little remains of the medieval town which prospered on its cloth trade and which occupied a prime position at the head of the Orwell estuary. The names of the streets on the town map, however, are a clue to its historic development – Corn Hill, Franciscan Way, Friar's Street, Greyfriars Road and the Butter Market.

The Danes landed here before their victory at Maldon and returned again in AD1010. The Normans recorded 110 burgesses and 100 poor men in Domesday (today the population is over 130,000). A castle was destroyed by Henry II, never to be rebuilt, and under King John there was a mint here.

Cardinal Wolsey was born in the town, and in 1527 he founded a College in Black Friar's Street, but it was not finished before his fall from grace, and today only a brick gateway remains. Charles Dickens used the hostelry, the Great White House, as a setting for Mr Pickwick's adventures; the inn remains.

The Ancient House, beautifully restored as a bookshop, was a rich merchant's house dating from the 15th century. It stands on a street corner and the two fronts are elaborately embellished with oriel windows and magnificent coloured pargeting. The Tourist Information Centre is in the Town Hall, and a town trail sets out from there.

At the time of Domesday there were 21 churches in Ipswich; 12 medieval churches remain, along with several later places of worship, including the Old Unitarian Meeting House in Friar's Street, built in 1699 by a carpenter. The four pillars were probably ship's masts, and the great brass chandelier is Dutch.

St Margaret's, another fine

church, stands next to Christchurch Mansion, probably the town's greatest asset. Surrounded by an undulating park that was saved from the developer by a far-sighted local brewer, this Elizabethan mansion contains room after room furnished in various period styles. Much of the furniture has been recovered from town houses that are now demolished. The collection of treen ware is remarkable, and so is the small but fine Wolsey Art gallery, with paintings by Constable, Munnings and Gainsborough. The first Queen Elizabeth is known to have stayed here twice.

The Ipswich Museum of Archaeology and Natural History in the High Street has a display of a Roman villa, and a Mankind Gallery.

The A45 bypass is carried high over the docks and the river by a spectacular bridge. The western bypass is also complete, and these good communications help Ipswich's industries and docks to thrive. Now an airline operates from the airport to the Midlands and the Continent.

Ipswich may also be remembered for having the country's first spiral underground car park, the largest wet dock (1839) and the first grass-mowing machine.

Pin Mill, on the south shore of the Orwell estuary, can now be reached off Ipswich's eastern bypass. Follow the B1456 and, after Woolverstone, turn left down to the shore. Steep, mixed woodland backs the muddy foreshore, on which there is a variety of barges and hulks, used as houseboats by marine squatters. Even the sleek hull of a 6-metre yacht now makes a snug berth. A circular footpath from the public car park at Pin Mill runs through the wood and over the adjoining fields, before conveniently finishing by the Butt and Oyster, arguably one of the finest East Anglian pubs. Old Thames sailing barges are often moored to the jetty, their rust-coloured sails furled along massive spars. Here there is an authentic tang of mud and salt water in the air.

AA recommends:
Hotels: Belstead Brook, Belstead Rd, 3-star, *tel.* (0473) 684241
Ispwich Moat House, London Rd, 3-star, *tel.* (047386) 444
Marlborough, Henley Rd, 3-star, *tel.* (0473) 57677
Great White Horse, Tavern St, 2-star, *tel.* (0473) 56558
Restaurants: The À La Carte Restaurant, Orwell House, 4A Orwell Pl, 2-fork, *tel.* (0473) 230254
Mortimer's, Wherry Quay, 1-fork, *tel.* (0473) 230225
Guesthouses: Bentley Tower Hotel, 172 Norwich Rd, *tel.* (0473) 212142
Gables Hotel, 17 Park Rd, (0473) 54252
Campsite: Priory Park, Nacton, 2-pennant, *tel.* (0473) 77393

Kersey, Suffolk

Map Ref: 92TM0044

The one street of this picturesque village leads down to a shallow ford, where ducks are wise enough to avoid the cars of visitors who come in great numbers, attracted by the timber-framed cottages with their colour-washed walls and pantile roofs. Beyond, the street rises to a church that has watched over the community since Saxon times. The present building was begun in the 12th century; the original font was re-discovered in 1927, after it had been used as a cottage doorstep. Similarly, the six panels of the original rood-screen were rescued from a local farm. The flint tower,

Kersey, one of the prettiest of the Suffolk wool towns

the erection of which was halted by the Black Death in 1349, was finally completed in 1481.

There is no firm proof that the village gave its name to a coarse, ribbed cloth for which Suffolk weavers were famous in the 14th and 15th centuries. Cloth was certainly made here, however, and sheep farming was the main medieval industry. In 1844 more than 780 people lived here, and 12 traders were identified. An Augustinian Priory was once established at the north end of the village, but in 1444 it was disbanded and King's College, Cambridge, obtained its lands.

Oliver Cromwell

Oliver Cromwell was born in Huntingdon in 1599, in a house in the main street. The grammar school which he and diarist Samuel Pepys attended is now a museum devoted to Cromwell and the Great Rebellion of 1640–1660. Cromwell became MP for the town in the short-lived parliament of 1629, was made Justice of the Peace in 1630 and moved to St Ives a year later.

In 1640, Charles I assembled Parliament again, and Cromwell, a

OLIVARIVS CROMWELL EXERCITVVS ANGLIÆ REIPVBLICÆ DVX GENERALIS LOCVM TENENS ET GVBERNATOR HIBERNIÆ

respected landowner who had already stood up to the King over the controversial draining of the Fens, became MP for Cambridge both for the term of what became known as the Short Parliament, because it lasted just three weeks, and for the term of the Long Parliament, recalled by Charles I at the end of 1640. This Long Parliament lasted throughout the period of the Civil War and the Republic, until the restoration of the monarchy under Charles II in 1660.

Of Cromwell, parliamentarian John Hampden commented: 'That slovenly fellow which you see before us will be one of the greatest men of England'. Cromwell's strong views and forthright manner brought him to the fore very quickly, and through the bitter struggles of the Civil War, he proved an able military leader; some would say one of the most brilliant in English history. When Civil War was declared in 1642, East Anglia supported Parliament, and it was in Cambridge that Cromwell set up the headquarters for the Eastern Association, raising more cavalry forces for the Parliamentary cause from Trinity College. After the defeat and execution of King Charles I in 1648, Cromwell became Lord Protector of the newly-declared Protectorate until his death in 1658.

King's Lynn, Norfolk

Map Ref: 87TF6120

The best way to approach this seaport and town is up the Great Ouse from the Wash, so as to appreciate the waterfront, the docks and the frieze of colourful buildings that would not be out of place in Dutch or Belgian ports. Lynn, as it is commonly called, was for centuries a prosperous trading port, and continues to thrive on trade with both Europe and the large hinterland which is well-served by waterways.

Lynn has been the recipient of at least 15 Royal Charters and was once surrounded by a wall; only the south gate remains. King John was welcomed here on his way to Newark Castle, where he later died. His baggage train was lost attempting to cross the Wash, together with many royal treasures, which are still sought for today. While in King's Lynn, King John also left an embossed and enamelled cup with a silver-gilt cover, made about 1385, which is now on display in the Regalia Rooms of the Old Town Hall or Guildhall, together with some of the Royal Charters. This guildhall, one of the two surviving ancient town halls in the town, was built in Queen Street in 1421, for the Guild of Holy Trinity, and incorporates a large assembly room hung with full-length royal portraits.

St George's Guildhall in King Street, (once called Stockfish Row), was built in 1420 and is the oldest surviving medieval guildhall in England. The heavily beamed roof is splendid, and under the range of buildings that stretch down to the staithe on the river bank there is a wide tunnel, part of which has been converted into a coffee shop. Shakespeare is reputed to have visited Lynn with a travelling troop of players, and to have performed here. The Guildhall now houses the Fermoy Centre and is used for concerts, notably during the King's Lynn Festival.

Further along King Street is the elegant Customs House, built in 1683, overlooking the Purfleet. Many older buildings have been preserved in this quarter by the Lynn Preservation Trust.

St Margaret's Church was founded by Bishop Losinga 800 years ago and constructed from Northamptonshire limestone, which was brought by lighter down the Great Ouse. The twin towers of this large church are outstanding; the south-west one has a Norman base. The Early English chancel and its brasses are of national importance. St Nicholas' Church, in St Anne's Street, is nearly as large as St Margaret's and is remarkable for its south porch and great west window.

The Tuesday market is surrounded on three sides by some fine houses, the most prominent being the 17th-century Duke's Head Hotel, directly opposite the later and more prosaic Corn Exchange. Paved precincts branch off from here to a shopping centre.

Lynn has yet another outstanding building, Red Mount Chapel, in a public park called the Walks. Built in 1485, it is an octagonal red brick chapel with fine fan vaulting, set beside the ancient pilgrim's way to Walsingham.

The docks, the huge trading and industrial estate, the big hospital, and the polytechnic all confirm Lynn's importance as an active centre with a memorable history.

AA recommends:
Hotels: Duke's Head, Tuesday Market Pl, 3-star, *tel.* (0553) 774996

On Tuesdays in King's Lynn, shoppers enjoy the market, overlooked by imposing old houses

Rising Lodge, Country House, Knight's Hill Village, South Wootton, 3-star, *tel.* (0553) 675566

Guesthouses: Havana, 117 Gaywood Rd, *tel.* (0553) 772331

Maranatha, 115 Gaywood Rd, *tel.* (0553) 774596

Russet House Hotel, 53 Goodwins Rd, *tel.* (0553) 773098

Garages: Fenland s/sta, Clench Warton Rd, West Lynn, *tel.* (0553) 760606

Swan St Motors, Hardwick Rd, *tel.* (0553) 772644

Selection only: see page 4

Lavenham, Suffolk

Map Ref: 92TL9149

Edward III encouraged Flemish weavers to settle in England, giving impetus to the well-established cloth-weaving industry. Lavenham became a centre for the production of blue cloth which was widely exported, and in the Middle Ages there was a loom in nearly every house. Wealth created in this way was used to finance the building of many half-timbered houses along streets that were first laid out by the Saxons, and also to build the remarkable church of St Peter and St Paul. A smaller church once occupied the site; it was replaced between 1444 and 1525 by the present beautiful building, which has a tower 141ft high. The south porch is notable for its elaborate stone carving and fan-vaulting. This was the gift of John de Vere, Earl of Oxford, whose effigy is carved on the entrance porch to the Guildhall, on the south side of the market place.

This 16th-century half-timbered hall was built by the Guild of Corpus Christi, one of four guilds in Lavenham whose function was more religious than commercial. The guilds were eventually suppressed, like many others, and the Hall has been used over the years as a prison, store, shop and school. It is now a community centre, and houses a museum with a fine exhibition about the cloth trade which includes an original working loom.

Virtually every street is lined with timber-framed houses and several Tudor shops remain, with their original windows. Little Hall, dating from the 14th century, and the Old Priory – with a lovely herb garden – are both open to the public. The Swan Inn is a famous hostelry, which has been carefully preserved.

AA recommends:
Hotel: Swan, High St, 3-star, *tel.* (0787) 247477
Restaurant: The Great House, Market Pl, 2-fork, *tel.* (0787) 247431

The old white watermill at Lode (above), sitting astride the willow-hung canal, has been fully restored and is well worth a visit. These half-timbered Tudor houses in Lavenham (left) are typical of the well-preserved buildings in the town

Layer Marney, Essex

Map Ref: 95 TL9217

One of the glories of Essex is this magnificent Tudor gatehouse, rising 80ft from the ground. From the top there are unrivalled views towards the coast. Four towers make up the gatehouse, the outer ones each with eight storeys and the inner ones with seven. They are surmounted by superb Italianate terracotta parapets which, in the early 16th century, were an exciting architectural innovation.

The Marney family probably came over with William the Conqueror, but it was not until 1523 that Lord Henry Marney decided to erect a grand hall here, in keeping with his family's position. However, as both he and his son were dead by 1525, building had to stop, and today the gatehouse dominates the humbler range of buildings that flank it. To the south of the house is a long building, also from the 16th century, that once housed up to 30 horses and their grooms. The timbered roof is of special interest,

with its pincer-shaped beams.

The garden reflects the care which the present owners, the Charringtons, give to all the restoration work carried out here; griffins from their coat-of-arms are reproduced in Portland stone on the brick gateposts.

The church of St Mary the Virgin is contemporary with the gatehouse, and contains the tombs of several Marneys, including that of Lord Henry Marney, who started the building. He also gave the church the iron-bound chest which is now at least 500 years old; the wall painting of St Christopher is about the same age.

Little Walsingham, Norfolk
(see under Walsingham, page 71)

Lode, Cambridgeshire

Map Ref: 91 TL5362

This is a small village, 6 miles north-east of Cambridge, once surrounded by low-lying fenland and unremarkable except for the

Augustinian Priory, now known as Anglesey Abbey, established nearby. In keeping with many other ecclesiastical buildings in East Anglia, the priory was converted for domestic use in the 16th century, and only the Chapter House and vaulted monks' parlour survive from the 13th century. Among the many past owners of the Abbey was one Hobson, a carter from Cambridge, who gave our language the expression 'Hobson's choice'. In 1926 the estate was bought by Huttleston Broughton, who later became the first Lord Fairhaven. He bequeathed Anglesey to the National Trust in 1966 and his nephew now lives here.

The family was rich, and when money is allied to a love of the arts, the results can be stunning. Lord Fairhaven filled the Abbey with an extraordinary collection of *objets d'art*, all in perfect condition and of outstanding workmanship. The scale of the gardens created by Lord Fairhaven out of the flat fens surrounding the Abbey is even more impressive. Covering 100 stunning acres, the gardens have vistas and many trees, as well as classical statues, as carefully selected as the furniture in the house.

The old watermill across the lode, or canal, that skirts the gardens is now fully restored and grinds flour from local corn at weekends.

Long Melford, Suffolk

Map Ref: 92TL8646

Regarded as one of the best-preserved linear villages in the country, Long Melford's street is one mile long and lined by a succession of pleasing frontages. Not all of these are antique shops and tea rooms. At the south end is Melford Place, where the Martyn family lived for generations – one of them, Lawrence, was Lord Mayor of London in 1567. But the finest buildings are at the north end, where the vast, triangular village green slopes down to the River Stour, which was once navigable and brought wealth to the village long after the cloth industry declined. The isolated building on the green is an old conduit which supplied water to Melford Hall, whose four Elizabethan towers rise behind a high brick wall.

The first owner of the Hall, which is now a National Trust property, was William Cordell, an astute lawyer who became Speaker of the House of Commons and entertained Queen Elizabeth I here in 1578, together with 2,000 retainers. A fine stained-glass portrait of the Queen is in a window in the east gallery.

The property changed hands several times before Sir Harry Parker bought the Hall in 1786, and his descendants have lived here ever since. Admiral Hyde Parker served at the Battle of Copenhagen. The maritime flavour of the Hall is strengthened by a superb collection of Chinese porcelain, taken from a captured Spanish galleon in 1762. The banqueting hall retains original Tudor panelling. Two upstairs rooms are a reminder that the author of those inimitable books for children, Beatrix Potter, often came to stay here.

A few hundred yards up the road a three-quarter mile-long avenue of limes, planted in 1678, leads to **Kentwell Hall**. This moated Elizabethan mansion was rescued from mouldering oblivion in 1971 by a young lawyer, whose family has since restored it. Each summer, schoolchildren take part in re-enactments of everyday life of the Tudor period here. In 1985, the front courtyard was transformed into a brick-paved mosaic maze,

Melford Hall, a turreted brick Tudor mansion, has changed little since 1578; it retains its original panelled banqueting hall
Above right: Kentwell Hall's amazing Tudor rose brick mosaic maze

representing a perfect Tudor rose.

The Clopton family, who built Kentwell in 1563, has a beautiful Chantry in the great parish church of Holy Trinity that commands the green. Perhaps the loveliest of the wool churches, it was built in the late 15th century using flushwork – knapped flints within a stone framework – and its 97 windows give an impression of lightness inside. Only the tower is of a later date. The various memorials in brass and stone bear witness to medieval dress and style.

AA recommends:
Hotels: Bull, 3-star, *tel.* (0787) 78494
Crown Inn, Hall St, 2-star, *tel.* (0787) 77666
Restaurant: Chimneys, Hall St, 2-fork, *tel.* (0787) 79806

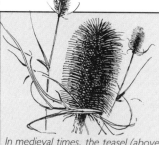

In medieval times, the teasel (above) was used for combing wool

Medieval Industries

The Norfolk Broads are man-made peat pits, dug to meet the needs of an area which lacked any other kind of fuel; it seems that medieval Broadland was the equivalent of a major coalfield today.

Thaxted, in Essex, was the centre of the medieval cutlery trade. It declined towards the end of the Middle Ages, but the church and magnificent guildhall remain, as symbols of the town's wealth when trade was at its height.

The small port of Maldon, at the head of the Blackwater Estuary in Essex, is home to a flourishing

Lowestoft, Suffolk

Map Ref: 89TM5493

Once a Royal Demesne that attracted great privileges, Lowestoft now successfully combines the role of a leading holiday resort with that of a modern fishing and commercial centre. There are two towns, north and south of the swing bridge that spans the entrance to the River Lothing and, further inland, to the lake and Oulton Broad. Visitors head towards South Town where the broad sands, twin piers, parks and hotels cater for their enjoyment.

Most of the commerce and shops are centred north of the bridge, around the main street that rises towards the bluff, or ness, which is the most easterly point in England. From this street the narrow lanes, or scores, run steeply down to the Denes; in the last century the slopes were covered by hanging gardens. One such garden remains, below the old Martello lighthouse. The latter stands on the site once occupied by a 40ft tower, erected in

crystal sea-salt industry, which started in medieval times. Here, sea water flowing over the marshes and mudflats is concentrated by the drying action of the sun and wind. In times past, salt was essential for preserving fish and meat; today, salt is more often used for cookery.

Up until the 14th century, English wool was mainly exported as raw material to the Continent. Very little was woven here, and what cloth was, tended to be rough material, for local consumption. In 1326, Edward III encouraged the home trade by banning the import of foreign cloth and offering franchises to weavers and dyers.

Enterprising Flemish weavers settled in East Anglia, where raw materials and markets for cloth products existed. They settled mainly in areas where they had trading contacts, around Ipswich and Colchester, and also inland along the Stour valley. Thus the famous wool towns of Lavenham, Long Melford, Kersey and Lindsey became increasingly wealthy. Many of them celebrated their prosperity by building magnificent churches.

1676 to contain a light, fuelled by coal, for guiding vessels into the harbour. The Maritime Museum is on the esplanade immediately below, and gives a good insight into the fishing industry that made Lowestoft prosperous. There are also two other interesting museums.

Herrings that swam south in the autumn provided great catches which were smoked and then sent to Billingsgate. In the summer, mackerel kept the fishermen busy. When trawlers were able to venture further afield, catches of cod and sole replaced herrings; now voluntary quotas set to restrict overfishing limit the numbers of boats.

There are several boat-building yards; on their slips pleasure craft and powerful trawlers can be seen, the latter able to withstand the worst weather on the Newfoundland Banks. The first lifeboat was stationed here in 1801, and six years later the first lifeboat in the world to use sails, as well as oars, was kept here. The famous sailing club in the outer harbour proudly calls itself Royal, and in the summer Dragon-class yachts race under its burgee.

Out on the Oulton road is St Margaret's Church, set purposefully well back from the sea. It is a

The Hythe at Maldon (right), for centuries an important fishing and boating centre. Lowestoft is another town owing its prosperity to the sea; below, its lifeboat rides at anchor in the harbour

spacious 15th-century building, containing memorials to men who distinguished themselves in the Royal Navy. Admiral Sir John Ashby's marble tomb is suitably inscribed; next to it is that of his nephew, Captain Mighells, remembered chiefly as a comptroller of the Navy in 1723.

AA recommends:
Hotels: Broadlands, Bridge Rd, Oulton Broad, 3-star, *tel.* (0502) 516031
Victoria, Kirkley Cliff, 3-star, *tel.* (0502) 4433
Wherry, Bridge Rd, Oulton Broad, 2-star, *tel.* (0502) 3521
Denes, Corton Rd, 1-star, *tel.* (0502) 64616
Garage: John Grose, Whapload Rd, *tel.* (0502) 65353

Maldon, Essex

Map Ref: 95 TL8507

Commanding good anchorages in the Blackwater and Chelmer estuaries, Maldon has been a port for 1,000 years and is now an important yachting centre. The Saxons came here to fend off marauding Danes who, by force of numbers, finally triumphed in August 991 when they landed on Northey Island, out in the estuary, and defeated Brytnoth's army. In 1991, Maldon will stage a great re-enactment of that battle. In 1171 Henry II granted the town a Royal Charter, a copy of which hangs in the Moot Hall. First built by the d'Arcy family in the 15th century,

this has been the centre of local government since 1570. The Mayor still has his parlour here; his mace, 53in long, was made from silver-gilt in 1687. A circular brick newel staircase with a built-in handrail is the Moot Hall's showpiece.

Down the street and marked by the tower of the old church of St Peter, is the Plume Library, founded by Dr Thomas Plume in the 17th century. It contains some unusual royal portraits. A steep hill leads from here down to the harbour, where warehouses, chandlers and boat repair yards crown the quays. There are pleasure craft everywhere, and the marine parade leads down to the marshes at Northey.

All Saints Church is notable for its unique triangular tower and for its south aisle, built in the early 14th century, which is full of elaborate carving.

AA recommends:
Hotel: Blue Boar, Silver St, 2-star, *tel.* (0621) 52681
Restaurant: Francine's, 1A High St, 1-fork, *tel.* (0621) 56605
Garages: Champion Motors, Unit 5, C & D West, Station Yard, Spit Rd, *tel.* (0621) 5744
Doe Motors, 1 Spital Rd, *tel.* (0621) 52345
Quest Motors (Gozzett), 127-131 High St, *tel.* (0621) 52424

March, Cambridgeshire

Map Ref: 86TL4196

This early Saxon settlement has been a strategic centre for centuries. The Old River Nene running through it once formed the ancient boundary, or *merche*; today it is an important junction for the web of fenland railway lines. At the south end is the glory of March, St Wendreda's Church, named after a daughter of the 7th-century Christian King of the East Angles. A Norman church once stood here, but only its mutilated font remains. Across the flat fens the 140ft tower of the medieval church, built between 1350 and 1380, is a welcome landmark. Inside, the double hammerbeam roof can justifiably claim to represent the summit of the medieval woodcarver's art – 118 angels, several half life-size and with outstretched wings, look serenely down. Even a grinning devil has been carved into a spandrel by the craftsman.

At Manea to the south-east, where a high-level drain flows 20ft above the surrounding farmland, more than 2,000 acres of washland have been flooded to form a wetland nature reserve.

AA recommends:
Hotel: Olde Griffin, High St, 1-star, *tel.* (0354) 52517

Mersea Island, Essex

Map Ref: 95TM0314

The island is strategically placed at the confluence of the Blackwater and Colne rivers; it is separated from the mainland by the Pyefleet, a broad channel in which the tiny island of Ray forms an oasis of scrub and stunted trees. A causeway, the Strode, spans the creek and is occasionally flooded by spring tides.

The Romans were here, and tesselated floors have been found around the site of the Norman Church of St Peter and St Paul in West Mersea, the main village. The brass ring from a pouch carried by a Roman has also been found. A font of 13th-century Purbeck marble can be seen in the church. Beyond it are the boatyards, where serried rows of yachts are drawn up in the winter. Oysters, for which this coast has always been famous, are kept in tanks and can be eaten fresh in a small restaurant on the quay. West Mersea is now both a centre for yachtsmen and a dormitory for Colchester. There is a small but interesting museum in the town.

AA recommends:
West Mersea
Restaurant: Le Champenois (Blackwater Hotel), 20-22 Church Rd, 1-fork, *tel.* (0206) 383338

Nayland, Suffolk

Map Ref: 92TL9734

Nayland is a delightful village on the left bank of the River Stour. It is off the well-beaten Constable track, which is a pity, as the parish church of St James contains one of the painter's only two religious works. Completed in 1809, it depicts Christ blessing the bread and wine. The church itself is mainly Perpendicular, with a 14th-century

tower, and is full of monuments to wealthy clothiers. Once such was William Abel, who paid for the handsome tower porch.

A one-arched bridge over the river joins Suffolk and Essex, and in Church Street is a Georgian obelisk milestone. There are several timber-framed buildings including the inevitable inns; the Queen's Head retains its old coaching yard. The most notable building is, however, Alston Court. Situated near the church, it has a 15th-century east wing but is otherwise Tudor, with great leaded windows.

Newmarket, Suffolk

Map Ref: 91TL6463

Because of the racing tradition and the power of the Jockey Club, Newmarket Heath remains an oasis of grassland. Across it, for nearly 8 miles, sweeps Devil's Ditch or Dike, a massive defensive earthwork built in the troubled years after the Roman occupation. The Icknield Way (now the A1304), cutting through the Dike at right-angles and running straight through the town, was once trodden by pilgrims on their way to shrines at Ely and Walsingham. James I came here in 1605 to course the hare, and it was the nobles of his court who first appreciated that the Heath's springy turf was ideal for horse racing. Under the patronage of Charles I, racing became well-established, and the famous Rowley Mile is named after Charles II's hack of that name. The Jockey Club was founded in

At any one time, more than 2,000 horses are in training at Newmarket; colourful displays in the National Horse Racing Museum in the High Street (right)

1751; it is now based in the
impressive building at 101 High
Street. On the other side of the
Club is the horse racing museum,
where all the great jockeys are
portrayed in gaudy silks. The
National Stud is housed in fine
buildings built in 1964.

AA recommends:
Hotels: Newmarket Moat House,
Moulton Rd, 3-star, *tel.* (0638) 667171
Bedford Lodge, Bury Rd, 2-star, *tel.*
(0638) 663175
Rosery Country House, 15 Church St,
2-star, *tel.* (063877) 312
Rutland Arms, High St, 2-star, *tel.* (0638)
664251
Campsite: Caravan Club Site, 3-pennant,
tel. (0638) 663235

Norwich, Norfolk

Map Ref: 89TG2309

Norwich is a medieval city. Once
surrounded by a great wall 4 miles
long, with 12 gates, it originated as
three small Anglo-Danish settlements
on the River Wensum. Shortly after
1066, the Normans built a castle at
the highest point of the small town.
The Cathedral's foundation stone
was laid by Bishop Losinga in 1096;
a site near the river was essential as
the building stone came, in part,
from Caen in France.

The textile industry was the most
important one in medieval
Norwich, nurtured by skilled
Flemish weavers who taught the
manufacture of worsted cloth. The
wealth that was generated expressed
itself in the construction of splendid
churches in the Perpendicular style,
in town houses, and in other
buildings, like the early 15th-
century Guildhall beside the present
market place. Thirty-three medieval
churches remain within the walls of
the old city, the finest of which is
St Peter Mancroft, dominating the
market place with a great tower and
spire, and floodlit at night.

Textiles continued to be the main
industry in Norwich until the early
19th century, when a whole range
of new industries grew up. Shoe-
making then, as now, employed
thousands; breweries flourished, the
last one closing as recently as 1985.
The railway came in 1845, and this
encouraged the company of J J
Colman to build a mustard mill on a
new site at Carrow. To mark its
150th anniversary, Colmans opened
a mustard shop in Bridewell Alley,
next door to the present Bridewell
Museum. Victorian in decor, the shop
also houses an interesting museum
that shows how the company has
grown to its present size.

Services to traders, manufacturers
and farmers were developing
meanwhile, and the local Gurneys'
Bank, first established in 1775,
joined forces with three other
country bankers to form Barclays
Bank in 1896. The main city
branch of the bank, in Bank Plain

*Norwich Market, a patchwork of
awnings known locally as tilts.
Flint-cobbled Elm Hill (right)*

near the Castle, has an impressive
gilded banking hall, and is still called
Gurneys' Bank.

The Norman castle, with its early
12th-century keep, served as a
gloomy prison until the late 19th
century, and a visit to the dungeons
gives some idea of the misery of its
unfortunate inmates. A fine view
from the battlements looks out over
what was once the second most
important city in the country. In
1894 the castle was converted into
a fine museum and art gallery. For
centuries the open bailey of the
castle was used for the livestock
market, which was finally moved to
the southern outskirts in 1960. A
re-development of the whole area
has now begun, after a careful
archaeological excavation of the site.

There are several other museums
portraying Norwich's historic past.
In Bridewell Museum there is a
nostalgic collection of exhibits about
the city's industries and varied crafts;
in Stranger's Hall, once a medieval
merchant's house, there is a series
of rooms furnished in a variety of
period styles, from early Tudor to
late Victorian. St Peter Hungate's
Church is now a centre for
ecclesiastical art and brass-rubbing.

Next door are St Andrew's Hall
and Blackfriars Hall, which are now
used for a range of functions.
Originally the Halls were the choir
and nave of the Convent Church of
the Blackfriars, founded in Norwich
in 1226. The barrel-vaulted crypt
and Becket's Chapel of an earlier
building, survive under the present
buildings. Portraits of early Lord
Mayors line the walls of Blackfriars
Hall; St Andrew's has a magnificent
hammerbeam roof.

The Cathedral, best seen from
Mousehold Heath where George
Borrow met his gipsies, or from the
river, has an impressive spire,
second only to that of Salisbury
Cathedral. The building has a
Norman plan, which calls for an
apse behind the altar and a throne
for the Bishop, both unique to
Norwich. The vaulting in the nave,
the great cloisters, and the

bewildering array of flying
buttresses, make this one of the
finest ecclesiastical buildings in the
country. The Cathedral Close,
which is entered through two
magnificent gates, remains a
medieval precinct, and contains the
old Bishop's Palace, which is now
part of the King Edward VI School.

The City Council has undertaken
some imaginative developments,
both in new building work, and in
preserving some historic corners.
The City Hall that towers over the
Market Place is well-designed and
functional; the old quarter of Elm
Hill retains its cobbled streets and
shady trees. People are encouraged
to live in the city through the
provision of quiet streets lined with
pleasant houses.

AA recommends:
Hotels: Sprowston Hall, Wroxham Rd,
Sprowston, 3-star, *tel.* (0603) 410871
Hotel Norwich, 121-131 Boundary Rd,
3-star, *tel.* (0603) 787260
Hotel Nelson, Prince of Wales Rd, 3-star,
tel. (0603) 760260
Guesthouses: Grange Hotel, 230 Thorpe
Rd, *tel.* (0603) 34734
Marlborough House Hotel, 22 Stacey Rd,
tel. (0603) 628005
Wedgewood, 42 St Stephens Rd, *tel.*
(0603) 625730
Garages: High Level S/sta, Hammond
Rd, *tel.* (0603) 408180
Spruce Hawlett & Co, Trowse, *tel.* (0603)
615100

Selection only: see page 4

Some fine old buildings survive in Orford, including elegant Orford Farm

Orford, Suffolk

Map Ref: 93TM4250

From the top of Orford Castle's 90ft-high keep – one of the finest in England – there is a magnificent view over the once-thriving medieval port, and the 10-mile long shingle bank of Orford Ness. Orford has documentary evidence, in the form of Pipe Rolls, which enables the construction of the castle to be dated exactly, to 1165. Built by Henry II as part of a network of coastal defences, it was the first castle keep built with 18 sides on the outside, yet with a cylindrical inside. The keep was reinforced by three battlemented turrets.

AA recommends:
Hotels: Crown & Castle, 2-star, *tel.* (0394) 450205
King's Head Inn, Front St, *tel.* (0394) 450271

At the Wildfowl Trust in Peakirk you can see over 112 kinds of wildfowl, many of them rare

Oulton, Suffolk

Map Ref: 89TM5294

Oulton, the most southerly of the Broads, is in the Waveney Valley, adjacent to Lake Lothing. A cut made in 1831 gave access to the lake from the sea, and then into Oulton Broad by a new lock. It is now difficult to appreciate that this Broad, like all the others, was created by the cutting of peat in the 13th and 14th centuries; more than 300,000 turves were said to have been exported from Oulton in 1341 alone. The River Waveney forms the boundary with Norfolk.

The North Landing has been developed in imaginative style, and the Broad supports a flourishing holiday industry of pleasure craft and boat-building. In August, a water carnival presents a colourful display. Fritton Lake, further downstream, 6 miles south-west of Great Yarmouth, consists of 230 acres of wood, grassland and water, providing every possible diversion for the holiday maker.

Peakirk, Cambridgeshire

Map Ref: 86TF1606

Off the beaten track, this village on the edge of the Fens has many unpretentious but charming houses built of Barnack 'rag', from the ancient quarries near Stanford. The church is the only one in the country dedicated to St Pega, whose cell became a hermitage. The restored remains of the cell can be seen nearby, to the east. Much of the church itself is of Norman origin, but the unusual lectern and wall paintings are from the 14th century.

The Car Dyke, built by the Romans to gain access to the Fens, runs through the osier beds to the east of the village. In this wetland the Wildfowl Trust has established 17 acres of water gardens which provide a sanctuary for more than 100 different species of exotic waterfowl, among them Chilean flamingoes, Andean geese and West African tree-ducks.

In **Crowland**, 6 miles north-east, are the ruins of a Benedictine Abbey founded in 716. The north aisle is now the parish church, and the abbey is reported to have had the first ringable peal of bells in the world.

Peterborough, Cambridgeshire

Map Ref: 86TL1998

This strategically placed provincial city has taken full advantage of its good communications, to become an important centre in Cambridgeshire, with a population of 149,000, growing rapidly. The A1 skirts the western boundary, the A47 linking the Midlands and East Anglia runs around the city, and the 'new' River Nene is navigable to the Wash. Industry at all levels has been attracted here by bold incentives and easy access, so that what little remains of old Peterborough is now rather overwhelmed by new developments.

The city still retains the great market square, now at the hub of the Queensgate shopping complex, which has traffic-free precincts and multi-storey car parks. The Guildhall (1671) commemorates the restoration of Charles II. The gothic church of St John the Baptist also survives. It incorporates the nave of a church that was once part of the Cathedral Close.

The City Museum and Art Gallery is in Priestgate. It is a late Georgian house, with some illuminating displays that explain the city's growth. They include fossils found in local clay at Fletton. This clay was found to be ideal for brick manufacture, and Fletton bricks are found in countless buildings in areas like Essex, where there is no local stone. Another display is devoted to the needlework of Mary, Queen of Scots, worked during her final captivity (see also Oxburgh Hall in Norfolk).

The Cathedral, rising in Norman splendour (in marked contrast to the concrete buildings around it), was completed in 1238. It was built on the site of a monastery founded in 655 by the Christian King of Mercia, Penda. Built of Barnack limestone 'rag', the present building was once the church of the former Benedictine Abbey, and was only raised to a Cathedral by Henry VIII in 1541. One of Henry VIII's wives, Catherine of Aragon, is buried in front of the Retrochoir. The later version of the *Anglo-Saxon Chronicle* was written here in 1155. The Cathedral is justly famed for its painted wooden nave ceiling, rich in colour and decoration, and for its fan-vaulted apse ceiling in the Retrochoir beyond. The Hedda Stone sculpture dates from the early

Peterborough Cathedral's painted wooden ceiling is the biggest in Europe

Saxon period. Mary, Queen of Scots was interred here after her execution at Fotheringhay. Her body was later removed to Westminster Cathedral by her son, James I of England.

The precinct is entered through a gateway flanked by a chapel and the old prison. It opens out into a great garden – a peaceful setting for such a fine Cathedral. Not far distant, by the river, is another open space, the Ferry Meadows Country Park, where the new theatre overlooks the Nene.

At **Longthorpe**, a few miles west, there is a late 13th-century hall, which had a three-storey tower added at a later date; the builder was the Abbey's Steward. The medieval interior decoration is said to be the finest in England.

Just to the south-east of the city, at **Flag Fen**, there is a very exciting excavation. It is the only place in the country where the wooden walls of a Bronze Age house can be seen. There is a reconstruction, to one-tenth scale, of a village which was discovered here beneath the peat, showing how the Fens appeared 3,000 years ago.

AA recommends:
Hotels: Bull, Westgate, 3-star, *tel.* (0733) 61364
Peterborough Moat House, Thorpe Wood, 3-star, *tel.* (0733) 260000

Garages: Cartell Autocare, Dukes Mead, Werrington, *tel.* (0733) 77444
Marshall's, 7 Oundle Rd, *tel.* (0733) 66011

Saffron Walden, Essex

Map Ref: 91TL5338

'A town surrounded by fields smiling with pleasant saffron': this is how Saffron Walden was described in Tudor times, when it boasted the ruins of a Norman castle at one end, and a commanding parish church at the other, with seven streets in

The Norman cathedral is the focal point of Peterborough; built of local limestone, it has a fine west front

between. St Mary's Church is pure Gothic, and dates from the 16th century; its spectacular tower and spire are as high as the building is long – 190ft. The interior is rich with carvings and ornamented roofs; the crypt and some arcades are from an earlier building.

On the green beside the castle is a rare maze of concentric circles. Cut in the chalk, these may once have been used by soldiery for exercise. West of the town are the banks and ditches of an Iron Age fort, formerly called Repel Ditches.

The cloth trade brought prosperity to the town, which became a centre for the cultivation of meadow saffron in medieval times. This was used as a natural dye, and for medicines. The Sun Inn, now a book dealer's shop, is renowned for its pargeting and carved timbers, and the present youth hostel is a fine 16th-century building with a great room on the first floor. The Fry Gallery of Contemporary Art is in Bridge End Gardens. There is also an excellent museum.

Lord Audley, who died in 1544, has a black marble tomb in the church. His home was at **Audley End**, a mansion on a grand scale, just west of the town. Above ground, nothing remains of his first house, built on the site of a Benedictine Abbey; what we see today is a splendid Jacobean-style house, which has been remodelled over several centuries. The Great Hall and the moulded ceilings are especially notable, and the elegant park was landscaped by Capability Brown. It is cared for by English Heritage.

AA recommends:
Hotel: Saffron, 10-18 High St, 2-star, *tel.* (0799) 22676
Garages: Cleales, Station Rd, *tel.* (0799) 23203
Saffron Automotive Eng, Shirehill Industrial Estate, Thaxted Rd, *tel.* (0799) 21273

The rare and very old earth maze on the Common in Saffron Walden

St Ives, Cambridgeshire

Map Ref: 90TL3171

This populous town on the left bank of the Great Ouse was established in 1110, when Henry I granted a charter for an annual fair. Sea-going barges once navigated up to the six-arched bridge that was built about 1415; the two-storey chapel on it was consecrated 10 years later. There are only two others like it in the country. One of the keys to the chapel is kept in the Norris Museum and Library, a new building on the riverbank upstream, that contains some interesting collections.

Further up is All Saints' Church with its tall, 15th-century steeple, ornate porches, and colourful rood-screen by Cowper, who was responsible for similar work at Eye in Suffolk. The 'dole' is distributed to needy parishioners in the form of groceries each January, according to the instructions of a 17th-century benefactor. Around the church are period buildings, some with fine Venetian windows. In the market place stands a pensive statue of Oliver Cromwell, who once owned a farm over the bridge.

AA recommends:
Hotels: Dolphin, Bridge Foot, London Rd, 3-star, *tel.* (0480) 66966
Slepe Hall, Ramsey Rd, 3-star, *tel.* (0480) 63122
Golden Lion, Market Hill, 2-star, *tel.* (0480) 63159
Pike & Eel, Overcote Lane, Needingworth, 1-star, *tel.* (0480) 63336
Guesthouse: Oliver's Lodge Hotel, 50 Needingworth Rd, *tel.* (0480) 63252
Garage: Riverside, London Rd, *tel.* (0480) 62952

Sandringham, Norfolk

Map Ref: 87TF6928

As their son Bertie approached his twenty-first birthday, Queen Victoria and Prince Albert searched for an estate which would be a healthy country retreat for him, as Osborne and Balmoral were for them. Even Albert's death could not delay this project, and the Sandringham Estate was bought some two months afterwards, in 1862. A railway had been in operation here since 1847, and Wolferton became a royal station until road transport killed the railway. Today the main station buildings and the signal box are lovingly preserved by an enthusiast who has created a fascinating display of royal memorabilia in them, from train tickets and letters, to furniture and children's toys. This museum is also the owner's home, and is open to visitors.

When the Prince of Wales married Princess Alexandra, Sandringham House, despite its many additions, became too small for them. The main block was demolished, and a new house, in the Jacobean style, replaced it. At the same time the grounds were replanted, and the result is a water landscape that follows the traditions of great landscape designers such as Capability Brown. Fringed with rockeries, shrubs and trees, both exotic and native, the lakes are perfect mirrors for the house. The house and grounds are open to the public except when a member of the Royal Family is in residence.

Outside the grounds is a country park, where there is free access to nature trails, walks and a picnic

Nearby Ramsay Abbey financed the building of St Ives' medieval bridge and chapel across the Ouse

area. Of perhaps almost as much interest as the house is the church of St Mary Magdalene, which is resplendent with gifts from royalty and other distinguished visitors. The altar and reredos are of solid silver, and the oak pulpit is covered in the same metal.

Sheringham, Norfolk

Map Ref: 88TG1543

Four miles west of Cromer, the old fishing village here has become almost a fossil within an outer circle of seaside villas and hotels. Real fossils may, indeed, be found in the cliffs backing the sandy shore. The fishermen, once known as shannocks, still tend their crab pots and long-lines, but summer tourists, first lured by the railway, have now become a major industry in this part of Sheringham. There are now two railways – the main line that connects at Norwich for London, and the more leisurely North Norfolk Railway, a steam service that will soon puff its way from here to Holt, via Weybourne. There are various entertainments provided for tourists during the season.

Upper Sheringham to the west, bypassed by road and railway, is the residential area. It remains small and secluded, but the church and enormous surrounding churchyard are witness to its former importance. Many graves here record those lost at sea. All Saints is notable for its 15th-century rood-

screen and loft, a very rare survival, and for its cambered tie beam that carries the pulley and counterpoise required to raise and lower the wooden font cover. The handsome memorials are to the Upcher family, responsible for the building of Sheringham Park and Hall to a design by Humphry Repton in 1812. The Park has a lower entrance drive, leading off the village square, and is now National Trust property. It is open daily for walkers. There are several viewing platforms, or gazebos, which command fine views of this hilly coast and, in May and June, there are acres of rhododendrons and azaleas in the woods. The Hall is only open by appointment.

AA recommends:

Hotels: Beaumaris, South St, 2-star, *tel.* (0263) 822370

Southlands, South St, 2-star, *tel.* (0263) 822679

Two Lifeboats, Promenade, 1-star, *tel.* (0263) 822401

Guesthouses: Beacon Hotel, Nelson Rd, *tel.* (0263) 822019

Camberley House Hotel, 62 Cliff Rd, *tel.* (0263) 823101

Melrose Hotel, 9 Holway Rd, *tel.* (0263) 823299

Campsite: Woodlands Caravan Park, Holt Rd, Upper Sheringham, 2-pennant, *tel.* (0263) 823802

Garages: Central, 49 High St, *tel.* (0263) 823168

Sheringham, 46 Cromer Rd, *tel.* (0263) 822022

Somerleyton Hall, Suffolk

Map Ref: 89TM4897

Somerleyton spells exuberance. Some country houses are refined, some are grandiose, others are historical, but Somerleyton and its grounds convey a sense of

enjoyment, and even its architecture contributes to this feeling. The present house is Victorian. Its wealthy (and later bankrupt) railway-building creator spared no expense in bringing stone from France which was then blended with red brick to form a house reminiscent of English architecture some 300 years ago, with strong Italian overtones.

The present building encloses an earlier house, built some seven years after the first Queen Elizabeth's death. Contemporary pictures show that the original Hall had beautiful, curved gables; this was obviously not apparent to Oliver Cromwell when he sacked the house in 1642.

There is a maze in the grounds, and some unusual animals are to be seen in the children's farm which occupies part of the walled garden. Nearby there is an aviary and a miniature railway. The gardens, which are beautifully kept, have changed little since Victorian times, and are complemented by greenhouses which contain fine displays of hot-house plants.

Sheringham is still a flint-built fishing village at heart, despite attractions like the North Norfolk Railway, where steam trains run most days in summer

Southend-on-Sea, Essex

Map Ref: 95TQ8885

At the beginning of the 19th century this was a small village, fast earning a reputation as a bathing place. In those days, the air here was thought to be dry and salubrious. The railway opened up the town, first to day-trippers from London, and then to commuters. Several villages like South Church and Prittlewell – the Saxon for pretty well or spring – were swallowed up to form a resort several miles long. The remains of the Priory at Prittlewell, founded for Cluniac monks by Robert of Essex in Henry II's reign, now house the town museum of local and natural history. The church on top of the hill has a Norman embattled tower.

Visitors come to Southend, however, to enjoy themselves rather than to study what few historical buildings remain. There is the famous pier, the longest in the world at 1½ miles, with its own train service. For children, there is Never-Never Land, set in 2 acres of Cliff Gardens, and for shoppers the paved pedestrian precincts give access to department stores and shops on various levels. The airport is increasingly important as a springboard for European feeder services.

At **Rayleigh**, 6 miles north-west, is the great motte of a Norman castle, surrounded by earthworks, and a tower windmill which houses a local history museum.

AA recommends:
Hotel: Balmoral, 34 Valkyrie Rd, Westcliff-on-Sea, I-star, *tel.* (0702) 342947 **Rayleigh**
Garage: Mac's, 235-243 Eastwood Rd, *tel.* (0268) 774311

Southwold, Suffolk

Map Ref: 93TM5076

A heady mixture of hops and salty breezes pervades this uncommercialised seaside town, whose Charter was granted by Henry VII in the 15th century. Adnams brewery is in the centre, a mecca for all local beer drinkers. The great church of St Edmunds, splendid even by Suffolk standards, is arguably the finest medieval seaside church in England. It rose during the 15th century from the ashes of an earlier church built in 1202. Inside, all is light and space; the original rood-screen glows with paintings, and glorious carving enlivens the choir stalls. Secure on one of the soaring perpendicular columns is the colourful effigy of 'Southwold Jack', a medieval striker of the bell, used to herald the start of the services.

Little survives of the medieval town due to a fire in 1659 which destroyed no less than 238 houses. As a result the town is a happy amalgam of Georgian dwellings set

Southwold is a lovely cliff-top town, with a white lighthouse and colourful bathing huts

around greens and squares. Later, gracious Regency and Victorian villas were added, and houses with a distinct Dutch flavour, a sign of the prosperous time in the mid-18th century when Southwold was the base for the Free British Fishery. The staid line of beach huts along the promenade are packed with visitors in summer.

The 1892 lighthouse overlooks the town and Sole Bay Inn, whose beer is supplied by horse-drawn drays from the brewery nearby. Along the banks of the River Blyth is a colourful medley of pleasure craft and longshore fishing boats. The footbridge over the river leads to Walberswick on the right bank, a happy hunting ground both for artists and for amateur naturalists, who can wander in the 1,000-acre nature reserve established by the Nature Conservancy Council.

AA recommends:
Hotels: Swan, Market Pl, 3-star, *tel.* (0502) 722186
Crown, High St, 2-star, *tel.* (0502) 722275
Pier Avenue, 2-star, *tel.* (0502) 722632
Randolph, 41 Wangford Rd, Reydon, 2-star, *tel.* (0502) 723603
Garage: Southwold Motor Co, Station Rd, *tel.* (0502) 722125

Stoke-by-Nayland, Suffolk

Map Ref: 92TL9836

On a clear day it is possible to see the majestic church of St Mary's from Harwich, 20 miles away. This 15th-century wool church sits on a hill, and its tower, built largely of brick, with four pinnacles, is 120ft high. The great south doors display wonderful carved figures and inside are memorial brasses to the Howard family. Katherine Howard, first wife of the John who was killed at

Bosworth while fighting for Richard III, is buried in the chancel. John Constable has immortalised St Mary's in several paintings now hanging in the Victoria and Albert Museum. In School Street near the church are two outstanding timber-framed buildings, the Guildhall and the Maltings, matched by two old inns, the Black Horse and the Crown.

The Rowley family own the Tendring estate that embraces much of the land and buildings in and around the village, and all is convenanted to the National Trust. The park is all that remains of Tendring Hall, designed in 1784 by Sir John Soane and once one of the greatest houses of England. Outside the village, Thorington Hall, beside the road, is an important 18th-century house with a fine 16th-century frontage. It is owned by the National Trust and open to visitors by appointment.

AA recommends:
Garage: L S Eaves, High St, *tel.* (0206) 262123

Stowmarket, Suffolk

Map Ref: 92TM0458

Nearly in the middle of Suffolk, and happily bypassed by the A45, this busy market town was a noted centre of the woollen industry and owes much of its growth to the canalisation of the River Gipping; the waterway was opened in 1793 to carry the town's trade directly to Ipswich. Hops were once grown in the valley and today the old towpath has become a popular and delightful walk. The railway came in 1849, taking away the canal trade, and Stowmarket remains one of the stops on the main Norwich–London line, the railway station being mock-Elizabethan.

The church of St Peter and St Paul has a tower surmounted by a wooden steeple, and inside are some fine memorials in verse and an unusual metal wig-stand.

In an attractive 30-acre riverside site in the centre of Stowmarket, the Museum of East Anglian Life is dedicated to the re-creation of local country life during the last 150 years. Steam ploughing engines made in Thetford work alongside Remus, a Suffolk Punch horse. Buildings include a watermill, smithy and windpump rescued from other places in Suffolk, all shown in original working order. In the new Boby Building are industrial and craft displays.

Three miles west, up the A45, is Haughley Park, a Jacobean manor house with a fine collection of 17th-century Dutch paintings, in attractive gardens and woodland, open at certain times.

AA recommends:
Hotel: Cedars, Needham Rd, 2-star, *tel.* (0449) 612668

Sudbury, Suffolk

Map Ref: 95TL8741

An ancient market town mentioned in Domesday and situated on the River Stour, Sudbury was once called Southburgh to distinguish it from Northburgh (which became Norwich). One of its various claims to fame is for being described as 'Eatanswill' by Charles Dickens in *The Pickwick Papers*. Flemish weavers settled here in the reign of Edward III and instructed local people in the art of weaving all types of cloth, including crêpe. A crêpe maker called Gainsborough lived at No 46, Sepulchre Street, and had nine children. The youngest child was Thomas, the portrait and landscape painter. There is a bronze statue of him on Market Hill, and his birthplace is now a museum and art gallery. Also on Market Hill is the handsome early-Victorian Corn Exchange, now used as a library and venue for civic functions, and the redundant church of St Peter, one of three churches in Sudbury. St Gregory's, at the west end of the town, was rebuilt in the 14th century by Simon of Sudbury, Archbishop of Westminster. He was later murdered in the Peasants' Revolt.

Down Stour Street, towards the river, there are some historic half-

A windmill and windpump are among the re-erected buildings at the Museum of East Anglian Life

timbered houses, including The Chantry and Salter's Hall, dating from the time Sudbury was the largest of the Suffolk wool towns.

To the north-east is a large and expanding trading estate, and there are firm plans to bypass Sudbury entirely to rid the town centre of excessive traffic.

AA recommends:
Guesthouse: Hill Lodge Private Hotel, 8 Newton Rd, *tel.* (0787) 77568
Campsite: Willowmere Caravan Park, Bures Rd, 3-pennant, *tel.* (0787) 75559
Garages: Ipswich Co-op Society, Cornard Rd, *tel.* (0787) 72301
D J Molkenthin, Recovery Unit 9, Mills Rd, Chilton Industrial Estate, *tel.* (0787) 74840

Sutton Hoo, Suffolk

Map Ref: 93TM2849

On a sandy ridge overlooking the Deben estuary, downstream from Woodbridge, is Sutton Common. Excavation work began in 1938 on four of the 11 long barrows or burial mounds that are a feature of this heathland. The first three yielded few remains, but in the fourth, opened a year later, a great ship was discovered, 89ft long, which had been used for the burial of a Saxon chieftain. The ship's timbers had rotted away, but much metalwork had survived, as well as a great hoard of jewellery and all the totems befitting an important warrior. Most of the treasure is now on display in the British Museum and includes a gold mounted harp, an iron battle standard, a great sword, and buckles, brooches and mounts, all of which are gold. Research has dated the burial to the middle of the 7th century, but excavation will continue for years to come in an effort to discover who was buried in such state there. There are guided tours of the dig in season, and replicas of some of the finds are on display in the Ipswich Museum.

Swaffham, Norfolk

Map Ref: 87TF8108

Once described as the finest Regency town in East Anglia, Swaffham was for many years the social centre of the surrounding district. Prosperous farmers had town houses here, used in the winter months for parties and soirées. The town was an important stop on the flourishing theatre circuit, and in 1806 the Nelsons, with Lady Hamilton in their party, attended a performance of *She Stoops to Conquer*. The elegant market cross, built in 1783, is a central feature in a great triangular area. Here an open market, of ancient origin, is held every Saturday.

In a small shop on the Fakenham road, baskets are still woven from local withies and osiers by an octogenarian. Perhaps the most famous son of Swaffham is John Chapman, a 15th-century pedlar who, so the story goes, dreamt that 'something to his advantage' would happen to him if he stood on London Bridge. He went and met a shopkeeper who told him that if he went to Swaffham and dug in the garden of a pedlar, he would find a crock of gold. He returned to his own home, and there, under a tree, he discovered the gold. With his new-found riches he repaired the north aisle of the parish church, memorable for its lofty narrow nave and roof, resplendent with angels carved in wood and stone.

AA recommends:
Swaffham
Hotels: George, Station Rd, 2-star, *tel.* (0760) 21238
Grady's Country House, Norwich Rd, 2-star, *tel.* (0760) 23355
Fakenham
Hotels: Crown, Market Pl, 2-star, *tel.* (0328) 51418
Old Mill, Bridge St, 2-star, *tel.* (0328) 2100
Campsite: Caravan Club Site, 2-pennant, *tel.* (0328) 2388
Garage: English, Greenway Lane, *tel.* (0328) 2200

Below: a memorial to the Pedlar in Swaffham parish church

Thaxted, Essex

Map Ref: 94TL6131

First the Romans and then the Saxons settled here. The pattern of the town, established in the 14th century, has altered little since, and civic pride has ensured the survival of some remarkably well-preserved historic buildings. Approach from any quarter and the parish church, begun in 1380 and finished 170 years later, dominates the scene; its construction took place during the reigns of 10 monarchs, encompassing the Black Death, the Peasants' Revolt and the violent deaths of three kings. The spire is 181ft high, and the whole building is 183ft long.

Under its shadow is the most important civic building, the Guildhall, built by the Cutlers' Guild in 1390. Here the Trustees of the Yardley charity meet. This is one of the many charities that have contributed much to Thaxted's communal life. Near the Guildhall is the Recorders' House, now a restaurant, with two bay windows on the second storey resting on oak coves, carved with the arms of Edward IV. Gustav Holst, the composer, lived next door, at the manse.

The windmill of 1804, approached by going along the ridge past a range of restored almshouses, is now a local museum; much of the original machinery is intact.

Thetford, Norfolk

Map Ref: 88TL8783

Thetford has been a thriving community since before the Norman Conquest, and was at one time the most important city in East Anglia, until the removal of the Bishop's throne to Norwich in the 11th century. Many traces of its fascinating past remain, from the Iron Age ramparts surrounding the Norman castle, of which only the mound survives today, to the fine buildings of the town centre's conservation area.

Thetford Priory, founded by the Norman warrior Roger Bigod, 1st Earl of Norfolk, dates back to the 12th century. From then until the

Although not much now remains of Thetford Priory, it should not be overlooked by the visitor

Dissolution, it was an important religious centre, but little remains today of one of the country's finest examples of Norman architecture.

The 15th-century timber-framed Ancient House Museum in White Hart Street has beautifully carved beam ceilings, and houses an exhibition depicting the story of Breckland man, with examples from local Neolithic settlements. Near the museum is the birthplace of Thomas Paine, Thetford's most famous son. A gilt statue of him stands in front of King's House.

AA recommends:
Hotels: Bell, King St, 3-star, *tel.* (0842) 4455
Anchor, Bridge St, 2-star, *tel.* (0842) 63925
Historical Thomas Paine, White Hart St, 2-star, *tel.* (0842) 5631
Garage: Canon's Motor Services, Brandon Rd, *tel.* (0842) 2976

Thornham Parva, Suffolk

Map Ref: 92TM1071

One of the greatest treasures to be seen in an English parish church is the altarpiece, or retable, in the tiny thatched building here. The retable dates from the very early 14th century and was only discovered in 1927, in the stables of Thornham Hall. There are nine panels showing eight saints and the Crucifixion, painted in brilliant colours on a fine patterned background. The figures include St Edmund and two Dominican saints. This masterpiece may have been designed for a Dominican Friary in East Anglia – Dunwich, perhaps, or even Norwich. The gilded background appears in a similar altarpiece in the Cluny Museum in Paris.

Tilbury, Essex

Map Ref: 94TQ6476

With an echoing Victorian railway station on one hand and an ugly power station on the other, Tilbury Fort is in a quiet, windy spot, where it is possible to ponder over the past history of this strategically vital section of the Thames. The Fort is a fine surviving example of late 17th-century military engineering, its shape a giant star, and its overall plan scarcely altered. The handsome Water Gate bears the royal cipher of Charles II. The landward approach has been restored to its former intricate and formidable design. The Fort has never been tested in battle. The only unusual events to have taken place near here were a fracas following a cricket match in 1776, and the shooting-down of a German Zeppelin in World War I.

An expensive ferry plies between Tilbury and Gravesend across the murky waters of the Thames, and the main industry, apart from the bustling docks upstream, seems to be breaking up old cars.

Walsingham, Norfolk

Map Ref: 88TF9336

For 900 years pilgrims have flocked to Little Walsingham. In 1061, Mary, the mother of Jesus, is said to have appeared in a vision to Richeldis, the Lady of the Manor, and to have bidden her build here a replica of the Holy House of Nazareth, where Gabriel spoke to the Virgin Mary. An Augustinian Priory was founded in 1153 to house the Shrine of Our Lady of Walsingham, and its size can be gauged today by the romantic ruins in the garden of Abbey House, and by the 15th-century gatehouse standing at the north end of the main street.

Pilgrims used to stop at Houghton St Giles, the last wayside shrine before Walsingham, and many removed their shoes and walked the remaining 1½ miles barefoot. This is how the Slipper Chapel got its name. It is now part of a large Roman Catholic shrine. The small parish church nearby, reached by a ford, has a well-preserved rood-screen, complete with panels in original colours. The Anglican Shrine of Our Lady is at the north end of Little Walsingham; the route to it passes the impressive ruins of a Franciscan Friary (not open), as well as many period houses in the High Street, before continuing through the Common Place, which has a 16th-century conduit topped by a metal brazier. Set between the two competing shrines is the parish church of St Mary, where Anglo-Catholicism is preached and the finest stepped font in the county can be admired. The Shirehall Museum, off the High Street, is housed in a Georgian courtroom, complete with original fixtures.

The 14th-century Slipper Chapel at Houghton St Giles is part of the RC National Shrine

Waltham Abbey, Essex

Map Ref: 94TL3800

The ceaseless murmur of traffic on the M25 can be shut out in the lofty nave of the Abbey Church of Waltham Holy Cross, first established by King Harold, who prayed here for the victory that eluded him at Hastings in 1066. His remains are supposed to rest outside the east end of the present, truncated building, which was once 400ft long. The simplicity of the great Norman piers and arches compares well with other great cathedrals. There are two

Altar panel in the Shrine of Our Lady of Walsingham, to which pilgrims still flock each year

marvellous 17th-century tombs that say a lot about the social history of the time, and above the altar, in the 14th-century Lady Chapel, there is a 15th-century Doom painting.

The ruins of the original Abbey (that include the gateway of 1370), are now being 'landscaped', and the Lea Valley Park Visitor Centre has opened here, on the banks of the Lea. The waters of this river once powered the Abbey corn mills. What remains of the ancient market town south of the church is interesting; Sun Street is closed to vehicles, and at the east end there are some Tudor buildings, including the library and a good museum.

AA recommends:
Garage: Nick Mason Eng, 51 Cartersfield Rd, *tel.* (0992) 713487

The Pastons

The tiny hamlet of Paston was once the home of the influential Paston family, who made their fortune from the wool trade and, later on, from farming. In the 15th and 16th centuries they owned extensive lands in north Norfolk and were one of the richest families in the county, owning several manors including Caister Castle. The great house which they

North Walsham Grammar School, formerly the Paston Grammar School, was founded in 1606, and is still flourishing

built at Paston has since been demolished.

The family name is best-known for the famous *Paston Letters*, written by various members of the family to one another, which now provide us with a valuable commentary on 15th-century life.

Many of the letters were written by Margaret Paston to her husband John, who practised as a lawyer in London. Margaret managed the family estates in his absence, negotiating with neighbours and dependents, collecting rents and defending family properties against everything from violence to law-suits. All these activities are faithfully reported in her letters, along with news of local events and people. When John fell from the King's favour and was imprisoned, Margaret wrote that this had evoked much sympathy from the people of Norwich.

Sir William Paston, a grandson of John and Margaret, founded a grammar school in North Walsham in 1606 which still bears his name. The school has survived to this day, and one of its former pupils was Lord Nelson. The Pastons fought for the Royalist cause in the Civil War, and were rewarded with the Earldom of Yarmouth. When the family fortunes and estates were squandered by the second Earl, the family sank into obscurity.

Wells-Next-The-Sea, Norfolk

Map Ref: 88TF9143

The patron saint of sailors and children, St Nicholas, was chosen as the namesake of the parish church here. This delightful town has been, and remains, largely dependent on the sea for its trade. Along the quay there are always coasters with holds full of grain, fertiliser and timber, while pleasure craft are dotted about the muddy creeks, waiting for the tide to turn. Fishing boats continue to bring in their catches of whelks, crabs and sprats. In season tourists come to the area which was once the harbour, where there are now

caravan sites out on the pine-covered dunes, and entertainments along the quay. At all seasons you can admire the High Street, lined with colourful houses full of character, which leads to the church, rebuilt after destruction by fire and lightning in 1879. A street similarly closed to traffic leads to the Buttlands, a large green that is shaded by trees and surrounded by Georgian houses. The Wells Centre in the old maltings dispenses information, music and good food.

Two miles west, along the coast, Lady Anne's Drive provides access to superb stretches of sand and pines, all part of the vast **Holkham** estate. In the centre of it all sits

Holkham Hall, built between 1734 and 1759 by William Kent for the Coke family, whose name is synonymous with progressive agricultural practice. The Hall is a beautifully balanced, monumental mansion, faced with sand-coloured brick made on the estate. The Marble Hall is arguably the finest Palladian room in the country, and the rooms that lead off from it are in exuberant colours, with crimson velvet hangings and gilded ceilings. The Statue Gallery reflects 18th-century taste at its purest, with its chilly marble and elaborate furniture.

The estate became an agricultural success under the hand of Thomas Coke, 'Coke of Norfolk'. The park was landscaped on a grand scale by Capability Brown, who created the lake and had planted the thousands of ilex trees. Humphry Repton wrote one of his famous Red Books about Holkham. The stable block is home for an extensive exhibition of bygone equipment, and in the old walled garden, designed by Samuel Watt in the 1780s, the plant nursery has an excellent reputation.

AA recommends:
Hotel: Crown, The Buttlands, 1-star, *tel.* (0328) 710209
Restaurant: Moorings, Freeman St, 1-fork, *tel.* (0328) 710949
Guesthouse: Scarborough House, Clubbs Lane, *tel.* (0328) 710309
Garage: BE & SM Ayton, Warham Rd, *tel.* (0328) 710397

Wells-Next-The-Sea is a delightful old-fashioned port, where a small fleet of whelk and shrimp boats (left) operates from the harbour, and where ships of up to 300 tons can also often be seen unloading

Wimpole Hall is Cambridgeshire's most spectacular mansion. The South Drawing Room (left) was added to the earlier house between 1713 & 1718. The great barn of the Farm houses a museum of agricultural equipment

Wimpole, Cambridgeshire

Map Ref: 90TL3350

There are now two Wimpoles: the new one, built in the 1840s as a model village along the Cambridge–Sandy road, and the old one, whose emparkment by a series of landscape architects caused the population shift. Wimpole Hall is now surrounded by 360 acres of historic parkland, with trees and avenues laid out by Charles Bridgeman, Capability Brown and Humphry Repton. Under permanent pasture are the remains of a medieval village, and ancient tracks can be traced to areas of ridge-and-furrow cultivation. The present parish church is Georgian, but built on the site of a medieval one, and in the graveyard lie the remains of Mrs Elsie Bambridge, the daughter of Rudyard Kipling, who undertook the restoration of the estate and gave it to the National Trust in 1976.

The contrast between the park and the surrounding windswept arable land is remarkable. The home farm at Wimpole, a cluster of thatched and timber buildings with some modern additions, was designed by Sir John Soane in 1792 for the third Earl of Hardwicke. The visitor can now see in and around the farm a wide selection of rare breeds of domestic livestock, as well as a commercial flock of sheep; the black-and-white Bagot goat is one breed that has been rescued from extinction. The great barn has a complete collection of agricultural implements on show, similar to those used on the farm here 150 years ago. The restored Victorian stable block now echoes once again to the clatter of the hooves of heavy Suffolk Punch horses, now a rare breed.

A double avenue of elms, planted in 1721, once led south for 2½ miles. Disease killed the trees, but limes have now taken their place, and the avenue again provides a fitting approach to the Hall, which remains one of the grandest mansions in mid-Anglia despite the removal of its Victorian wings. The core of the existing house dates back to 1640, but the facing is Georgian. The inside was created by a number of celebrated architects; Soane built stately rooms here inspired by Palladio's designs. There is also a superbly proportioned library of 1730 by James Gibbs, and Sir James Thornhill's *trompe l'oeil* decoration in the Chapel is stunning.

Wisbech, Cambridgeshire

Map Ref: 86TF4609

Much is written about the trade once enjoyed by East Anglian merchants with the low countries, especially the export of wool and grain. At Wisbech it is possible to see at first hand the fruits of that trade; elegant Georgian houses and multi-storied warehouses line the river banks, although the River Nene now runs along an artificial course from Peterborough.

The finest houses are along the Brinks, and in one, on the South Brink, Octavia Hill was born in 1838. The National Trust, which she helped found, now owns the fine house opposite, Peckover House. It is named after the country banker who bought it in 1777. His bank merged with two others locally, and in 1896 it was one of the founder members of Barclays Bank. The glories of the house include its wood and plaster decorations, and its 2-acre garden. The garden is striking as it has retained its 19th-century layout of trim lawns, borders and rare shrubs. In the traditional greenhouse are fruiting orange trees, which are more than 250 years old; they were transplanted from an earlier garden. The ginkgo, or maidenhair tree, was the tallest in the land until dismasted by a storm.

Further down the Brink is a classical Georgian brewery, which still keeps local pubs supplied with real ale, and under the Rose and Crown Hotel in the market place there are barrel vaults built in early Tudor times. Two crescents of fine Georgian houses run north and south of the old castle. The castle was built by the Normans, and then replaced by a mansion. Today, though, only the gate piers of this building remain. The museum is housed here, and contains some fascinating collections, including Parish registers and more than 10,000 books. There is also a working Georgian theatre in Wisbech.

AA recommends:
Hotels: Queen's, South Bank, 2-star, *tel.* (0945) 583933
Rose & Crown, Market Pl, 2-star, *tel.* (0945) 583187
White Lion, South Bank, 2-star, *tel.* (0945) 584813
Guesthouse: Glendon, Sutton Rd, *tel.* (0945) 584812

The town centre of elegant Wisbech

Wymondham's wooden Market Cross (above), built in 1617. The Tide Mill on the Deben in Woodbridge (top) was the last working mill of its kind in the country

Woodbridge, Suffolk

Map Ref: 93TM2648

A natural site for a settlement beside an estuary, Woodbridge must always have been, as it is now, a pleasant riverside town. The history of this area spans over 3,000 years. The Romans had a large camp at Burgh, and the Anglo-Saxons were also here in force, as we know from the stunning finds made in burial mounds across the Deben estuary, at Sutton Hoo.

In Elizabeth I's reign local industries flourished – weaving, rope-making, salt manufacture and ship building. Much business was conducted in the churchyard where, to accommodate traders, one of the first public lavatories was built!

The name of Thomas Seckford occurs in any history of Woodbridge; he was Master of the Court of Requests in Elizabethan times and, with his trading fortune, became a leading benefactor of the town. He established almshouses which gave way to the present Elizabethan-style hospital bearing his name, and his endowment still benefits schools here. He also financed the building of the Shire Hall, where magistrates still dispense justice.

Elegant Georgian porches and façades can be discovered in the narrow, medieval streets that lead down to the quays and modern marinas, where the boat industry reigns supreme. Silting up of the River Deben halted the building of large vessels long ago, but meeting the demands of the sailing fraternity now keeps the locals busy; sail lofts, ship brokers and chandlers are everywhere.

Overlooking this bustle is the symbol of Woodbridge, the old tide mill with its white clapboard sides and tidal mill pond. The water from this pond drives the new water wheel, installed in 1976. There has been a mill here since 1170. There is a short walk up the Deben to Kyson Hill, 4 acres of historic parkland with a pleasant view over the river valley.

AA recommends:
Hotels: Seckford Hall, 3-star (country house), *tel.* (0394) 385678
Crown, Thorofare, 2-star, *tel.* (03943) 4242
Garage: Jewell, Barrack Corner, 60 Ipswich Rd, *tel.* (03943) 3333

Wymondham, Norfolk

Map Ref: 88TG1101

Wymondham is a charming market town with many fine houses. The octagonal wooden Market Cross, built in 1617, survives, as does the Guild Chapel dedicated to Thomas à Becket and rebuilt in the 14th century; it now houses the County Library.

Wymondham Abbey has a curious history, and its surviving twin towers are a legacy of the division between the monasteries and the townspeople. In the 13th century, the monks of the Benedictine priory here quarrelled to such an extent with the people that the Pope awarded the nave, north-west tower and north aisle to the people, and the rest to the monks! The monks walled off their portion, while the people built the present Great West Tower in 1445. The monks retaliated with a lovely octagonal tower of their own. This survived the destruction of the east end of the church during the Dissolution. The townspeople's part, with its Norman nave and 15th-century towers is classed as one of the great buildings of Norfolk.

AA recommends:
Hotels: Abbey, Church St, 2-star, *tel.* (0953) 602148
Sinclair, 28 Market St, 3-star, *tel.* (0953) 606721
Restaurant: Adlards, 16 Damgate St, 1-fork, *tel.* (0953) 603533

Directory

This directory of places to visit and things to do and see in East Anglia introduces you to a selection of the best-known attractions in the area. Tourist information centres can provide additional and more detailed information.

CRAFTS

There are many small craft shops all over East Anglia. Several museums have a craft shop, as well as craft demonstrations. From the wide selection, you should not miss the thriving **Dedham Centre** (Essex) on three floors in a converted church *Tel.* (0206) 322666, (open all year, Mon-Sun; closed Mon Jan-Mar). In Norfolk, **Wroxham Barns Ltd**, a collection of 18th-century barns, has workshops and courtyards displaying rural crafts *Tel.* (06053) 3762, open daily. **Snape Maltings** in Suffolk consists of a remarkable old collection of buildings on the bank of the River Alde converted into shops, galleries and an activity holiday centre *Tel.* (072888) 303, open all year.

ACTIVITIES

Angling
With the Broads, rivers, small lakes for freshwater fish and the coast for sea-angling, you are never far away from excellent fishing in East Anglia. General information, licences and leaflets are available from Anglian Water (see useful addresses).

Beaches
There are some wonderful sandy beaches in East Anglia, and some that are shingle. On the north Norfolk coast, there are wide beaches where the tide goes out for miles; on the east coast, they tend to be narrower and shelve steeply. Those in Suffolk are always more attractive and safer at low tide when they shelve less steeply. The majority of Essex beaches are sandy. When bathing, remember that the current flows south on the flood and north on the ebb and can run quite strongly, especially when the wind is in the same direction.

Although East Anglia has more sunshine than most parts of the country, there are sometimes onshore easterly winds, so a windbreak may be useful.

Seaside resorts can be busy and lively with the usual holiday entertainments – for example, at Great Yarmouth and Clacton-on-Sea – or quiet, out-of-the-way places, some with nature reserves, as at Winterton-on-Sea in Norfolk and Walberswick in Suffolk.

Birdwatching
The varied coast from the Wash, along the soft cliffs down to the sand and shingle beaches, provides excellent viewing, especially at the coastal reserves of Snettisham, Titchwell Marsh, Minsmere and Havergate Island. The river estuaries – particularly the Stour, Blackwater and Orwell – are well worth visiting. Inland, Fowlmere, Strumpshaw Fen and the Ouse Marshes are home to a variety of waterside breeding birds. Wolves Wood (Suffolk) and Stour Wood and Copperas Bay (Essex) are the habitat of several woodland species. The following list of nature reserves is only a selection: more information may be found in the feature on page 12, and leaflets are obtainable from naturalist organisations (see useful addresses). The reserves in the following list are open all year, unless otherwise stated; the best visiting seasons are given where applicable.

Norfolk
Cley Marshes (Norfolk Naturalists' Trust): 5 miles NW of Holt. Coastal wetland. Waders, wildfowl, rarities, bittern, bearded tit. Access at all times on footpaths, beach and roads; most hides always open, but for some a permit is required (available from information centre, at a fee).
Strumpshaw Fen (RSPB): near Brundall, E of Norwich. Grazing marsh, fen. Fen flowers, marsh harrier, Cetti's warbler. (Open 9am-9pm or dusk, whichever is earlier. Best visited in spring, early summer.)
Titchwell Marsh (RSPB): 5 miles E of Hunstanton. Coastal wetland. Marsh harrier, waders, rarities, little tern, wildfowl.
Welney Wildfowl Refuge (Wildfowl Trust): 5 miles NW of Littleport. Wetland. Bewick's and whooper swans, wigeon, pintail. Permit from Wildfowl Trust, fee to non-WT members. (The classic time to visit is winter, but a summer trail is also open.)

Suffolk
Bradfield Woods (Suffolk Wildlife Trust): Bradfield St George, near Bury St Edmunds. Ancient coppice woodland. Herb paris, oxlip, nightingale, warblers. (Best visited in spring, early summer.)

Havergate Island (RSPB): Orford. Lagoons on shingle spit. Avocet, shingle flowers. Access by boat from Orford Quay; book in advance with RSPB warden, 30 Mundays Lane, Orford; fee. (Best visited in spring, summer.)
Minsmere (RSPB): near Westleton. Wetland, woodland and heathland. Avocet, marsh harrier, bittern, little tern, rarities. Fee for non-members of RSPB. Central reserve closed Tue, but free public hides always open. (Access from Dunwich cliffs NT car park.)
Walberswick (Nature Conservancy Council): S of Southwold. Coastal reed-bed, heath. Marsh harrier, bearded tit, wintering birds of prey.

Cambridgeshire
Fowlmere (RSPB): Near A10 Cambridge–Royston road. Old watercress beds, reed-bed, scrub. Reed warbler, sedge warbler, kingfisher. (Best visited in spring, early summer.)
Hayley Wood (Cambridgeshire Wildlife Trust): S of B1046, W of Cambridge. Coppice woodland. Oxlip, bluebell, primrose; fungi; fallow deer. Permit from CWT, but bridleway skirts reserve. (Best visited in spring.)
Wicken Fen (National Trust): 3 miles SW of Soham. Fen, scrub. Rich wetland flora, including southern marsh orchid. Small fee. (Best visited in spring, summer; closed Xmas.)

Essex
Danbury Ridge (parts National Trust, Essex Naturalists' Trust): around Danbury, E of Chelmsford. Woodland, heathland. Nightingale, warblers, woodland flowers. Many access points. (Best visited in spring, early summer.)
Epping Forest (Corporation of London): Loughton and Epping area. Ancient woodland. Beech, oak and hornbeam; warblers, woodpeckers. Numerous public car parks. (Best visited in spring, early summer.)
Fingringhoe Wick (Essex Naturalists' Trust): SE of Colchester. Scrub, saltmarsh, estuary. Nightingale, brent geese, dragonflies. (Access at all times, but some restrictions for non-members of ENT.)
Stour Wood and Copperas Bay (RSPB): W of Harwich. Sweet chestnut coppice, intertidal flats. Waders, wildfowl, woodland birds and flowers. (Spring best for woodland, winter for estuary birds.)

Boat Excursions
Essex
Harwich: morning and afternoon cruises on the Rivers Stour and Orwell, and Harwich harbour. *Tel.* (0255) 502004.

Norfolk
Burnham Overy Staithe: trips to Scolt Head Bird Sanctuary and Overy Beach. *Tel.* (0328) 711053.

Great Yarmouth: Broads cruises daily. *Tel.* (0493) 844772 (evenings).
Horning: Broadland trips on Mississippi paddle boat. *Tel.* (0692) 630262.
Hunstanton: trips to Seal Island and coastal cruises. *Tel.* (04853) 2342.
Norwich: Broadland river cruises and city cruises. *Tel.* (0603) 501220.
Potter Heigham: from Haven Bridge to Great Yarmouth. *Tel.* (0692) 670711.
Stalham: Broads cruises. *Tel.* (0692) 670530.
Wroxham: Broadland tours. *Tel.* (06053) 2207.

Suffolk
Oulton Broad: Broads trips. *Tel.* (0502) 4903.
Snape: trips of River Alde. *Tel.* (072888) 303.
Waldringfield: From the Deben estuary to Woodbridge. *Tel.* (047336) 260.

Boat Hire
There is ample opportunity for a water based, do-it-yourself holiday in East Anglia, particularly on the Broads and Fenland Waterways. You can hire a rowing boat for an hour or a luxury cruiser for a fortnight. A list of boat hire addresses is available from the East Anglia Tourist Board (see useful addresses). Please observe the waterway code: obey speed limits, keep to marked channels, do not enter the reed-beds and moor only at the places provided.

Golf
Links golf courses abound, some with hotels. A list of clubs that welcome visitors can be obtained from the East Anglia Tourist Board, or see *The AA Guide to Golf in Great Britain*, an annual publication which gives descriptions, telephone numbers and local arrangements for courses in the region.

Walking
There is a lot of easy walking in East Anglia – on the coast, by rivers, in woods and in the countryside. Several country parks have signposted paths and produce their own leaflets describing the walks, as do the many local nature trails; there are also several long-distance footpaths. The East Anglia Tourist Board can supply addresses.
Picnic sites are to be found in the parks, on Forestry Commission land and in Areas of Outstanding Natural Beauty.

Watersports
Boardsailing
Boardsailing has become more popular of late in this region. The following schools, all recognised by the Royal Yachting Association, can teach the basics in a day and hire out equipment to the more experienced.

Cambridgeshire
Peterborough Sailboard Club: *Tel.* (0778) 346342.

Essex
Bradwell Field Studies & Sailing Centre: *Tel.* (0621) 76256.
Channels Windsurfing Centre (Chelmsford): *Tel.* (0245) 441000.
Point Clear Windsurfing (St Osyth): *Tel.* (0255) 820651.

Norfolk
Surf 55 (King's Lynn): *Tel.* (0553) 764356.

Suffolk
Suffolk Water Park (Ipswich): *Tel.* (0473) 830191.
Windsurfing Seasports (Felixstowe): *Tel.* (0394) 284504.

Sailing
An extensive list of launching sites for small craft is available from the East Anglia Tourist Board. Always make sure of permission from the landowner, or obtain a licence where necessary (see Anglian Water – useful addresses). There are numerous marinas and harbours for larger craft along the coast. Of particular interest to both large and small craft are the Broads, which provide navigable waters in pleasant scenery; for more information, contact the Broads Authority (see useful addresses).

PLACES TO VISIT

Many of these places have full descriptions within the gazetteer section of this book.
BH = Bank Holiday

Ancient Sites and Buildings
Cambridgeshire
Flag Fen Bronze Age Excavation, Peterborough: *Tel.* (0733) 313414. (Open end Mar-Oct, daily.)

Essex
Hedingham Castle, Castle Hedingham: *Tel.* (0787) 60261. (Open May-Oct, daily.)
Mountfitchet Castle, Stansted (3m NE Bishops Stortford): Reconstructed Norman motte and bailey castle and village, on the original site. (Open mid Mar-mid Nov, daily.)
Priors Hall Barn, Widdington (4m S Saffron Walden): One of the finest surviving medieval barns in SE England. *Tel.* (0223) 358911 *ext.* 2964 for opening times.

Norfolk
Caister Roman Town, nr Great Yarmouth: (Open all year, daily.)
Castle Rising: Fine 12th-century keep with notable history, set in centre of massive earthworks. *Tel.* (0223) 358911 *ext.* 2964 for opening times.
Cockley Cley Iceni Village and Museum (3m SW Swaffham): Reconstruction on original site of Iceni encampment. *Tel.* (0760) 21339. (Open Apr-Oct, daily.)
Grime's Graves, Weeting (1½m N Brandon): *Tel.* (0223) 358911 *ext.* 2964 for opening times.

Suffolk
Framlingham Castle: *Tel.* (0223) 358911 *ext.* 2964 for opening times.
Guildhall, Lavenham: *Tel.* (0787) 247646. (Open Apr-Oct, daily.)
Orford Castle: *Tel.* (0223) 358911 *ext.* 2964 for opening times.
Sutton Hoo, nr Woodbridge: Excavations continue. *Tel.* (039 43) 3397. (Open Apr-Oct, Sat, Sun & BH – guided tours only.)
West Stow Anglo-Saxon Village (in West Stow Country Park): Thoroughly researched site; 5 buildings reconstructed. *Tel.* (028484) 718. (Open Apr-Oct, Tue-Sun & BH, pm.)

Historic Houses and Gardens
Cambridgeshire
Anglesey Abbey, Lode (6m NE Cambridge): 13th-century abbey, later a Tudor house. Fairhaven collection of paintings and furniture. Outstanding 100-acre garden. (House open Apr-mid Oct, Wed-Sun & BH, pm; gardens open Apr-Jun, Wed-Fri; Jul-mid Oct, daily, pm.)
Cambridge University Botanic Garden: (Open all year, Mon-Sat; May-Sep, also Sun pm.)
Island Hall, Godmanchester: (Open mid Jun-mid Sep, Sun pm.)
Kimbolton Castle (7m NW St Neots): (Open Easter, Spring BH & mid Jul-Aug, Sun pm.)
Peckover House, Wisbech: (Open Apr-mid Oct, Sat, Sun & BH; May-Sep, Sat-Wed; pm.)
Wimpole Hall, nr New Wimpole: (Open Apr-Oct, Tue-Thu, Sat, Sun & BH, pm.)

Essex
Audley End House, Saffron Walden: *Tel.* (0799) 22399. (Open mid Apr-Oct, Tue-Sun, BH; house pm only, gardens 12 noon-6.30pm.)
Hyde Hall Gardens, Rettendon (3m NE Wickford): Garden with interest throughout the year. (Open Apr-Sep, Wed, Sun & BH.)
Layer Marney Tower (6m SW Colchester): (Open Apr-Sep, Thu & Sun; Jul & Aug, also Tue; pm.)
Paycocke's, Coggeshall: (Open Apr-early Oct, Tue, Thu, Sun & BH, pm.)
St Osyth's Priory, nr Clacton: (Open May-Sep, daily.)
Saling Hall Garden, nr Braintree: 12 acres, including 1698 walled garden and small park. (Open mid May-Jul, Sep-mid Oct, Wed, Thu & Fri, pm.)

Norfolk
Blickling Hall (1½m NW Aylsham): (Open Apr-Oct, Tue, Wed, Fri-Sun, BH, pm.)
Bressingham Gardens, nr Diss: (Open May-Sep, Sun & BH; Jun-Aug, also Thu; Aug, also Wed.)
Felbrigg Hall (3m SW Cromer): (Open Apr-Oct, Sat-Mon, Wed & Thu, pm.)
Holkham Hall (2m W Wells-Next-The-Sea): *Tel.* (0328) 710733. (House open Jun-Sep, Sun-Thu; BH, pm. Garden open all year, daily – Sun, pm only.)

Houghton Hall (14m E King's Lynn): Built for Robert Walpole in early 18th century. Original William Kent furnishings. *Tel.* (048522) 569. (Open Apr-Sep, Thu, Sun & BH, pm.)
Mannington Hall and Gardens, Saxthorpe: 15th-century small moated manor house. Lake, gardens, woodland. *Tel.* (026 387) 284. (House open by appt; gardens open Apr-Oct, Sun pm; Jun, Jul & Aug, also Wed, Thu & Fri.)
Norfolk Lavender, Caley Mill, Heacham: Distillery can be visited during harvest, mid Jul-mid Aug. (Shop and grounds open all year, daily, Oct-Easter, Mon-Fri only.)
Oxburgh Hall (7m SW Swaffham): (Open Apr-Oct, Sat & Sun, pm; May-Sep, also Mon-Wed, pm.)
Sandringham House, Grounds and Museum: (Open Apr-Sep, Mon-Thu, Sun. Closed when Royal Family in residence, usually mid Jul-early Aug.)
Sheringham Park, Upper Sheringham: (Open all year, daily.)

Suffolk
Akenfield, 1 Park Lane, Charsfield: Half-acre council house garden; vegetables, many varieties of flowers, including dried ones. (Open mid May-Sep, daily.)
Christchurch Mansion, Ipswich: (Open all year, daily; Sun, pm only, some BH.)
Helmingham Hall Gardens (between Ipswich and Debenham): Lovely moated Elizabethan gardens; possibly the best kitchen garden in England. Highland cattle and safari rides in deer park. *Tel.* (047339) 363. (Open May-Sep, Sun pm.)
Ickworth, Horringer: (Open Apr-Oct, weekends; May-Sep, also Tue, Wed, Fri; BH; pm.)
Kentwell Hall, Long Melford: *Tel.* (0787) 310207. (Open Apr-Sep.)
Melford Hall, Long Melford: (Open Apr-Sep, Wed, Thu, Sat, Sun & BH.)
The Priory, Water Street, Lavenham: *Tel.* (0787) 247417. (Open Apr-Oct, daily.)
Somerleyton Hall (5m NW Lowestoft): (Open Apr & May, Thu, Sun & BH; Jun-Sep, also Tue, Wed & Fri; pm.)
Wingfield College (7m SE Diss): *Tel.* (037 984) 505. (Open Apr-Sep, Sat, Sun & BH, pm.)

Abbeys, Churches and Priories
Cambridgeshire
Bridge Chapel, St Ives: (Open all year. Key from Town Hall or Norris Library.)

Essex
St Botolph's Priory, Colchester: (Open all year, daily.)
St Osyth's Priory, Clacton: (Open May-Sep, daily.)

Norfolk
Binham Priory (5m SE Wells): (Open all year, daily.)
Burnham Norton Friary: (Open all year, daily.)

Castle Acre Priory, nr Swaffham: *Tel.* (0223) 358911 *ext.* 2964 for opening times.
St Faith's Priory, Horsham St Faith: (Open Apr-Sep, Sun pm & BH.)
St John's Cathedral, Norwich: (Open all year, daily. Tower tours May-Sep, Sat pm.)
St Peter Mancroft Church, Norwich: (Open all year, Mon-Fri.)
Shrine of Our Lady of Walsingham: (Open all year, daily.)
Slipper Chapel, nr Houghton St Giles (1½m SW Little Walsingham): (Open all year, daily.)
Walsingham Abbey Grounds (5m N Fakenham): *Tel.* (032 872) 259. (Open Apr, Wed; May-Sep, Wed, Sat, Sun; Aug, also Mon and Fri; all BH; pm.)

Suffolk
Bury St Edmunds Abbey: (Open all year, daily.)
Leiston Abbey: (Open all year, daily.)

Mills
Cambridgeshire
Downfield Windmill, Soham: 1726 mill in working order. (Open Sun & BH.)
Great Chishill Mill: 19th-century open-trestle post mill. (Open Apr-Oct, daily. Key at PO.)
Great Gransden Post Mill: Dated 1674, restored 1984. (Open Apr-Oct, daily. Key at PO.)
Houghton Mill, Huntingdon: Mid 17th-century mill, in use until 1930. (Open Apr & first half Oct, Sat & Sun, pm; May-Sep, Sat-Wed, pm.)
Lode Water Mill: Corn grinding BH and 1st Sun in month. (Open Apr-Oct, Sat, Sun & BH, pm.)
Sacrewell Water Mill, Farming & Country Life Centre: Working mill. *Tel.* (0780) 782277. (Open Apr-Oct, Sun pm, and Mon-Fri.)

Essex
Bourne Mill, Colchester: 16th-century fishing lodge converted into mill, in working order. *Tel.* (0206) 72422. (Open Apr-early Oct, Sat, Sun & BH, pm; Jul-Aug, also Tue.)
John Webb's Windmill, Thaxted: (Open May-Sep, Sat, Sun, BH.)
Mountnessing Windmill: 19th-century post mill, fully working. *Tel.* (0277) 215777. (Open May-Sep, certain weekends.)
Rayleigh Windmill: Non-operating Tower mill with museum. *Tel.* (0268) 775768. (Open Apr-Sep, Sat am.)
Stansted Mountfitchet Windmill: 1787, best-preserved tower mill in Essex. *Tel.* (0279) 812096. (Open Apr-Oct, 1st Sun in month, BH; Aug, every Sun; pm.)

Norfolk
Berney Arms Mill: Splendid 70ft-high marsh mill in full working order. (Open Apr-Sep, daily–Sun, pm only.)
Billingford Windmill: Fully-restored cornmill. (Open all year.)

Bircham Mill: (Open Apr-mid May, Sun, Wed, BH; mid May-Sep, Sun-Fri.)
Boardman's Mill, How Hill: Open-framed timber trestle windpump with working turbine. (Open all year, daily.)
Cley Windmill: 166-year-old tower mill converted to guesthouse. (Open Easter w/e and Jun-Sep, daily.)
Denver Windmill: 6 storeys with original machinery. *Tel.* (0366) 3374. (Open Mon-Sat by appt.)
Foulden Watermill: (Open Mar-Oct, Tue-Sun, BH.)
Horsey Windpump: (Open Apr-Aug, daily.)
Letheringsett Watermill: Working mill, demonstrations. (Open all year, Tue, Thu, Sun (not winter) & BH, pm.)
St Olave's Windpump, nr Great Yarmouth: Working. (Open all year, daily.)
Snettisham Watermill: Restored 18th-century machinery. Demonstrations. *Tel.* (0485) 42180. (Open May, Sat, Sun, Thu, BH; early Jul-early Sep, am only, also Wed.)
Starston Windpump: *Tel.* (0379) 852393. (Open all year, daily.)
Stow Mill: Working order. *Tel.* (0263) 720298. (Open all year, daily.)
Stracey Arms Windpump: Restored drainage pump. Exhibition. (Open Apr-Oct, daily.)
Sutton Windmill: Tallest mill in the country. *Tel.* (0692) 81195. (Open Apr-mid May, Sun-Wed, am; mid May-Sep, all day.)
Thurne Dyke Windpump: Fully restored. Exhibition. (Open Apr-Oct, daily.)
Wicklewood Mill: Restored tower mill. *Tel.* (0953) 603694. (Open all year, daily.)

Suffolk
Bardwell Windmill: Working mill producing stone-ground flours. *Tel.* (0359) 51331. (Open all year, Tue-Fri, Sun pm.)
Buttrums Mill, Woodbridge: Restored 6-storey tower mill. *Tel.* (0473) 230000 *ext.* 6519. (Open all year by appt.)
Pakenham Watermill: 18th-century working mill. *Tel.* (0787) 247179. (Open May-Sep, Wed, Sat, Sun & BH, pm.)
Saxtead Green Windmill: (Open Apr-Sep, Mon-Sat.)
Thelnetham Windmill: *Tel.* (0473) 76996. (Open Apr-Oct, Sun & BH.)
Thorpeness Windmill: Working mill. Exhibitions. (Open Easter, May, Jun & Sep, Sat, Sun & BH: Jul & Aug, Tue-Sun; pm.)
Woodbridge Tide Mill: Working machinery. *Tel.* (03943) 2548. (Open May-Oct, most days.)

Museums and Art Galleries
(See also page 28.)
Cambridgeshire
Cambridge
The University Museums cover most subjects, including Classical Archaeology (Sidgwick Avenue), Zoology and Archaeology & Anthropology (Downing Street).

Fitzwilliam Museum,
Trumpington St: Outstanding art collection, furniture, antiquities including Egyptian collection and MSS. (Open all year, Tue-Sun & BH.)
Duxford
Imperial War Museum, Duxford Airfield: (Open all year, daily.)
Ely
Stained Glass Museum, Ely Cathedral: Extensive displays, 14th century to present day. *Tel.* (0223) 60148. (Open Mar (w/e only), Apr-Oct, daily; Sun pm only.)
Huntingdon
Cromwell Museum: Also other Civil War items. (Open all year, Tue-Sun; times vary.)
Peterborough
City Museum and Art Gallery: Local history, folk life, industry, costume, Victorian rooms. (Open all year, Tue-Sat.)

Essex
Billericay
Barleylands Farm Museum: Vintage farm machinery. (Open all year, Wed-Sun & BH.)
Colchester
Colchester and Essex Museum, Colchester Castle: (Open all year, Mon-Sat; Apr-Sep, also Sun pm.)
The Hollytrees, High St: 1718 house with costume and social history displays. (Open all year, Mon-Sat.)
Minories Art Gallery: Changing exhibitions including painting, sculpture, printmaking, craft workshops. (Open all year, Tue-Sat & Sun pm.)
Dedham
Sir Alfred Munnings Art Museum, Castle House: *Tel.* (0206) 322127. (Open May-Oct, Sun, Wed, BH; Aug, also Thu & Sat; pm.)
Takeley
Aklowa African Traditional Heritage Village (3m E Bishops Stortford): Reconstructed African village where drumming, dancing, etc. can be experienced. *Tel.* (0279) 871062. (Open Apr-Oct by appt.)

Norfolk
East Dereham
Bishop Bonner's Cottage: Domestic and agricultural exhibits in early 16th-century cottage. (Open May-Sep, Tue-Sat pm.)
Glandford
Shell Museum (3m NW Holt): *Tel.* (0263) 740081. (Open Dec-Feb, Mon-Thu am; Mar-Nov, Mon-Thu all day, Fri & Sat pm.)
Great Yarmouth
Old Merchant's House, South Quay: (Open Apr-Sep, Mon-Fri for guided tours only. Apply custodian's office at Row 111.)
Elizabethan House Museum, South Quay: Displays of Victorian domestic life. (Open Jun-Sep, Sun-Fri; Oct-May, Mon-Fri.)
The Tolhouse Museum, Tolhouse St: Local history, dungeons, brass rubbing centre. (Open Oct-May, Mon-Fri; Jun-Sep, Sun-Fri.)

Great Yarmouth Museum's Exhibition Galleries, Central Library: Paintings and other arts and craft. (Open all year, Mon-Sat.)
Maritime Museum for East Anglia: (Open Oct-May, Mon-Fri; Jun-Sep, also Sun.)
Gressenhall
Norfolk Rural Life Museum (2m NW East Dereham): *Tel.* (0362) 860563. (Open Apr-Oct, Tue-Sun & BH.)
King's Lynn
Fermoy Centre and Art Gallery: Regular exhibits in the gallery of a thriving arts centre. Craft and Art Fair, Sep. (Open all year, Mon-Sat.)
Norwich
Castle Museum: Archaeology, natural history, geology, fine and applied art collections, including Norwich School. (Open all year, Mon-Sat & Sun pm.)
Strangers' Hall Museum of Domestic Life: Displays covering 16th to 19th centuries in late medieval town house. (Open all year, Mon-Sat.)
Royal Norfolk Regiment Museum, Brittania Barracks: (Open all year, Mon-Fri.)
Bridewell Museum, Bridewell Alley: Norwich trades and industries from the 17th century. (Open all year, Mon-Sat.)
St Peter Hungate Church Museum and Brass Rubbing Centre, Princes St: (Open all year, Mon-Sat.)
Sainsbury Centre for Visual Arts, University of East Anglia: Collections of modern and ethnographic art. *Tel.* (0603) 56060. (Open all year, Tue-Sun, pm.)
Walsingham
Shirehall Museum: Almost perfect Georgian courtroom. Local history and pilgrimage displays. (Open Apr-Sep, daily; Oct, weekends.)
Wolferton
Station Museum (6m NE King's Lynn): (Open Apr-Sep, Sun-Fri–Sun pm only.)

Suffolk
Bury St Edmunds
The Gershom Parkington Collection of Clocks and Watches, Angel Corner: *Tel.* (0284) 60255. (Open all year, daily.)
Bury St Edmunds Art Gallery, Market Cross: Robert Adam's only public building in the east of England. (Open all year, Tue-Sat; Sun by appt.)
Moyses Hall Museum: Local history, archaeological and natural history displays. (Open all year, daily.)
Suffolk Regiment Museum, Gibraltar Barracks: *Tel.* (0284) 2394. (Open all year, Mon-Fri, ex BH.)
Ipswich
Ipswich Museum: Local archaeology including replicas of the Sutton Hoo and Mildenhall treasures. (Open all year, Mon-Sat, ex BH.)

Lowestoft
Lowestoft and East Suffolk Maritime Museum, Whapload Rd: Ship models, paintings, tools. (Open May-Sep, daily.)
Lowestoft Fishing Industry and Harbour Tour: A tour of the working harbour and fishing industry. *Tel.* (0502) 565989 *ext.* 125. Board a trawler Mon-Fri am by appt.
Newmarket
National Horse Racing Museum, High St: The great story of the development of horse racing. Tours of the National Stud can be arranged. *Tel.* (0638) 667333. (Open Apr-Nov, Tue, Sat, Sun, BH; Aug, daily.)
Stowmarket
Museum of East Anglian Life: Attractive 30-acre riverside site with re-erected buildings including watermill, windpump and smithy. Demonstrations and special events at weekends. *Tel.* (0449) 612229. (Open Apr-Oct, daily.)
Sudbury
Gainsborough's House: Paintings by Gainsborough; also changing exhibitions. (Open all year, Tue-Sat all day, Sun & BH pm.)

Animal Collections
Cambridgeshire
Home Farm, Wimpole Hall: (Open Apr-Oct, daily, ex Mon & Fri.)
Linton Zoo: (Open all year, ex Xmas.)
Wildfowl Trust, Peakirk, Peterborough: (Open all year, daily, ex Xmas.)
Willers Mill Wild Animal Sanctuary & Fish Farm, Shepreth: (Open Mar-Oct, daily; Nov-Feb, Sat & Sun.)

Essex
Basildon Zoo: (Open all year, daily.)
Colchester Zoo: (Open all year, daily.)
Hayes Hill Farm, Waltham Abbey: Working farm. (Open all year, daily.)
Hobbs' Cross Dairy Farm, Theydon Garnon: Working farm. (Open all year, daily.)
Marsh Farm Country Park, South Woodham Ferrers: *Tel.* (0245) 321552. (Open all year, daily.)
Mole Hall Wildlife Park, Widdington: *Tel.* (0799) 40400. (Open all year, daily.)

Norfolk
Badley Moor Fish, Bird & Butterfly Centre: (Open all year, daily.)
Banham Zoo & Monkey Sanctuary: *Tel.* (095387) 476. (Open all year, daily.)
Kelling Park Aviaries, Holt: *Tel.* (0263) 712235. (Open all year, daily.)
Kilverstone Wildlife Park, Thetford: *Tel.* (0842) 5369. (Open all year, daily.)
Norfolk Shire Horse Centre, West Runton: (Open Apr-Oct, daily ex Sat.)

Norfolk Wildlife Park & Play Centre, nr Norwich: (Open all year, daily.)
Otter Trust, Earsham: (Open Apr-Oct, daily.)
Park Farm, Snettisham: Guided tours by tractor or landrover; farm trails. (Open Apr-Sep, Sun-Fri.)
Pettits of Reedham Feathercraft & Falabella Miniature Horse Stud, Reedham: (Open Apr-Oct, Mon-Fri, Sun pm.)
Redwings Horse Sanctuary: (Open Apr-Dec, Sun pm.)
Thrigby Hall Wildlife Gardens: Tel. (049377) 477. (Open all year, daily.)
Tropical Butterfly Farm, Great Yarmouth: All-weather gardens. (Open Mar-Oct, daily.)

Suffolk
Easton Farm Park, Wickham Market: Tel. (0728) 746475. (Open Easter-Oct, daily.)
Kentwell Hall, Long Melford: (Open Apr-Sep – see also Historic Houses.)
National Stud, Newmarket: Tours at certain times. (Open Apr-Sep, Mon-Sat.)
Norton Tropical Bird Gardens: (Open all year, daily.)
Suffolk Wildlife and Rare Breeds Park, Kessingland: Tel. (0502) 740291. (Open Apr-Oct, daily.)

Steam Railways
Cambridgeshire
Audley End Miniature Railway, nr Saffron Walden: (Open Apr-Sep, Sat, Sun, BH, pm; school summer holidays, Tue-Sun.)
Nene Valley Railway, Stibbington: Tel. (0780) 782854. (Open Apr-mid Oct, weekends.)

Essex
Colne Valley Railway, Castle Hedingham Station: Tel. (0787) 61174 for steam days. (Open Mar-Xmas, Tue-Sun.)
East Anglia Railway Museum, Chappel Station (6m W Colchester): Tel. (07875) 2571. (Open all year, daily; steam days, 1st Sun in month.)

Norfolk
Barton House Railway, Wroxham: (Open Apr-Oct, 3rd Sun in month, Easter Mon.)
Bressingham Live Steam Museum (2¼m W Diss): Tel. (037988) 386. (Open Apr, Sun; May-Sep, Sun & BH; Jun-Aug, also Thu; Aug, also Wed.)
North Norfolk Railway, Sheringham Station: Tel. (0263) 822045 for steam days.
The Thursford Collection (6m NE Fakenham): Tel. (032877) 477. (Open Apr-Oct, daily, pm.)
Wells and Walsingham Light Railway: (Open Apr-Sep, daily.)

Suffolk
Pleasurewood Hills American Theme Park Miniature Railway, Lowestoft: (Open mid May-mid Sep, daily.)

Suffolk Miniature Light Railway, Suffolk Wildlife Park, nr Lowestoft: Tel. (0502) 740291. (Open mid Apr-Oct, daily.)

Seaside Attractions
Essex
Clacton Pier: 23 rides, swimming pool and water chutes, side-shows, sea-lions, aquarium. Tel. (0255) 421115. (Open all year. Attractions open Jun-Sep & school holidays, daily; Oct-May, weekends & BH.)
Never-Never Land, Southend-on-Sea: 2 acres of magical scenery. A unique children's adventure park where fantasy becomes a living, animated reality.
Peter Pan's Playground, Southend-on-Sea: Over 20 rides and attractions. Tel. (0702) 68023. (Open most of the year.)

Norfolk
Great Yarmouth Pleasure Beach: Over 70 rides, side-shows and attractions. Tel. (0493) 844585. (Open Apr & May, weekends & BH; Jun-Sep, daily.)

Suffolk
Charles Mannings Amusement Park, Felixstowe. Many rides and attractions. Tel. (0394) 282370. (Open Easter-Sep, weekends & school holidays.)
Pleasurewood Hills American Theme Park, Lowestoft: East Anglia's first theme park. Rides, trains, shows and many other attractions. Tel. (0502) 513626/7. (Open May, weekends & BH; Jun-mid Sep, daily.)

USEFUL ADDRESSES

Anglian Water: Ambury Rd, Huntingdon, Cambs PE18 6NZ. Tel. (0480) 56181.
Broads Authority: Thomas Harvey House, 18 Colegate, Norwich NR30 2RE. Tel. (0603) 610734.
Cambridgeshire Wildlife Trust: 5 Fulbourn Manor, Fulbourn, Cambridge CB1 5BN. Tel. (0223) 880788.
Churches:
Cambridgeshire
Cambridge Historic Churches Trust, Little Gidding, Huntingdon, Cambs.
Essex
Secretary, Friends of Essex Churches, Sparrow Hall, Twinstead Green, Sudbury, Suffolk CO10 7NB.
Norfolk
The Norfolk Churches Trust, The Old Rectory, Holt, Norfolk.
Suffolk
Hon. Secretary, Suffolk Historic Churches Trust, The Old Rectory, Chattisham, Ipswich IP8 3PY.
Countryside Officer: Department of Property, Cambridgeshire County Council, Cambridge. Tel. (0223) 317446.
East Anglia Tourist Board: Toppesfield Hall, Hadleigh, Suffolk IP7 5DN. Tel. (0473) 822922.

(EH) English Heritage: Govt Bldgs, Cambridge. Tel. (0223) 358911.
Essex County Council (Tourism Section): Planning Dept, Globe House, Chelmsford CM1 1LF. Tel. (0245) 352232 ext. 323.
Essex Naturalists' Trust: Fingringhoe Nature Reserve, Nr Colchester. Tel. (020628) 678.
Forestry Commission: Santon Downham, Brandon, Suffolk. Tel. (0842) 810271.
Great Yarmouth Port and Haven Commission: 21 South Quay, Great Yarmouth NR30 2RE. Tel. (0493) 855151.
Inland Waterways Association: 114 Regents Park, London NW1 8UQ. Tel. 01-586 2556.
National Anglers' Council: 5 Cowgate, Peterborough PE1 1LR. Tel. (0733) 54084.
National Trust: Blickling Hall, Blickling, Norfolk. Tel. (0263) 733084.
Nature Conservancy Council: 60 Bracondale, Norwich NR1 2BE. Tel. (0603) 620558.
Norfolk and Suffolk Yachting Association: Spring Cottage, Mill Lane, Horning, Norfolk NR12 8LL. Tel. (0692) 630831.
Norfolk County Council: Dept of Planning and Property, County Hall, Martineau Lane, Norwich. Tel. (0603) 611122 ext. 5247.
Norfolk Museums Service: Castle Museum, Norwich. Tel. (0603) 611277 ext. 24.
Norfolk Naturalists' Trust: 72 Cathedral Close, Norwich NR1 4DF. Tel. (0603) 625540.
Norfolk Windmills Trust: c/o County Hall, Norwich. Tel. (0603) 611122 ext. 5124.
Royal Society for the Protection of Birds: Aldwych House, Bethel St, Norwich NR2 1NR. Tel. (0603) 615920.
Suffolk County Council: Planning Dept, County Hall, Ipswich. Tel. (0473) 230000 ext. 6516.
Suffolk Wildlife Trust: Park Cottage, Saxmundham IP17 1PQ. Tel. (0728) 3765.
Youth Hostels Association: Ely, Cambs. Tel. (0353) 67351.

TOURIST INFORMATION CENTRES

Tourist Information Centres can provide further information about local accommodation, the opening times and admission charges of tourist attractions, ideas for places to visit and things to do, and up-to-date information on events. In addition to those in the cities listed below, there are centres in many towns and resorts in the region.
Cambridge: Wheeler St. Tel. (0223) 322640.
Colchester: 1 Queen St. Tel. (0206) 712233.
Ipswich: Town Hall, Princes St. Tel. (0473) 58070.
Norwich: The Guildhall, Gaol Hill. Tel. (0603) 666071.

CALENDAR OF EVENTS

This list is just a selection of the many annual events taking place in East Anglia. Actual dates may vary from year to year, so contact the East Anglia Tourist Board or any Tourist Information Centre for full details and information on local events.

March
National Shire Horse Show,
   Peterborough

April
Thriplow Daffodil Weekend, Cambs

May
Hadleigh Show, Suffolk
Air Fête, RAF Mildenhall, Suffolk
Stilton Cheese Rolling, Stilton, Cambs

June
Suffolk Show, Ipswich
Essex County Show, Chelmsford
Colchester Summer Show
Royal Norfolk Show, Norwich
Dunmow Flitch Trials, Essex
*Aldeburgh Festival of Music and the
   Arts*, Snape Maltings, Suffolk

July
Tendring Hundred Show, Essex
*North Norfolk and Norwich Horse
   Show*, Norwich
East of England Show, Peterborough
Mannington Rose Festival,
   nr Norwich
Sandringham Flower Show, Norfolk
Cambridge Folk Festival

August
Oyster Festival, Essex

September
East Anglia Antiques Fair, Bury St
   Edmunds, Suffolk

*The Red Arrows are always a popular
event at air fêtes*

EAST ANGLIA
Atlas

The following pages contain a legend, key map and atlas of East Anglia, three motor tours and sixteen coast and countryside walks.

Above: getting out and about at Newmarket

Legend

GRID REFERENCE SYSTEM

The map references used in this book are based on the Ordnance Survey National Grid, correct to within 1000 Metres They comprise two letters and four figures, and are preceded by the atlas page number.

Thus the reference for NORWICH appears 89 TG 2309

89 is the atlas page number

TG identifies the major (100km) grid square concerned (see diag)

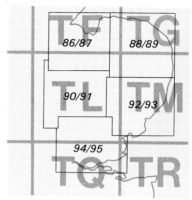

2309 locates the lower left-hand corner of the kilometre grid square in which **NORWICH** appears .

Take the first figure of the reference 2, this refers to the numbered grid running along the bottom of the page.
Having found this line, the second figure 3 tells you the distance to move in tenths to the right of this line. A vertical line through this point is the first half of the reference.

The third figure 0, refers to the numbered grid lines on the right hand side of the page, finally the fourth figure 9 indicates the distance to move in tenths above this line. A horizontal line drawn through this point to intersect with the first line gives the precise location of the places in question.

TOURIST INFORMATION

Ӽ	Camp Site		Nature reserve
⚏	Caravan Site	☆	Other tourist feature
ⓘ	Information Centre		Preserved railway
Ⓟ	Parking Facilities		Racecourse
	Viewpoint		Wildlife park
✕	Picnic site		Museum
	Golf course or links		Nature or forest trail
	Castle	m	Ancient monument
	Cave	✆ ✆	Telephones : public or motoring organisations
	Country park		
❀	Garden	PC	Public Convenience
⌂	Historic house	▲	Youth Hostel

ORIENTATION

Diagrammatic   Only

True North

At the centre of the area is 2°14'W of Grid North

Magnetic North

At the centre of the area is about 6½°W of Grid North in 1989 decreasing by about ½° in three years

KEY-MAP   1:625,000   or 10 MILES to 1"

ROAD INFORMATION

Motorway with service area, service area (limited access) and junction with junction number

Motorway junction with limited interchange

Motorway, service area and junction under construction with proposed opening date
Mid 1989

Primary routes ⎱ Single and dual carriageway with service area
Main Road ⎰

Main Road under construction

Narrow Road with passing places

Other roads ⎰ B roads (majority numbered)
B 1134 ⎱ Unclassified (selected)

Gradient:14% (1 in 7) and steeper, and toll

Primary routes and main roads ⎱
24   15

Motorways ⎰
24   15

Primary Routes

These form a national network of recommended through routes which complement the motorway system. Selected places of major traffic importance are known as Primary Route Destinations and are shown on these maps thus NORWICH . This relates to the directions on road signs which on Primary Routes have a green background. To travel on a Primary Route, follow the direction to the next Primary Destination shown on the green backed road signs. On these maps Primary Route road numbers and mileages are shown in green.

Motorways

A similar situation occurs with motorway routes where numbers and mileages, shown in blue on these maps correspond to the blue background of motorway road signs.

Mileages are shown on the map between large markers and between small markers in large and small type

1 mile = 1·61 kilometres

GENERAL FEATURES

Passenger railways (selected in conurbations)

AA..A   RAC..R   PO..T   Telephone call box

+-+-+-+-+-+-+-+-+-+-+   National Boundary

------------------   County or Region Boundary

Large Town   Town / Village

⊕   Airport

427.   Height (metres)

WATER FEATURES

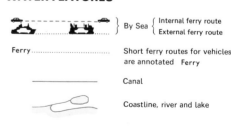

By Sea ⎰ Internal ferry route
         ⎱ External ferry route

Ferry..................................   Short ferry routes for vehicles are annotated   Ferry

——————   Canal

Coastline, river and lake

ATLAS 1:250,000 or 4 MILES to 1"
TOURS 1:250,000 or 4 MILES to 1"

ROADS   Not necessarily rights of way

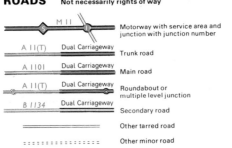

M 11 — Motorway with service area and junction with junction number

A 11(T) Dual Carriageway — Trunk road

A 1101 Dual Carriageway — Main road

A 11(T) Dual Carriageway — Roundabout or multiple level junction

B 1134 Dual Carriageway — Secondary road

Other tarred road

Other minor road

Gradient: 14% (1 in 7) and steeper

RAILWAYS

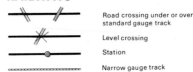

Road crossing under or over standard gauge track

Level crossing

Station

Narrow gauge track

WATER FEATURES

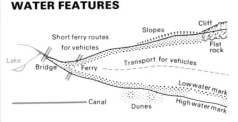

Cliff

Slopes

Flat rock

Short ferry routes for vehicles

Lake

Bridge   Ferry   Transport for vehicles

Low water mark

Canal   Dunes   High water mark

ANTIQUITIES

☼ Native fortress

----- Roman road (course of)

Castle • Other antiquities

CANOVIVM • Roman antiquity

GENERAL FEATURES

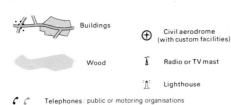

Buildings

Wood

⊕ Civil aerodrome (with custom facilities)

Ⅰ Radio or TV mast

Lighthouse

C C   Telephones : public or motoring organisations

RELIEF

Feet	Metres	
		.274
		Heights in feet above mean sea level
3000	914	
2000	610	
1400	427	
		Contours at 200 ft intervals
1000	305	
600	183	
200	61	
		To convert feet to metres multiply by 0.3048
0	0	

WALKS 1:25,000 or 2½" to 1 MILE
ROADS AND PATHS   Not necessarily rights of way

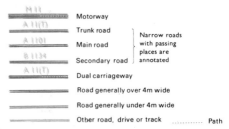

M 11 — Motorway

A 11(T) — Trunk road

A 1101 — Main road

B 1134 — Secondary road

} Narrow roads with passing places are annotated

A 11(T) — Dual carriageway

Road generally over 4m wide

Road generally under 4m wide

Other road, drive or track   .... Path

RAILWAYS

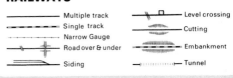

Multiple track

Single track

Narrow Gauge

Road over & under

Siding

Level crossing

Cutting

Embankment

Tunnel

GENERAL FEATURES

♦ Church
or
♦ Chapel
+

{ with tower
{ with spire
{ without tower or spire

Electricity transmission line
pylon   pole

Gravel pit

Sand pit

Chalk pit, clay pit or quarry

Refuse or slag heap

NT   National Trust always open

NT   National Trust opening restricted

FC   Forestry Commission pedestrians only (observe local signs)

National Park

HEIGHTS AND ROCK FEATURES

Contours are at various metre vertical intervals

50 }   Determined   { ground survey
285 ·   by   { air survey

Surface heights are to the nearest metre above mean sea level. Heights shown close to a triangulation pillar refer to the station height at ground level and not necessarily to the summit.

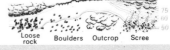

Vertical Face

Loose rock   Boulders   Outcrop   Scree

PUBLIC RIGHTS OF WAY

Public rights of way shown in this guide may not be evident on the ground

-------- }
-------- }   Public Paths   { Footpath
   { Bridleway

+ + + + +   By-way open to all traffic

Road used as a public path

Public rights of way indicated by these symbols have been derived from Definitive Maps as amended by later enactments or instruments held by Ordnance Survey between 1st Aug 1976 and 1st Mar 1987 and are shown subject to the limitations imposed by the scale of mapping

Later information may be obtained from the appropriate County Council.

The representation on these maps of any other road, track or path is no evidence of the existence of a right of way.

WALKS AND TOURS (All Scales)

7   Start point of walk

→   Route of walk

Line of walk

Alternative route

3   Start point of tour

→   Route of tour

Featured tour

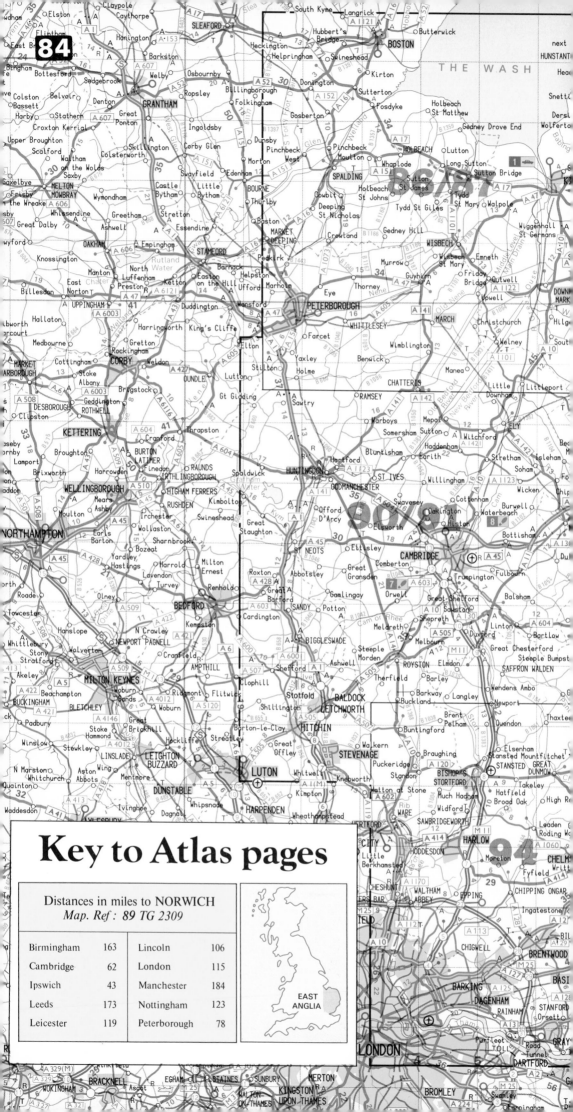

Key to Atlas pages

Distances in miles to NORWICH
Map. Ref : 89 TG 2309

Birmingham	163	Lincoln	106
Cambridge	62	London	115
Ipswich	43	Manchester	184
Leeds	173	Nottingham	123
Leicester	119	Peterborough	78

EAST ANGLIA

HARLESTON

Withersdale
Street
Weybread
Mendham
B 1123
Brockdish
Syleham
Wingfield
Athelington

Pixey Green
Stradbroke
Wilby
Worlingworth
B 1117
Bedfield
Monk
Soham
B 1119
Earl Soham
Brandeston
Cretingham
Kettleburgh
Hoo
Monewden
Charsfield
Dallinghoo
Debach
Clopton
Bredfield
Burgh
Hasketon

B 1123
Fressingfield
Metfield
B 1116
Silverley's
Green
Ashfield Green
Huntingfield
Laxfield
Tannington
Saxtead
Saxtead
Green
Brabling
Green
FRAMLINGHAM
Easton
Letheringham

St James
South Elmham
Rumburgh
All Saints
South Elmham
St Lawrence
Cox
Common
Brampton Sta

Spexhall
Wissett
HALESWORTH
Cookley
Walpole
Bramfield
Heveningham
Ubbeston
Green
Abbey
Peasenhall
Sibton
Yoxford
Badingham
Bruisyard
Cransford
Rendham
Swefling
Great
Glemham
Knodishall
Coldfair
Green
Friston
Snape
Gromford
Farnham
Stratford
St Andrew
Parham
Hacheston
Marlesford
Campsey Ash
Tunstall
Rendlesham

Brampton Sea
Stoven
Frostenden
South Cove
Covehithe
Wrentham

Westhall
Holton
Blyford
Wangford
Reydon
SOUTHWOLD
Blythburgh
Walberswick

Darsham
Westleton
Middleton
Theberton
Eastbridge
Leiston
Abbey
Sizewell
LEISTON
Aldringham
Thorpeness

ALDEBURGH
Aldeburgh Bay

River Alde

NORTH SEA

TOUR *1* 74 MILES
North-west Norfolk

This tour of the resorts of north-west Norfolk also takes in Castle Acre, Sandringham and Castle Rising.

From King's Lynn *(see page 58), follow the A47, signed Swaffham, to reach Narborough, where there is an old church containing monuments. At the end of the village, turn left on to an unclassified road, signed Narford and West Acre, and in 1 mile pass, on the left, the early 18th-century and partly Georgian Narford Hall (not open).*

Go on, and 1 mile further, turn left at a crossroads signed West Acre. Cross the River Nar, then skirt the hamlet of West Acre before turning right at a T-junction, signed Castle Acre. In 2½ miles turn right, to enter Castle Acre (see page 40). The motte and the imposing bailey gate of the 11th-century castle can be seen, and included in the remains of the 11th-century priory is a 12th-century church noted for its arcaded west front.

Follow signs to Swaffham, to leave through an archway. In ¼ mile cross the River Nar, then branch left along a narrow by-road signed Sporle. In a further ¼ mile, at some crossroads, turn left onto the A1065, signed Cromer. Pass through the village of Weasenham to East Raynham, where the 17th-century Raynham Hall (not open) lies in a splendid park. In 2½ miles branch right on to an un-classified road, signed town centre, and in ½ mile join the B1146 to reach Fakenham, a pleasant market town situated on the River Wensum. From the town centre follow the through traffic signs, and in ¼ mile turn left on to the A148, signed King's Lynn. In ½ mile turn right on to the B1105, signed Walsingham. In 2 miles pass through East Barsham. On the left, there is a fine Tudor brick and terracotta Hall with very fine chimneys and an imposing gateway (not open).

One mile further on pass through Houghton St Giles. Off to the left is a Slipper Chapel, which has been restored and now serves as a Roman Catholic shrine. *In 1½ miles, you reach Little Walsingham (see page 71). Follow signs to Wells on the B1105 and later skirt Wighton, to reach the junction with the A149. Turn left here and immediately right, signed Beach, into Wells-next-the-Sea (see page 72). The drive continues left alongside the attractive Quay, signed Hunstanton.*

In ¾ mile join the A149 to Holkham. Holkham Hall, once the home of the agriculturalist Coke of Norfolk, is the most splendid Palladian mansion in the county. Dating from 1734, it is situated in a magnificent park and is open at certain times in the summer.

Keep on the A149 passing, on the left, the road to Burnham Thorpe, birthplace of Lord Nelson. Continue to Burnham Overy Staithe (see page 37), and in ½ mile pass, on the left, a restored tower windmill. In another ¼ mile, you pass an attractive old mill while crossing the River Burn. Keep forward through the villages of Burnham Deepdale and Brancaster Staithe. Scott Head, a bird sanctuary nearby, can be reached by boat. *Pass through Brancaster, Titchwell and Thornham to Old Hunstanton, where there is a 14th-century church. In ½ mile turn right, signed seafront, on to the B1161 (no sign) to enter Hunstanton,* a seaside resort developed in the 19th century, with famous red and white chalk cliffs and excellent conditions for bathing.

From the seafront, keep forward, then bear right into Westgate. In ½ mile, at a roundabout, take the first exit signed King's Lynn, then at the main road turn right on to the A149 to skirt Heacham (see page 54). Here to the left of the A149 is Caley Mill, the largest grower and distiller of lavender in Britain. The harvest is during July to mid-August.

Continue through Snettisham, where the 14th-century church has a west front resembling Peterborough Cathedral, then pass Ingoldisthorpe to Dersingham. Turn left here on to the B1440, signed Sandringham, climbing through attractive woodland scenery. In 1½ miles you reach the gates of Sandringham House (see page 66). The grounds of the royal residence are open regularly in the summer, and Sandringham Church contains royal memorials. *Turn right here on to an unclassified road (no sign) and in ¾ mile bear right again and continue through well-wooded country.*

In ¾ mile, a detour can be made by crossing the main road and, ½ mile further on, branching right to reach Wolferton Station. Here the station's former Retiring Rooms can be seen, built in 1898, specifically for kings and queens and their guests *en route* to Sandringham.

The main tour turns left on to the A149, signed King's Lynn. In 2½ miles, on an ascent, turn right on to an unclassified road to reach Castle Rising. The castle has a fine restored Norman keep with impressive earthworks. The 17th-century Trinity Hospital almshouses are of note, and there is a restored Norman church. *Continue through the village (one way), then turn left and cross the wooded Ling Common to reach South Wootton. Go forward at the traffic signals on to the A148 for the return to King's Lynn.*

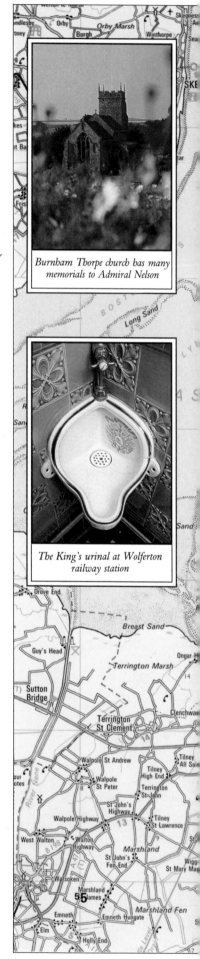

Burnham Thorpe church has many memorials to Admiral Nelson

The King's urinal at Wolferton railway station

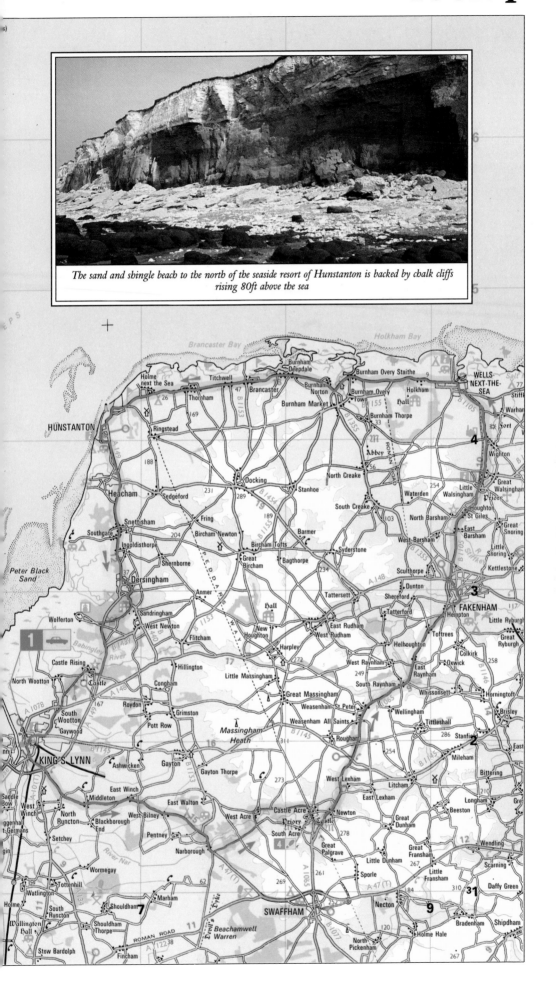

The sand and shingle beach to the north of the seaside resort of Hunstanton is backed by chalk cliffs rising 80ft above the sea

TOUR 2 79 MILES
Norwich and north-east Norfolk

This tour begins and ends in Norwich, ancient capital of East Anglia and the county town of Norfolk. Time should be allowed for discovering some of the many fine old buildings in the city, including the 12th-century keep of the Norman castle – which now houses a museum – the 15th-century Guildhall and St Peter Hungate, a 14th-century church containing a museum of church art and antiquities.

Leave Norwich *(see page 63) by the Yarmouth road, the A47, and pass through Thorpe St Andrew to reach Acle (bypass under construction). Here the road enters flat marshland, and after 2¾ miles it passes Stracey Arms wind pump on the left.* This stretch of the road is below sea level in places, and the numerous windmills in the area bear witness to the need for draining the marshes.

Continue along the A47 to the town of Great Yarmouth (see page 50). Formerly a busy herring-fishing port, it is now a popular seaside resort with two piers and many amenities. The restored 14th-century Tollhouse, the Fishermen's Hospital of 1702, the 114ft-high Nelson's Tower and the Maritime Museum of East Anglia are among the buildings of interest here.

Leave Great Yarmouth by the A149, signed Caister, and in 2 miles take the second exit at a roundabout, into an unclassified road, to enter Caister-on-Sea (see page 39). From the town centre turn left, signed Acle and Norwich, and pass on the right the excavated ruins of Caister Roman Town. At the next roundabout take the second exit on to the A1064, then in ¾ mile you will pass, on the left, the road to Caister Castle. The 15th-century moated ruins contain an interesting collection of vintage cars.

Take the next turning right on to an unclassified road, signed Ormesby. A mile further on, at a T-junction, turn left on to the A149 to enter Ormesby St Margaret. At a memorial turn right, signed Scratby, on to an unclassified road alongside the green, then turn left. At the following T-junction turn right, signed Hemsby. Continue to Hemsby and at the end of the village turn left on to the B1159, signed Mundesley. A winding road then leads through Winterton-on-Sea – a wind-swept little place of much character – to West Somerton. Continue with signs for Cromer and pass, on the left, Horsey Windpump, from the top of which there are fine views across Horsey Mere (NT), situated off to the left. Horsey stands where the Broads come to within a couple of miles of the sea, and it is here that the sea has broken into the Broads and flooded thousands of acres at very high tides.

After skirting Horsey, you see high coastal dunes on the right before reaching Sea Palling, the scene of severe flooding in 1953. In 1¾ miles, turn right, and continue through Lessingham to reach Happisburgh (pronounced 'Haisboro'). This small resort is dominated by a tall red-and-white lighthouse. The 15th-century church has a fine rood-screen and a magnificent carved font.

In 1½ miles, at some crossroads, turn right for Walcott, from where there are fine marine views. At Bacton pass, on the left, the remains of a priory which was, in the Middle Ages, one of the holy places of Europe. In ¼ mile turn right, and in a further 1¼ miles pass through the installations of the North Sea Gas Terminal. Later, pass Stow Windmill before entering the small resort of Mundesley.

Follow signs for Cromer, crossing higher ground with occasional views before passing through Trimingham and skirting Overstrand to reach Cromer (see page 43). Cromer is a popular resort with a pier and good bathing from a sandy beach. There are high cliffs nearby. The 15th-century church tower of St Peter and St Paul, once used as a lighthouse, rises majestically over the town. At 160ft, it is one of the highest in Norfolk, and there are breathtaking views from the top. *Leave the town on the Norwich road, the A149, and in 2¼ miles bear left, signed North Walsham. Continue through Thorpe Market to the outskirts of North Walsham.*

At the traffic signals, a diversion can be made by going forward on to an unclassified road, into the attractive town centre. North Walsham was pretty much wiped out in a great fire of 1600, and the little town is now suggestive of Georgian prosperity. The parish church is the second largest in Norfolk and was built in the 13th century. The market cross dates from the 16th century, but has been restored.

The main drive turns right at the traffic signals, and in ½ mile, at the next traffic signals, turn right again, signed Norwich, along the B1150. Continue through some wooded countryside to Coltishall on the River Bure. Here the large church has a fine thatched roof. *Cross the river to its twin village of Horstead. The drive continues through pleasant country on the return to Norwich.*

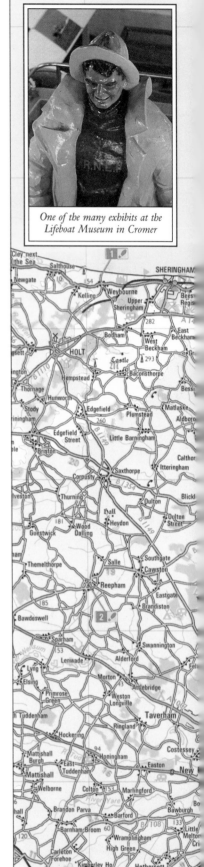

One of the many exhibits at the Lifeboat Museum in Cromer

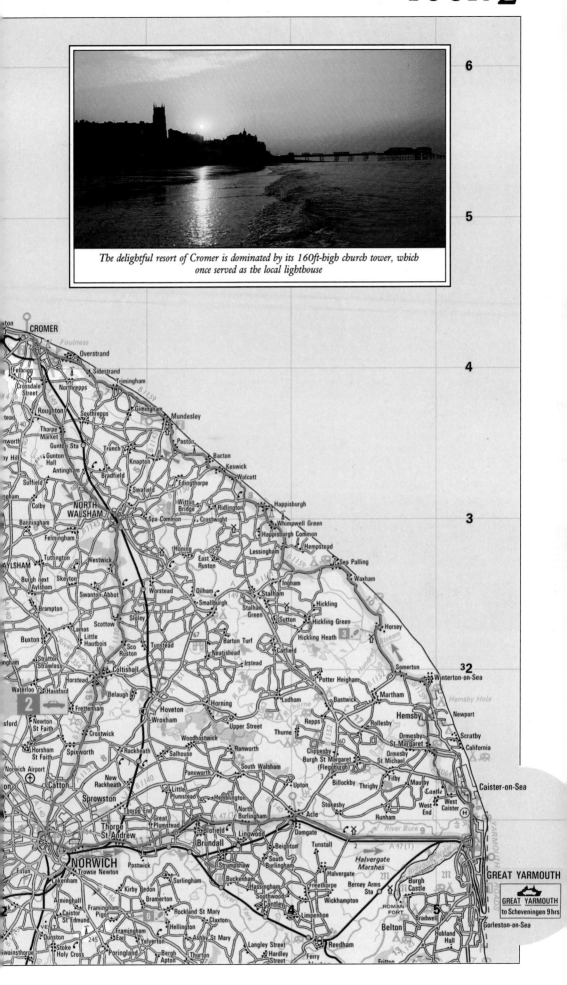

The delightful resort of Cromer is dominated by its 160ft-high church tower, which once served as the local lighthouse

TOUR 3 64 MILES
Old Suffolk Weaving Villages and Constable Country

John Constable wrote of the valley of the River Stour: 'I love every stile and stump and lane . . . as long as I am able to hold a brush, I shall never cease to paint them.' Places such as Flatford Mill and Willy Lott's Cottage, Lavenham and Long Melford have only changed superficially since Constable's time, and there are still places along this drive where you can leave the car and appreciate the beauty of the Suffolk countryside, which Constable captured in his paintings.

The drive starts at Ipswich. *Follow signs Colchester, A12, to leave by the London Road, A1214. In 2 miles, at the traffic signals, turn right on to the A1071, signed Hadleigh. Half a mile further, go forward at the roundabout. Later, pass through Hintlesham, then in 3¾ miles turn left on to the B1070 and enter the attractive market town of Hadleigh, which retains a variety of Suffolk architecture (see page 52).*

At the T-junction turn right, signed Lavenham. Keep left across the river bridge, then bear right. Almost ½ mile further on, turn left, then immediately right, to join the A1141. In ¾ mile turn left on to the unclassified Kersey road, then in another ¾ mile turn right and enter Kersey (see page 57). This beautiful old former weaving village of colour-washed cottages is considered one of the prettiest in Suffolk.

Descend through the watersplash, then ascend. Almost 1 mile further on, turn left to rejoin the Lavenham road, A1141. In 3½ miles, at the crossroads, keep left to Monks Eleigh, then continue past the edge of Brent Eleigh to reach Lavenham (see page 58). Lavenham is one of the most famous historic wool towns in England and is rich in old timbered houses, such as the Guildhall (NT), dating from 1529. The parish church is one of the finest in East Anglia, and there are several interesting old inns, notably the Swan and the Angel.

Follow signs Sudbury, to leave by the B1071. In ½ mile, at the outskirts of the town, turn right on to the unclassified Long Melford road. After 2¾ miles turn right again, and continue to the interesting large village of Long Melford (see page 60). At the northern end there is a large green, beside which stands the fine 15th-century church. Old buildings here include the Tudor red brick Melford Hall, and the Elizabethan Kentwell Hall. The Bull Inn dates from the 15th century.

Leave by the Sudbury road, A134. In 1¾ miles at the roundabout, take the second exit, A131, and enter the pleasant Stour Valley market town of Sudbury (see page 69). The artist Thomas Gainsborough was born here in 1727 and his birthplace is now an arts centre and museum.

Follow signs Bures to leave by the B1508, and head down the Stour Valley to Bures. To the north-east of the village is St Stephen's Chapel, a small thatched building thought to be on the site where St Edmund was crowned in 855.

In the village, turn left at the church on to an unclassified road, signed Nayland. Follow this by-road (narrow in places) for 4½ miles to the junction with the A134. Turn right here, and immediately left, on the B1087, to enter the attractive old village of Nayland (see page 62). Proceed to Stoke-by-Nayland and turn right, B1068, signed Ipswich. Continue through Thorington Street and Higham, then in 2 miles turn left on to the A12. Half a mile further on, branch left, B1070, signed East Bergholt, then turn left again. In another mile, at the Carriers Arms, turn right (unclassified) and enter the village of East Bergholt – Constable's birthplace. Although you can no longer see the house in which he was born, in 1776, his studio is still standing, as part of the Post Office.

On reaching the church, bear left, then in ½ mile pass the turning (on the right) which leads to Flatford Mill. The Mill, built in 1733, is now a field-study centre, owned by the National Trust. From the car park here, a path winds to a bridge over the Stour. Along the right bank you can see the side of the Mill, with its sluice gate and trees overhanging the river bank.

The drive continues on the Manningtree road, and in almost another ½ mile rejoins the B1070. In 1¼ miles, turn left on to the A137, signed Ipswich, and pass through Brantham. One mile further, at the Bull Inn, turn right on to the Holbrook road, B1080. Beyond Stutton the road runs through the grounds of the Royal Hospital School, to reach Holbrook. In 1¾ miles join the B1456, signed Ipswich, and later drive alongside the River Orwell to pass beneath the Orwell Road Bridge. At the roundabout, turn right on to the A137 for the return to Ipswich.

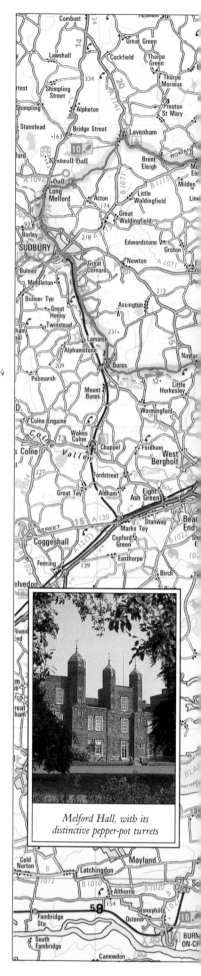

Melford Hall, with its distinctive pepper-pot turrets

FELIXSTOWE to

Zeebrugge............5-8 hrs

HARWICH to

Hook of Holland	6½-8½ hrs
Esbjerg	20 hrs
Kristiansand	22-24 hrs
Hamburg	21 hrs
Gothenburg	24 hrs
Hirtshals	27½ hrs
Oslo	35½ hrs

Flatford Mill, where John Constable spent much of his boyhood, was the inspiration behind many of the great artist's paintings

The North Norfolk Coast

Allow 2½ – 3 hours

'He who would old England win, must at Weybourne Hope begin.' Weybourne Hope, situated at the point where cliffs rise from the coastal marshland, was a deep-water port of some strategic importance. It was used as an embarkation point for troops off to France during World War I. Weybourne itself is very pretty, with flint-built cottages, typical of many villages in the District of North Norfolk, which is designated an Area of Outstanding Natural Beauty. The beach is more popular with fishermen than bathers, but wildlife abounds along the coast. South-east of the village lies the railway station, built in 1900, where steam trains from Sheringham stop.

From the free car park at the beach in Weybourne (TG110436), walk up Beach Road and turn left. Take the path through the churchyard, and go along the road, following the 'North Norfolk Railway' sign. The 11th-century All Saints Church has a brick and flint chequer-work porch, which was added in the 15th century. All around it are the extensive ruins of an Augustinian Priory, founded in 1200.

Leaving the village behind, cross over the railway bridge. It gives good views of the track, station and countryside. *Shortly afterwards, turn right on a wide track passing Springs Farm. The path narrows, entering woodland and leading to a picnic area. Just after the wildlife pond, turn right. The narrow path runs alongside a railway line. Go between the 'Ski' notice and tyres, and immediately bear right uphill on the narrow bracken and heather path.* There are panoramic views at the top over the coastline and the church, windmill and village of Weybourne. Often large ships can be spotted on the horizon.

Continue along the wide path to the white gate of the railway crossing. Stop, look and listen before crossing. Keeping the bungalow on your left, go straight ahead (north) across Kelling Heath, on the wide track and over the by-road. This heathland covers a wide area and is very pretty with the colours of wild flowers, especially when the gorse and heather are blooming. A mile down the road are Kelling Aviaries, which have a large variety of birds on show.

At the cross tracks on the heathland turn left, and after 10 paces, turn right down a narrow bracken-lined gorge. At the main road (A149), turn left. After 250yd turn right, passing Meadow View House and the playground of a flint school built in 1876, along the Norfolk Heritage Path. There are good views of the countryside and, further along by a shingle bank, bird reserves. Occasionally, common seal may be seen in the sea: they breed just along the coast at Blakeney Point. Boat trips are available to the Point from Blakeney and Morston.

At the fork turn right to the seashore, then, keeping the fence on your right, take the coastal path back to the car park. During World War II, remote-controlled target planes called 'Queen Bees' were flown from the now modern radar station on the coast. Terns may be seen diving for fish, perhaps catching the dab for which fishermen cast out their lines here.

The Town of Reepham

Allow 2 hours

This walk takes you around hedge-lined lanes and tracks and through the delightful old market town of Reepham.

Park in the free car park off Station Road (TG099229). Go to the far corner and turn left, away from the town, into hedged Chapel Walk, then turn right into Old Brewers Lane, strolling left into Ollands Road. At one time, Reepham was made up of three parishes, Hackford, Whitwell and Reepham, belonging to three sisters. Each had her own church. Two churches remain, built back to back, and you can see their towers above the rooftops.

At the main road junction, turn right over the railway bridge. Go straight ahead, signed Salle, then turn left into World's End Lane. Salle's magnificent 12th-century church has a 111ft tower, and connections with the family of Anne Boleyn.

At World's End Cottage keep right of the hedge and go over the stile into the meadow. Go straight down over the streams. At the high hedge, turn left, keeping the hedge on the right, and cross the stile. At the road, turn left under the railway bridge, then bear right. After 50yd, turn right into Catchback Lane.

(Or, if it is exceptionally wet, continue up the tarmac road, turning right into Smugglers Lane and right again, past the Police Station, left into Park Lane, and straight past Grosvenor House. At the end of the bungalows, the path narrows. Turn right at the T-junction. At the far end of a wire fence, turn left. Rejoin the walk at ** below.)

At the end of Catchback Lane, turn right into the road, then left opposite Winks Cottages into a rough track. Reaching the corner of the playing-field (**), turn right along the path in the meadow, keeping the tall hedge on your left. At the left-hand corner of the field, the path narrows, with woodland on the right. At the road, turn left uphill, and after 300yd turn right on to a grassy track. At a gap in the hedged track is a view of arable land sloping to the Wensum Valley. At the bottom of the track, a cluster of buildings includes Eade's water mill, on the River Eyn.

At the road turn left, signed Cawston. Turn right into a tree-lined path, emerging into Whitwell Street, with pretty cottages. *Turn into Bar Lane,* with Reepham church ahead. *Reaching Back Street, turn left.* This very old street has a timber-framed building among whitewashed cottages, some of whose names come from earlier trades, like Greyhound Inn and The Old Bakery. The old market square contains buildings of many different ages, including the Brewery House, dated circa 1700.

Turn right up Pudding Pie Alley. At Market Square, between the butcher's shop and The Chimes, take Fisher Alley back to the car park.

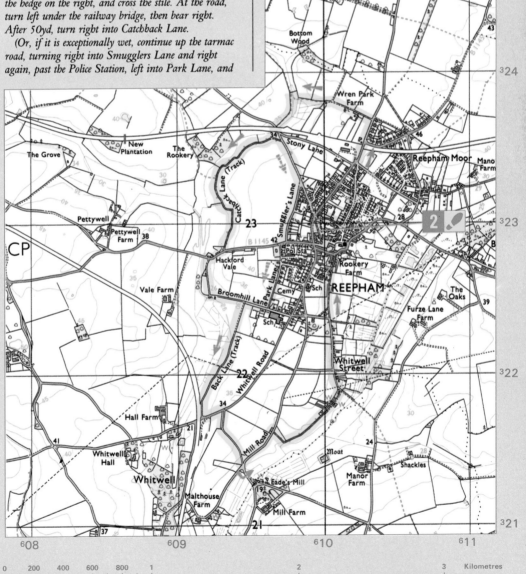

WALK 3
A Panoramic Landscape

Allow 2¼ hours

Horsey Mere, a Site of Special Scientific Interest because of its wide range of flora and fauna, is one of the largest areas of open water in Broadland. This is a favourite place for sailing boats. Horsey is thought to mean Horsa's Island; a Danish King named Horsa once settled here. Wet-weather footwear is essential in all but the driest spells.

Park at Horsey windpump (TG457222). Leave the car park, turning left into the road, past thatched houses. If you wish to make a detour to visit the 11th-century thatched church with its octagonal tower, turn left at the sign 'church'. Where the road bears sharp left, go straight up the signed by-road passing an old barn dated 1742 and the Nelson's Head public house. Go left at the fork, passing the nature reserve. Take the path through the dunes on to golden sands, or walk behind the dunes if it is windy. There have been serious invasions of the sea along this coast. In 1953 it broke through the dunes; in 1938 five feet of water was recorded at Horsey, and water travelled 10 miles inland. Two hundred years ago, before the marshes were drained, the only road to Horsey from Sea Palling was the track behind the dunes.

Continue along the beach for ¾ mile, then turn left through the concrete-walled opening in the dunes and follow the hedged path to the road. At the road, turn right for a few yards, then just after the 'bend in road' sign turn left into an arable field, keeping to the left edge. Where the fields join, turn right, keeping the hedge on your right. After the path bends left, at the electricity pole numbered 14, go through the gap in the hedge along the bedged lane between houses. Turn right at the metalled road, and after 10yd turn left, following the footpath sign to the bridge and stile. There is a disused windmill ahead. Go over the stile into the meadow, and keep on higher ground along the left boundary path, going over two stiles. Turn left along the path at the water's edge. This artificial waterway is called 'New Cut'. It links Horsey Mere to Waxham and Lessingham brickworks. Before the advent of the railways, barges and wherries used these waterways for trading between towns. On the other side of the water lie Brayden Marshes. From this marsh bed reeds are cut, stacked and then used in local thatching.

Continue along this path. The 1,700 acres of Horsey Mere, administered by the National Trust, are good for spotting winter wildfowl. The reed-beds, and the proximity of the sea, make it an attractive place for migrating birds. Grebes and marsh harriers are often seen, and you may hear the cry of bitterns over the reeds.

At a fence the path goes left. From the steps, follow the white discs back to the staithe, and Horsey wind pump. Horsey wind pump was built to help drain the surrounding marshes. The water was lifted by pump from the dykes into the river. This windpump is open to the public between April and October. The staithe, now used mainly as a mooring place for pleasure craft, is also the landing place for the thatching reeds and has been for over 150 years.

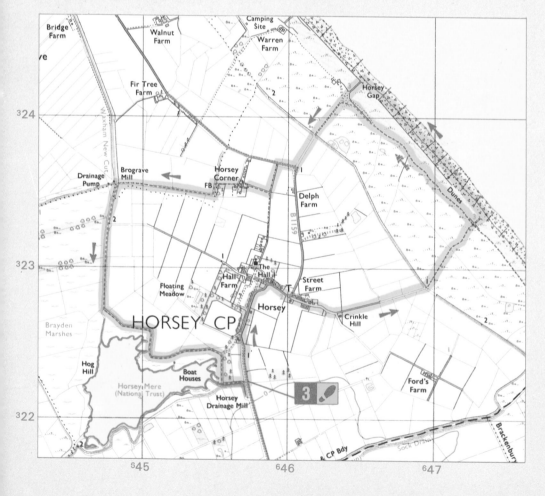

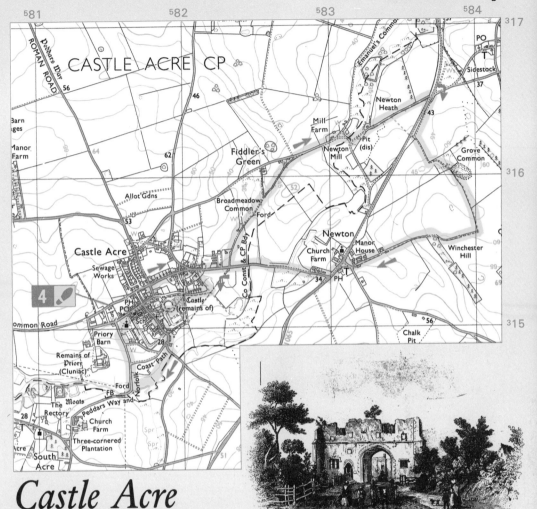

Castle Acre Priory, Norfolk. Gateway.

Castle Acre

Allow 2½ hours

Castle Acre is exceptional. On the green the village sign depicts a monk and priory; the priory ruins are to the west of the village. On the south side is a Norman castle, while a fine 13th-century church is at the other side. This walk is not suitable for young children, and wet-weather footwear is advisable.

From the free car park close to the village green (TF817151), take the Massingham road. Turn right towards Newton, passing wooden bungalows on your left. It is pleasant to stroll through Castle Acre, with its Bailey Gate and flint and brick buildings.

Passing East Green, turn left along a signed by-road. Keeping Breck House on your left, take the grass path over the common. At the fork, go right uphill, along a tree-lined path. At the metalled road, turn right to reach the hamlet of Fiddlers Green. Here ducks and geese rest after swimming in the River Nar. *Pass over the bridge and turn left along the public footpath. Keep straight ahead along the hedged path, with a flint cottage on your left.*

Cross the road and turn immediately right along the path parallel to the main road. At the track junction, turn left to reach a disused quarry. The workings are very deep and steep-sided, and this part of the walk may be dangerous for children. *At the quarry, turn right along the path between a field boundary and spoil mounds (this path can be a little overgrown at times). Go through the gap in the hedge, then along the field's edge, turning right on to a wide track.* Along most of this walk there are excellent views. From the quarry, Castle Acre church comes into view. The old workings of the quarry are now being reclaimed by nature, and wild flowers abound.

Go down Winchester Hill. After passing Newton Manor with its attractive fox door knocker, walk along the main road, passing the George and Dragon pub. Cross the main road and turn right into a road signed Castle Acre. North-west from the pub lies the Saxon St Mary and All Saints Church. The antiquity of the interior is not to be missed.

Opposite Footpath Cottage, cross the green to the left, and go over the stile into a meadow. Go through the gate into the second meadow, heading for the stile in the top right-hand corner. There is a good view here of the earthworks formerly used to flood the water meadows, to encourage an early crop of grass.

Bear left, taking the path over the moat, and cross the bridge, passing the castle ruins. Take the path to Bailey Street. Turn left, passing Malt House. Just after the road to your right, and before the bridge, turn right over the stile into a meadow. Follow the path to the road. Turn right uphill, and then go through the churchyard to the car park. The castle walls have stood for 500 years. The great square keep was converted in about 1140 from a late Norman country house. A footpath just opened by the Parish Council follows the River Nar. Heron are often seen here. There are fine views of the Cluniac Priory and St James's Church.

WALK 5

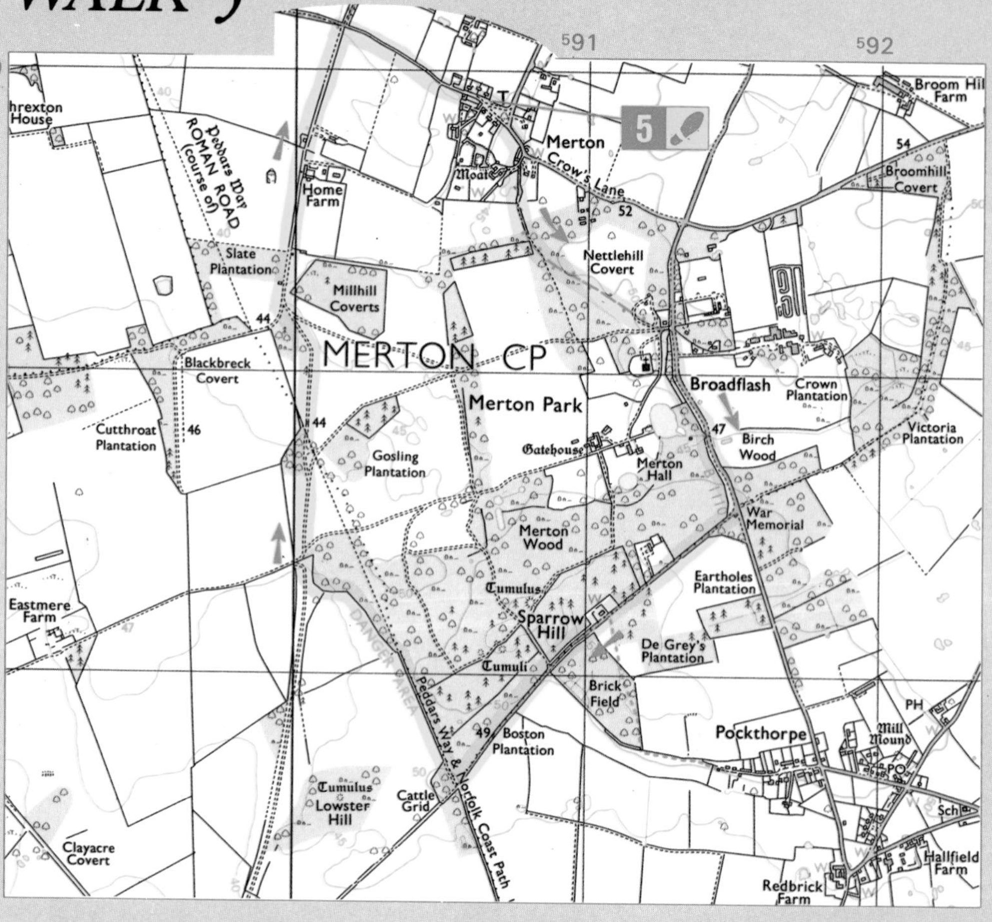

Paths of Neolithic Man

Allow 2 hours

This walk takes you through woodland and along by-roads where oak, ash and beech have stood for hundreds of years. Breckland is noted for its evidence of the Neolithic age. Grimes Graves Museum and the Stone Age flint mine are not very far away. Here prehistoric miners scraped hundreds of tunnels in the flint; the first workings have been dated to about 2900BC. From later times, an encampment of the Ancient Britons, the Iceni, has been reconstructed on its original site at Cockley Cley.

Leave the green in Merton, where parking is easily found (TL907989), and walk to the south-east corner, past a brick-pillared post box and 'road narrows' sign. The tranquil parish of Merton with its pink-thatched cottages appears tiny in comparison with the village green, on which stands a thatched circular bus shelter, erected by the villagers to commemorate the Queen's Jubilee in 1977.

About 200yd along a metalled road, opposite Flint Cottage, turn right on to a rough track, passing a thatched cottage on the right. Immediately bear left behind the white house, along a grass track with a fence on the right, which leads to natural woodland. At the T-junction with a wide dirt track, turn left. Merton church comes into view. Take the path right to the church lych gate. The 14th-century church of St James has a round tower. The Royal Arms of King William IV may be seen over the tower arch. There are fine stained-glass windows and a superb wood carving of the Last Supper. Keys to the church are available at the lodge. Stroll behind the church for a splendid view over Merton Hall, which has suffered badly from fire in the past. There are ponies in the park of the estate, and the lake is a favourite for many species of water fowl.

Retrace your steps to the track, passing the lodge with a blue clock. Turn right into a by-road, which can be quite busy and has no footpath. After 800yd, turn right into a lane signed 'road closed ahead', keeping the war memorial on your left. This memorial was removed from Tottington village when the area became the property of the Ministry of Defence. The plantation you pass on your right has some fine monkey-puzzle trees.

Passing Sparrow Hill House on the right, continue along the lane to the crossing of tracks. Turn right into the wood — along the Peddar's Way — following the blue arrow mark for 1¼ miles. This part of the walk can be very muddy, but is passable. Lord Walsingham, owner of the Merton Estate, provided this link in the Peddar's Way, a long-distance footpath. It starts at Thetford and ends at the north Norfolk coast. The Prince of Wales opened the now popular route in 1986. This area of unspoilt countryside is glorious, with abundant wildlife; in particular, pheasants in their colourful plumage are often seen.

The path becomes a wide track. A ¼ mile from farm buildings, at the crossing of tracks, turn right along the metalled road to Merton. On the Watton–Great Hockham road, a few miles from Merton, lies Wayland or Wailing Wood. Here the wicked uncle, from nearby Griston Hall, abandoned the original Babes in the Wood; their grave can still be seen here.

Green Lanes
and Villages

Allow 2½ hours

This walk takes you through the rural landscape of south Norfolk. Every turn brings rural scenes, quiet lanes and attractive houses with colourful gardens. The tree and hedge-lined tracks are a haven of wild flowers. However, sections may be muddy in wet weather.

Park in the well-defined lay-by with grass between it and the busy main road, just past the Gull Inn on the A146 (Norwich to Beccles road) (TG285037). Walk towards the Gull Inn. Cross to the road, and take the metalled lane, between white iron posts, passing houses with a stream on your left. After 200yd, fork right, signed Framingham Pigot, passing Scatterbrook Cottage. At the junction turn left towards the church. Framingham Pigot's knapped-flint church with its unusual spire and clock was built a hundred years ago. The ornamental ironwork on the entrance gates is particularly fine.

Turn left along the footpath, keeping the churchyard railings on your left. Just after the wooden garage go through a gate on the left into a meadow, and cross to the edge of the wood. Go over a broken stile into the field, and just after an old ivy-covered barn in the wood, turn right over the stile taking the path through woodland. Pass into the field, crossing over the stile into

Gull Lane. *Turn right, then after 50yd turn left into a path between trees leading into a field. At the road turn right towards Framingham Earl,* where the church has 15th-century stained-glass windows, a Saxon chancel, and a Norman tower and knave. The walk takes you through the modern part of Framingham Earl, with colourful gardens, hedges and trees.

At the road junction, turn left, signed Poringland. Go along Hall Road, leading into Upgate. As the road bends right, turn left, continuing along Upgate. Where the road turns left, turn on to the track, passing the entrance to the Roman Catholic Chapel of the Annunciation. Follow the bridleway sign along the sunken track. Just after Poringland Hall, turn left into a field, between posts. Follow it down the right-hand edge. Further along, rejoin the sunken path (it can be muddy in wet weather). At the T-junction, turn left. The path widens. Fox snares are used around here, so keep your dog on its lead. *Ignore the track to your left. After 700yd turn left into a field and follow the path uphill, around a small wood on the right, and down to the road. Turn left, passing Orchard Farm bungalow. When the road bends left, turn right on to the metalled farm track, and go through the farm. Turn right at the road, then left at Boundary Farm, going between farm buildings with a large pond on your right.* Here again, on a wet day mud may cause problems, but it is worth persevering for glimpses of the many beautiful birds on the pond.

Continue along the track to the brow of the hill, then swing left, keeping the field boundary hedge on your left. There is a fine view, and the white-faced Gull Inn can be seen across the valley.

At the far hedge, turn right with the hedge on your left. This path continues between trees to the road. Turn right to the main road to go back to the starting point.

SCALE 1:25 000

WALK 7

Grantchester & Trumpington

Allow 2½ hours

This walk criss-crosses the River Cam, taking you through the charming villages of Grantchester and Trumpington. Later it skirts the fine city of Cambridge.

Park in a lay-by close to the church in Grantchester (TL434555). Keeping the church on your right, walk towards Trumpington. Just after Rupert Brooke's Old Vicarage, turn left into the lane. At the bridge turn left. This is a quiet spot, with the River Cam gushing under the bridge, and a favourite place for a variety of ducks. The magnificent church has 14th-century tracery windows with a patchwork of medieval glass in the east window. A precious possession of the church is the portrait of Sir Roger de Trumpington, dated 1289. The second-oldest brass in England, it lies on a slab of Purbeck marble.

Leaving the church, cross the road into Campbell's Lane and then, almost immediately, bear left down a grass path with evergreen trees on your right. Continue along the path, and go through iron gates. Turn left and walk about ¾ mile down Trumpington Road, before turning right into Porson Road. Go to the end of the road, where there is a large hedge with a wooden gateway to its right. Go through the gate and follow the path to the end. Continue alongside the stream to the main road. At the road, turn left to the traffic lights, cross the road and go through an iron gateway into the

The lovely Dropwort thrives in rural Cambridgeshire

meadow. Note the fine old milestone on the bridge, 'To Great saint Marie's Church Cambridge'.

Keeping the stream on your left, take the wider path to the bridge. Cross this and the black footbridge. Continue to the main road. Turn left into Grantchester Street and then right into Grantchester Meadow Road. This becomes a rough track, and then a metalled path which goes through the famous Grantchester Meadows. At Grantchester, turn right through a wooden gate, passing the thatched Red Lion Inn, and then the Green Man pub. Cross the road back to the car.

Going through the Grantchester Meadows, look back to a fine view of the college spires in Cambridge. The church at Grantchester first stood on its site in Norman times. The present Parish Church of St Andrew and St Mary was built in 1877. It has fine stained-glass windows and visiting it completes a pleasant walk.

Reach – an Old Port

Allow 1½ hours

Reach in Cambridgeshire is extremely pretty, with pink- and white-washed cottages overlooking the large village green. From the 14th century, timber, iron and agricultural produce passed through the port down the river to King's Lynn. This walk has stupendous views and good paths.

Park on the village green close to the church (TL567662). Walk towards Chapel Lane. Turn left at the Chapel and then bear right past the Post Office, down The Hythe. Take the footbridge over the waterway (an old port). Turn left along the track and left again over the bridge to a metalled road. Turn right, away from Reach. After ⅓ mile, as the road bends right, go straight ahead along Barston Drove, a wide track. An earlier track, to the left, leads to the spot where, in the 14th century, chalky material (clunch) was dug for Ely Cathedral's Lady Chapel, and for some Cambridge colleges. Along the Drove, Swaffham Prior's windmill and church and the church at Swaffham Bulbeck can be spotted.

At the gas marker on your right before the hedge, turn left along a wide path between fields, with the railway bridge ahead. At the by-road turn right to cross

the railway bridge. After about 400yd turn left over the wire, and go back along the narrow path. Bear left through a fence gap and go downhill to the disused railway track. Turn right. The lofty tower of Burwell's magnificent church is ahead.

After 300yd, on reaching the earthworks of Devil's Dyke, turn left up a path on to the top of the Dyke. Go along a wide path, which narrows between trees. Continue back to the village green at Reach, passing The Kings and Dykes End pub. There are panoramic views from the top of the Dyke, including Ely Cathedral, 9 miles away. This Dyke was built by the Iceni people, and kept 'war out and peace in' for the Ancient Britons. Roman relics have been found in it. The end of the Dyke was demolished to create Fair Green at Reach. Reach's fair was first held in 1201; 787 years later, the Mayor of Cambridge still opens the annual fair on the Green. The church of St Etheldreda and Holy Trinity of 1378 was thought to stand on the same spot as the present church.

Two churches in one churchyard: Swaffham Prior

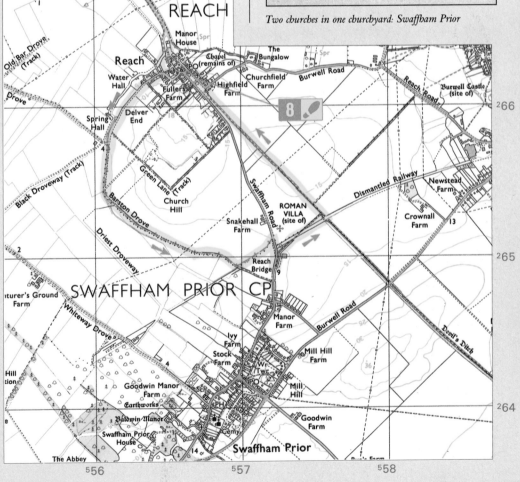

WALK 9

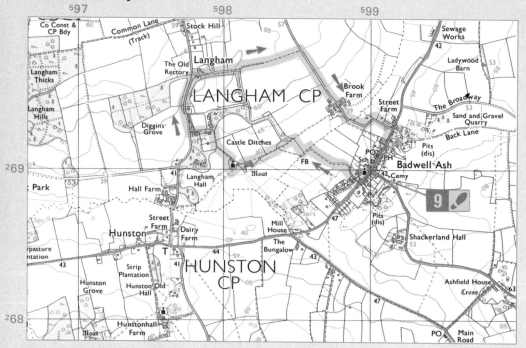

Tracks around a Charming Rural Village

Allow 1¼ hours

Badwell Ash, or Little Ashfield, is a picturesque village with a mixture of thatched, timber and white- and pink-washed dwellings. They stand cosily together, so peaceful and tranquil after the bustle of Bury St Edmunds a few miles away.

There is no official car park in this small community, but space is available close to the White Horse Inn/ Restaurant (TL990689). Start the walk from the church of St Mary, which stands in the centre of the village.

Go into the church, a fine structure with attractive stained-glass windows, and notice the porch, decorated all over with flushwork panelling. The tracery of the two-light windows inside has a four-petalled flower motif. A large old wooden chest and an old funeral bier stand in the church as memorials to the past. On leaving, notice the blacksmith's tools on the south-east buttress, and the flushwork on top of the tower.

Go southwards towards the village green. Turn right down a grass path with a footpath sign just before the green. Go over a stile into a meadow, following the yellow marker arrows. Cross the meadow diagonally and climb another stile. Keep to the right and walk along the field edge to a bridge. Cross the stream and continue along the field edge, with a hedge on your right, around the top of the field. Go through a wide open fence gap and walk between the hedge and a wooden fence, with Langham church straight ahead. Passing the moat of an old castle on your left, turn left over a stile and enter a meadow. Turn right, going

Horses graze in the peaceful fields around Badwell Ash – an example of country life at its most tranquil

through a gate on to the church path. This is an ancient walkway. Standing around the church are fine old beech trees, and to the left across the meadow is the attractive building of Langham Hall. The meadows, arable land with a meandering stream full of watercress, birds flying in and around the hedges and squirrels playing in the trees, all depict a truly rural scene.

Follow the path around the church inside the churchyard, to a second gate. Leave by this gate and turn right. Cross a wooden bridge and turn left along a wide grass path between a high beech hedge and a wooden fence. Pass through wooden barriers and continue along the tarmac path, passing the well-built stables for the stud horses with a lovely Pegasus weather vane. At a T-junction, turn left, going through a white gate to a by-road. At the by-road, turn right and after a short distance, at a grass triangle planted with trees, turn right along a track, passing the Old Rectory. The track continues along the edge of a field, then between fields to a by-road. Along this stretch of the walk there are extensive views of the countryside looking across to Stock Hill.

At the by-road turn right and walk towards Badwell Ash, passing Brook Farm. At the junction turn right. First pass a lovely thatched house and then the White Horse Inn, on your left, on the way back to the car park where the walk started.

The Medieval Town of Lavenham

Allow 2¼ hours

Strolling through Lavenham you have a pictorial view of history. The River Brett flows around the town, which was famous for the weaving of 'blue cloth'. Some of the buildings are decorated with pargeting, others have exposed timber-framing. The Guildhall in the Market Place has ornate carvings on its main timbers. The corner post is carved and a figure of an armed Knight can just be seen; it could be John de Vere, 15th Earl of Oxford, founder of the Guild of Corpus Christi, whose headquarters were at Lavenham.

Park at the free car park (TL915490) nearly opposite the church and next to the thatched Cock Inn. Turn right down Church Street passing the timber-framed houses, then right along Water Street, passing the Priory. Lavenham was a prosperous medieval town and the layout has altered little since the Middle Ages. The Priory has been carefully restored and is open to the public.

Turn left along a by-road, passing a postbox on a telegraph pole and keeping the playing field on your right. Turn right into the lane leading to Clayhill Farm. Cross the river by a bridge. Continue up the bridleway, passing a farm on your left and 1 mile or so further along, apple orchards on your right. At a by-

road turn right towards Brent Eleigh village. Go down the hill, passing Brent Eleigh Hall and the church on your right. Along this stretch there are tremendous views over the countryside. Clay Lane is an ancient routeway and the hedges contain a great number of plant species such as hazel, spindle, field maple, honeysuckle, dog's mercury and even some wetland species. As Spragg's Wood is approached, look out for primroses and bluebells in season, and other plants characteristic of ancient woodland. Brent Eleigh Hall is now a herb-growing centre. It is well worth visiting the church with its old box pews and fine medieval paintings on the east wall. The village of Brent Eleigh takes its name from *Illeleya*, derived from *leah*, the estate or land of a Saxon landowner.

After passing a thatched house on the left, keep the Tudor house on your left and go along a road signed Lavenham. Cross the main road and continue up a narrow lane, with the thatched Cock Inn on your right. Immediately after crossing the stream, turn right along a path at the field edge. Follow the yellow footpath markers. Ignore a stile on the right leading to the lake area. At a farm track, turn right then almost immediately left, keeping the hedge on your left and a plantation of poplar trees on your right. At the end of the plantation, a footpath crosses to the left bank of the stream. Continue along the edge of the stream for 650yd, ignoring the first footpath indicated to the right and taking the second one, turning sharp right uphill, then left along a track to a farm, ignoring the path ahead. At the pond turn right, skirting around the farm house to join a lane. At the lane turn right. Pass a pink thatched cottage, and then some new houses. As the lane bears right, turn left up a narrow metalled footpath to return to the car park. There are beautiful stained-glass windows in Lavenham church, and the carvings on the rood beams, chancel screen and the misericord seats are superb.

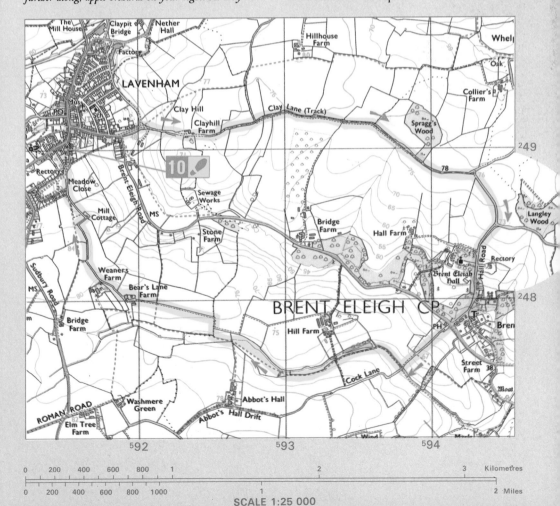

WALK 11
Walberswick —
the Suffolk
Nature Reserve

Allow 3 hours

This walk takes you into the Suffolk Nature Reserve, which covers mudflats, saltmarshes, reed-beds, heathland and woodland around Walberswick and the River Blyth. To the south lies Dunwich. The museum there contains many of the interesting relics that have been found in the area. Aldeburgh, just a few miles away, is renowned for its music festivals founded by Benjamin Britten.

Park at the Heritage car park on the outskirts of Walberswick (TM484745). Turn right along a metalled lane bordered by heathland. When the lane starts to go uphill, and at the crossing of tracks, turn right, taking the path over the heath towards woodland. Skirt the wood. At the end of the wood, the path bears right and continues to a road. At the road turn right. Shortly after passing a farmhouse, turn left along a signed Bridleway path, heading for the River Blyth. Excellent views appear over the heathland and surrounding countryside, and Walberswick church comes into view. This church dates back to the 14th century. The altar cross and candlesticks were carved out of driftwood in recent times by two members of the congregation. In the garden of the farmhouse peacocks and guinea fowl can be seen.

The water tower, church, lighthouse and houses in Southwold, on the far side of the Blyth, are clearly visible.

Continue along the path through heathland, ignoring all side tracks. At a metalled lane, turn left. Immediately before a footbridge over the river, turn right on to the river path. Continue along this path to Walberswick. The River Blyth is quite narrow, and landing stages to which small boats are moored run the whole length of it. Walberswick is an attractive village with houses standing around the Green. It was once a thriving port. Much trading took place with Iceland, and a few Icelanders settled in the village. In 1953 the sea invaded, and the Green was covered with 3ft of sea water.

At Walberswick, follow the path into the village, passing the Bell Hotel on the left. Soon after the village green, and just before the Anchor Inn, turn left through a gateway on to a path at the field edge, passing allotments on your left. Bear right along a path close to the marsh. At a pillar box turn left, down through scrubland. Turn right, following a path at the edge of a field. Turn left along a rough track, passing the old barns. Where the track leads into reed-beds, turn right up on to a path alongside another field edge. Follow the field edge round to the right, uphill and to the right of the pill box. As a wider track is reached, turn left over a stile. Follow the track across heath and scrubland, keeping to high ground away from the edge of the marshes at first. Continue along this winding path which eventually reaches a wooden sleeper path through the reeds. Along the marsh tracks a wide expanse of the North Sea can be seen. The boom of the bittern has been heard in the reed-beds. Other birds which have been spotted include the marsh harrier and bearded tits.

At end of the sleeper path, turn right and keep to the right-hand path through heathland to a metalled lane; turn right here and return to the car park.

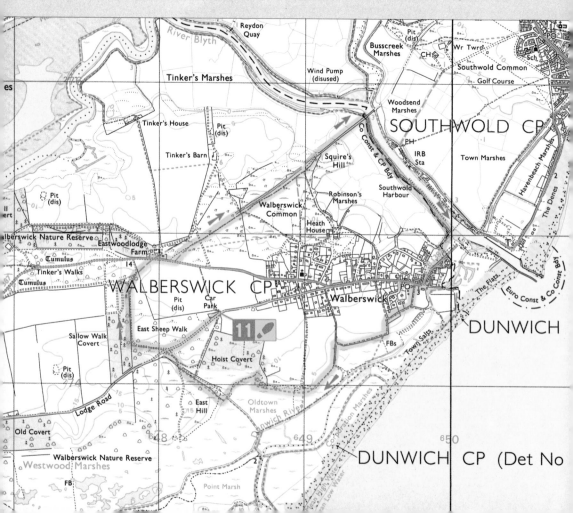

Map showing Orford, River Ore, Havergate Island and surrounding area. Map references include 641, 643, 249, 248. Labels: School, Orford, Chantry Farm, Chinese Wall Bridge, ORFORD CP, Pump House, Mast, FB, Ferry, Richmond Farm, Chantry Marshes, Sewage Works, Richmond Cottages, Tide Gauge, Chantry Point, Stonyditch Point, DGRAVE CP, Gedgrave Marshes, Cuckold's Point, The Crouch, RIVER ORE, HAVERGATE ISLAND CP, Havergate Island (Bird Sanctuary), Const Bdy, Mean High Water, Orford Beach.

Exploring Ancient Orford

Allow 2 hours

The River Ore is a valuable nature reserve, and the town of Orford has stood on its banks for centuries. The North Sea drift has built up a piece of land known as Orford Ness, on which stands the famous lighthouse. Two great buildings dominate the skyline — the remains of the massive 12th-century castle and the tower of the fine church — which, together with the market square and unspoilt houses, make Orford a most interesting town to explore.

Park at the pay car park close to the quay (TM424497), opposite the Jolly Sailor pub. Turn left out of the car park and walk to the quay. Turn right, taking the footpath along the side of the River Ore. Go through a gate up some steps on to the riverbank path. Turn left. After climbing two stiles, close together, the path continues in a curve along the river. Alternatively, at the stiles take the path down the bank over a wooden bridge, and across to the far bank. (Turn right at the top of the bank, if avoiding the loop). Continue along the path. There are very good views over the creeks, where in the 12th century a merman — or wild man — was thought to have been caught by local fishermen; the merman was kept at the castle, but later he escaped and fled back to the sea. Orford lighthouse and Havergate Island, a nature reserve, can be clearly seen. Look out for cormorants, herons and avocets, and listen for the calls of oyster-catchers and curlews. The tidal mudflats have many unusual plant species, and provide a unique opportunity for observing bird and animal tracks. Inland are the castle, church and town of Orford, which was important enough in 1135 to be granted a weekly market.

A fine keep is all that remains of Orford's castle

Near the end of Havergate Island, and at a footpath sign, turn right down the bank, through a gate and on to a wide track between fields to a by-road. At the by-road turn right, then at a public footpath sign turn left, up a sandy track. Just after an open barn, turn right up some steps on to a path at the edge of a field. Continue along the path until reaching the castle grounds. Good views appear over the coastline, including the radio masts of the BBC World Service station. In the same area Sir Robert Watson-Watt carried out his early experimental work on radar. Only the keep remains of Orford Castle; fine cannons guard the entrance. The castle was completed in 1173 in Henry II's reign, at a total recorded cost of £1,413.

From the castle's main entrance cross the road, and bear left uphill, passing the Crown and Castle Hotel. Cross Market Square. Go along the path to the church. St Bartholomew's Church is large and was built in the 12th century as a Chapel annexed to the mother church of All Saints Sudbourne (just up the coast towards Aldeburgh). It holds many interesting historic items, including the old parish stocks, a sturdy chest, three of the church bells, all dated 1639, and a superb 15th-century font.

From the church go down, through a gate and across the road. Continue down the road to the car park close to the quay. The houses in Orford are very attractive, especially those of the red brick, white-shuttered terrace along the road to the quay.

WALK *13*

A Walk along the Orwell

Allow 3 hours

Most of this walk follows the River Orwell. Cormorants can be seen, and there are fine views over the harbours of Felixstowe and Harwich.

Park in a side road behind Shotley Post Office (TM233351). Walk down the main street, with the Post Office on your right and Salisbury Villas on your left. Turn left along a metalled footpath between houses and the village hall, passing 1st Shotley Group HQ. Cross the road and turn right, then turn left between the bungalow numbered 26 and a row of four garages. The footpath continues between fields. At the field boundary, turn right, then left, over a footbridge. The footpath continues diagonally across the corner of a field, rejoining the boundary hedge, and eventually becomes a well-marked track running between hedges. There are good views of the countryside and over the River Orwell, and a handsome timber-framed house, Shotley Hall, can also be seen.

At the road turn right, passing first Shotley Hall, then the church on your left. The church has a Georgian chancel; in the churchyard hundreds of sailors are buried, including the entire ship's company of HMS *Gypsy*, which struck a magnetic mine in the Orwell.

Going downhill, turn right, and then climb over a stile into a meadow. Follow the path straight to the river estuary, go over a second stile and up on to the top of the river bank. Turn right and follow the path to Shotley Point and Shotley Gate. Coastal shipping travels up the River Orwell to Ipswich. A little further up river, on the opposite bank, there is a large marina. This stretch of water is a hive of activity. At Shotley Gate, the River Orwell meets the River Stour. At Shotley Point HMS *Ganges* was built as an onshore training centre for juniors wishing to join the Navy. The mast was used for a mast-manning ceremony, in which the Button Boy would climb the rigging to stand on the button of the mast, 140ft above ground. The base of the ship was used as a hospital in World War I, when two submarines collided in the harbour.

Take the path around the marina, passing the Bristol Arms. Bear left along a footpath beside the River Stour. After 750yd turn right up some steepish steps to the road; turn left here. At the end, go across a grassy area, and then take the path through a wood, along a field edge. After passing some cottages and caravans, turn right at cross tracks, up an unmarked wide rough track, passing Shotley Cottage on your right. Continue along this path to the road. At the main road turn left, passing Rose Inn, and return to the car park.

VEHICLE (V) & FOOT PASSENGER (F) FERRY SHIP	
Esbjerg (V/F) (Summer only)	20 hrs
Hamburg (V/F)	19-21½ hrs
Hook of Holland (V/F)	6½-8½ hrs
Gothenburgh (V/F)	23-25hrs

The Delights of the Stour at Stutton

Allow 2½ hours

Stutton lies close to the River Stour. The Stour Estuary has been designated an Area of Outstanding Natural Beauty. Flatford Mill is only a few miles away; John Constable's father, Golding Constable, and Samuel and John Gainsborough, were all Commissioners of Navigation on the River Stour in the late 1700s. The walk has superb views, and takes you along the banks of the Stour. It is an excellent area for bird-watching — many species of waders and water birds can be spotted. Over the farmland, hares chase one another.

Park at the Stutton Community Centre (TM143347). From the car park turn right into the road, passing the Gardeners' Arms on your left. Turn left into the driveway to Stutton Hall, passing the lodge cottage at the entrance. At cross tracks, turn right. At a junction, turn left and follow the winding lane to Stutton Mill and the River Stour. There are fine views over the rolling countryside. Stutton Mill, now a private house, stands proudly overlooking the river.

Go through the white gates. The path continues in front of the mill house. Go up on to the bank. The path goes either along the field edge at first, then down along the river shore; or immediately along the river shore,

going first through high reeds for a very short distance. Barges can be seen moored at low water in the Estuary. Looking across to Jacques Bay, trains can be seen (and heard) travelling to Harwich harbour. Oyster catchers, shelduck and redshank are among the many birds that can be spotted along this river walk. At Stutton Ness, the large clock tower of the Royal Hospital School can be seen towering over the trees — the chimes of the clock in the tower can be heard ringing out over the water.

About 20yd beyond a bird-watchers' hide, on the left, climb a bank and cross a wooden bridge. Follow the path at the edge of a wood, then enter a field. Before the next stretch of woodland, bear right down to a track beside the river. Go around the point at Stutton Ness, then turn left up on to a wide path, alongside the edge of a field. The track winds and turns left, leaving the river to go inland. Walk past farm buildings and Crepping Hall. The path continues along a driveway lined with poplars and holly trees. At a road, turn left and return to the Community Centre. Stutton is a very pleasant and friendly village. Its modern houses blend in well with the old timber-framed and pink-washed cottages, some with thatch. Stutton Hall was probably built in Tudor times, and the buildings were constructed of local brickearth found in Stutton. The Hall has fine spiralling ornamental chimneys. It is worth driving to St Peter's Church (which stands opposite Stutton Hall), passing cottages in Lower Street, which are very old and well-preserved. A church that stood on this site a thousand years ago is mentioned in Domesday. The present building was restored in the 18th century. There are excellent views over the River Stour from the top of the early 15th-century tower. The kneelers in the church are particularly fine, and at the west end are two large alabaster monuments dating back to the 1600s.

WALK 15
Around
Mersea Island

Allow 2 hours

Mersea is an oval-shaped island, 5 miles long by 2½ miles wide. It is connected to the mainland by a causeway, called the Strood. At very high tides the water covers the road. The island is a flat area of mixed farming, centred around the villages of West and East Mersea. It is well-known for its oyster fishing, and in the winter of 1962–63, millions of oysters were killed when the sea froze in the creeks. This walk takes you around the coastal area of Mersea, which is a National Nature Reserve, and through East Mersea, the smaller of the two villages.

Take the only road to East Mersea to its end. After parking in the lay-by (TM066153), walk away from the coastline, between the bungalows. A short distance along the road, just after Green Acre bungalow on your right, turn left into a public footpath. Turn left again with a house and fence on your left, on to a metalled road. The path now becomes a rough track. Go through the gates, turning left into Cudmore Grove Country Park. Turn left along the track with a horse-shoe sign, heading towards Brightlingsea Reach and the Colne Estuary. At the water's edge, go over the stile on your left, and follow the path at the top of the bank. The

Colne Estuary is a nature reserve, and an excellent area for spotting waders and other coastal birds. Craft of all kinds use these waterways. There are good views across to Brightlingsea and the famous Martello Towers, erected during the Napoleonic Wars against the threat of a French invasion.

Continue along the path towards the River Colne, passing the oyster farm on your left. Further along, the path curves inland for a short distance. At this point, go down the bank and cross an earth and grass bridge into the meadow. Bear right across the field towards the right-hand corner of the wood. Go over a flat wooden bridge into the wood. Turn left, continuing along the path to the lane. (If the woodland path is too obstructed, walk in the meadow alongside the wood to the lane.) At the lane, bear right, passing a superb tiled barn on stilts. At the T-junction, turn right, with a clapboard thatched cottage on your left. Opposite Black Water Cottage, turn left into the public footpath between fields. At the field boundary, turn right, then left, following the path to the road. At the metalled road, turn left, passing 'The Gables'. Reaching a thatched cottage where the road bends left, go right along the footpath. About 40yd from the bend in the field path, bear left into a narrow path. Where the path goes right at a house, keep left and follow the path to the road. At the road, turn right and return to the car.

There are panoramic views of the coastline throughout the whole of this walk. It is worth visiting the church of St Edmund, King and Martyr. The site is an ancient one; it is thought that both the Romans and Vikings used it. A moat once surrounded the manor house and church; part of it still remains. Among the interesting items in the church are the Arms of King George III.

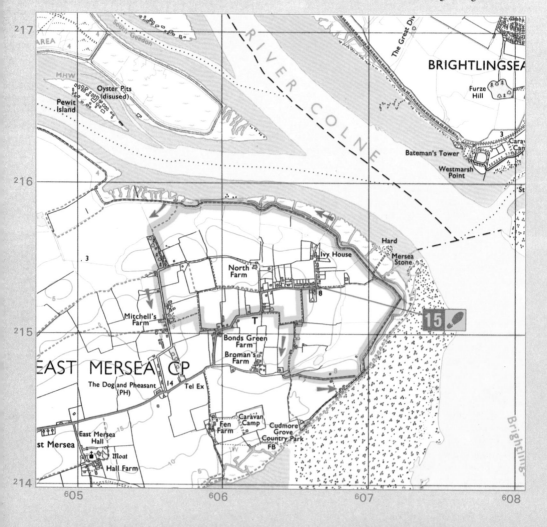

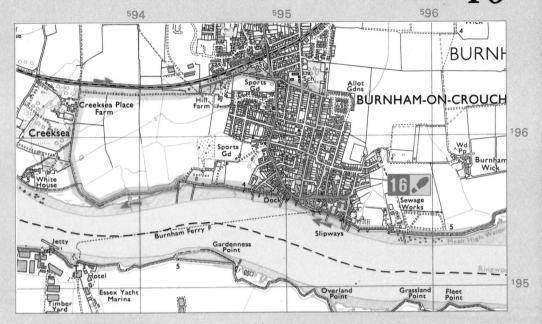

An Essex Riverside Walk

Allow 2 hours

This walk follows the River Crouch along some of its busiest and quietest stretches, turning inland and sauntering through the busy small town of Burnham-on-Crouch. Often known as 'the Cowes of the East', Burnham-on-Crouch is home to five yachting clubs, including the famous Royal Corinthian Yachting Club. The terrace of low red- yellow- and white-washed houses along the Quay is very pleasant. At the centre is The White Hart Hotel, with a porch on carved brackets. It is a lively place, with regattas and other yachting events there during the year.

Take the B1021 through the town. Just after the clock tower on your right, turn left into Ship Road, between the Ship Inn and Pymas' Estate Agents. Near the top of Ship Road is a free car park (TQ953958). Turn right out of the car park, walking back down Ship Road, with two clapboard houses on your right. At the main street, turn left. At the junction, with the Victoria Inn on the corner, turn right into Belvedere Road, and continue towards the river. At the end of the road, turn right into a narrow lane between the Duerr Engineering Office and a clapboard shipping office. This paved walk twists and turns beside the River Crouch. On one side of this river-walk, the river itself is a hive of activity, with craft of every description. On the other side, a host of merchants sell their wares; there are ships' chandlers, and boats being built and repaired. Further along, many kinds of house-boats are moored by the bank.

The path leads to a stile. Go over it, on to a grass path at the top of the river bank. Later on, this path forks; take the right fork down over a stile into a field. From here, there are magnificent views over the river. Across the water lies Wallasea Island, the home of the Essex Yachting Marina. Large boat-building yards can also be seen.

Passing a bungalow on your left, go towards the

The little town of Burnham-on-Crouch is a popular boating centre, often called 'the Cowes of the East'

railway line. Just before the level crossing, turn right along a wide path between the railway fence and a field. Go through the kissing-gate. Where a side path turns back to the left over the railway, keep straight ahead, on to a new road. The River Crouch, sometimes known as 'Battle River', can once again be seen from this higher ground. King Canute fought King Edmund Ironside further up the river at Fambridge. At the estuary of the river lies Foulness Island. In the 18th century, during the Napoleonic Wars, General Shrapnel's new explosive shell was tested there.

Continue along the pavement, with the Five Ways Stores on your left. At the main road, go straight across, keeping the Victorian Railway Inn on your right, and walk along Devonshire Road. Opposite Perkin Cottage, turn right into Mildmay Road, then along Dorset Road, and finally along Chapel Road. At the main road, turn left, and then left again, into Ship Road, for the return to the car park. The route back is through the quieter parts of town, with their Victorian houses. The new houses in Chapel Road blend in well with the old cottages. In the main street there are many clapboard houses, some dating from the 18th century. Looking down the alley-ways, you can catch glimpses of the river. The ornate clock and tower in the High Street were built in 1877 in memory of Lady Sweeting. Another plaque commemorates Sidney Harvey, who wound the clock by hand for 44 years.

Index

Page numbers in bold type indicate main entries

Acknowledgements

The publishers would like to thank the many individuals who helped in the preparation of this book. Special thanks are due to the East Anglia Tourist Board.

The Automobile Association also wishes to thank the following photographers, organisations and libraries for their assistance in the compilation of this book.

BBC Hulton 31 Benjamin Britten, 51 Flying Fortress, 57 Oliver Cromwell; *Cambridge Collection* 8 Slubbing out a drain; *East Anglia Tourist Board* 51 Gt Yarmouth; *Essex Record Office* 117 Burnham-on-Crouch; *Flatford Mill Field Centre* 21 Valley Farm, Flatford; *International Photobank* 5 River Ant; *Jarrolds Colour Library* 17 Norwich Cathedral; *Tom Mackie* Cover: Sailboat & Turf Fen Mill, R. Ant; *Mary Evans Picture Library* 47 Hereward the Wake, 113 Orford Castle; *National Gallery* 26 Mr & Mrs Andrews, 27 The Haywain; *Nature Photographers Ltd* 12 Parrot Crossbill, Common Seals (R Tidman), 13 Egyptian Geese (W Paton), Swallowtail (P Sterry), 14 Raft Spider, Military Orchid (R Tidman), 15 Norfolk Hawker (K Wilson), Fen Violet (R Bush), 16 Short Eared Owl (M Leach), Black tailed Godwit (F Blackburn); *Norfolk Museums Service* 27 Boats on the Medway, 27 Back of the New Mills, 28 Thorpe; *Norwich Central Library* 7 Reed Boathouse, 9/10 Harvesting, 23 Orford Castle, 37 Burnham Thorpe Rectory, 43 Unloading Wherry, 67 Sheringham Fisherman, 72 N Walsham Grammar School, 105 Castle Acre Priory; *Spectrum* 6 Windpump, Horsey Mere, 80 Red Arrows; *The Mansell Collection* 109 Swaffham Prior

The following photographs are from the Automobile Association's Photo Library:

M Adelman 19 Bures, St Stephen's Chapel, 22 Saffron Walden, 49 Finchingfield, 56 Huntingdon, 64 Peakirk Wild Fowl Trust, 66 St Ives' Bridge; *M Birkett* 8 Stretham Engine House, Beam Engine, 11 Grime's Graves, 17 Ely Cathedral, 21 Lavenham Guildhall, 39 Punting, King's College Chapel, 40 Castle Hedingham, Pedlar of Swaffham, 46 War Museum, Duxford, 47 Ely, 56 Godmanchester, 59 Lode Mill, 62 Jockey Colours, Racehorse Training, 65 Peterborough Cathedral, 69 Watermill Pump, Windmill Stowmarket, 73 Wisbech, 81 Racehorse Training; *P Davies* 3 Southwold, 68 Southwold; *S & O Mathews* 1 Norwich Cathedral, 6 Hickling Broad, 9 Fritton Village, 11 Breckland Forest, 16 Welney Wildlife, 17 Misericord Norwich, 18 Haddiscoe Church, 19 St Wendreda's Church, Greenstead Church, 19 St Wendreda's Church, Long Melford Church, 20 Grt Warley Church, 23 Oxburgh Hall, Paycocke's House, 24 Cley next the Sea, Sherringham Cottage, Burnham-on-Crouch, 25 Gainsborough's House, Sudbury, 29 Swanton Morley sign, 30 Tower Hse, Thorpeness, Blickling Hall, 32 Blakeney Salt Marshes, Bocking Pargeting, 33 Breckland Woodland, 34 Wicken Fen, Ranworth Broad, 36 Castle, Bungay, 37 Burnham Overy Mill, 38 Theatre Royal, 40 Cricket, 41 St Osyth's Priory, Clacton, 42 Kipper smoking, 43 Cromer, 44 Shermans Hall, Diss 45 Dunwich, 46 Bishop Bonner's Cottage, 49 Felixstowe Docks, 50 Glandford, Elizabethan House Panel, 52 Guildhall, Hadleigh, 53 Courtauld's Mill, Harwich Quay, 54 Norfolk Lavender, Hatfield Forest & Lake, 55 Cliffs at Hunstanton Bowls, 57 Kersey, 58 Market, King's Lynn, 60 Melford Hall, 61 Maldon, the Hythe, Lowestoft Harbour, 63 Norwich Market, Elm Hill, 65 Chancel Roof, Turf Maize, 67 Fisherman, North Norfolk Railway, 70 Thetford Priory, 71 Little Walsingham, 72 Shrimpboats, Wells, 74 Woodbridge Tide Mill, Market Cross, 96 Burnham Thorpe Church, 97 Hunstanton Cliffs, 98 Lifeboat Man, 99 Cromer, 100 Melford Hall, 101 Flatford Mill; *R Surman* 18 St Boltoph's, Colchester, 22 Ancient House, Ipswich, 38 Abbey Gardens gateway, Angel Hill, 42 Colchester Castle, 52 Plaque, Colchester, 56 Christchurch Mansion; *W Voysey* 45 Sign, 52 Dutch Quarter, 71 Slipper Chapel; *H Williams* 35 Horsey Mere, 73 Wimpole Hall, Wimpole Home Farm; *T Wood* 70 Swaffham Church; *T Woodcock* 7 Morston Salt Marshes, 21 Orford Castle, 31 Binham Priory, 36 Bressingham, 48 Hunting Lodge, 59 Lavenham, 60 Kentwell Maze, 64 Orford Farm, 96 Wolferton Railway Stn.

Other Ordnance Survey Maps of East Anglia

How to get there with Routemaster and Routeplanner Maps

Reach East Anglia from Birmingham, Southampton, London and Luton using Routemaster Sheet 9, or from Scarborough, Lincoln, Nottingham and Leicester using Routemaster Sheet 6. Alternatively, use the Ordnance Survey Great Britain Routeplanner Map, which covers the whole of the country on one sheet.

Exploring with Landranger and Holiday & Tourist Maps

Landranger Series
1¼ inches to one mile or 1:50 000 scale

These maps cover the whole of Britain and are good for local motoring, cycling and walking. Each contains tourist information such as parking, picnic places, viewpoints and public rights of way. Sheets covering East Anglia are:

131 Boston and Spalding
132 North West Norfolk
133 North East Norfolk
134 Norwich and the Broads
142 Peterborough
143 Ely and Wisbech
144 Thetford and Breckland
153 Bedford and Huntingdon
154 Cambridge and Newmarket
155 Bury St Edmunds and Sudbury

156 Saxmundham and Aldeburgh
167 Chelmsford and Harlow
168 Colchester and the Blackwater
169 Ipswich and the Naze

Holiday and Tourist Map Series
These maps cover popular holiday areas and are ideal for discovering the countryside. In addition to normal map details, ancient monuments, camping and caravan sites, parking facilities and viewpoints are marked. Lists of selected places of interest are included on some sheets, and others include comprehensive and useful guides to the area.

Holiday and Tourist Map Sheet 11 (The Broads)
covers the Norfolk Broads area
(1¼ inches to one mile or 1:50 000)

Other titles available in this series are:

Brecon Beacons	Forest of Dean & Wye Valley	Northumbria	Snowdonia
Channel Islands	Ireland	North York Moors	South Downs
Cornwall	Isle of Wight	Peak District	Wessex
Cotswolds	Lake District	Scottish Highlands	Yorkshire Dales
Devon & Exmoor	New Forest		